Žižek and Law

The very first book dedicated to Slavoj Žižek's theoretical treatment of law, this volume gathers widely recognized Žižek scholars as well as legal theorists to offer a sustained analysis of the place of law in Žižek's work. Whether it is with reference to symbolic law, psychoanalytical law, religious law, positive law, or human rights; to Lacan's, Hegel's, or Kant's philosophies of law; or even to Jewish or Buddhist law, Žižek returns again and again to law. And what his work offers, this volume demonstrates, is a radically new approach to law and a rethinking of its role within the framework of radical politics. With the help of Žižek himself – who here, and for the first time, directly engages with the topic of law – this collection provides an authoritative account of "Žižek and law." It will be an invaluable resource for researchers and students in the fields of law, legal theory, legal philosophy, political theory, psychoanalysis, theology, and cultural studies.

Laurent de Sutter is Professor of Legal Theory, Vrije Universiteit, Brussels, Belgium.

Nomikoi: Critical Legal Thinkers

Series editors
Peter Goodrich
Cardozo School of Law, New York
David Seymour
School of Law, City University, London

Nomikoi: Critical Legal Thinkers presents analyses of key critical theorists whose thinking on law has contributed significantly to the development of the new interdisciplinary legal studies. Addressing those who have most influenced legal thought and thought about law, the series aims to bring legal scholarship, the social sciences and the humanities into closer dialogue.

Other titles in the series

Judith Butler
Ethics, law, politics
Elena Loizidou

Evgeny Pashukanis
A critical reappraisal
Michael Head

Giorgio Agamben
Power, law and the uses of criticism
Thanos Zartaloudis

Niklas Luhmann
Law, justice, society
Andreas Philippopoulos-Mihalopoulos

Henri Lefebvre
Spatial politics, everyday life and the right to the city
Chris Butler

Carl Schmitt
Law as politics, ideology and strategic myth
Michael G. Salter

Althusser and Law
Edited by Laurent de Sutter

Deleuze & Guattari
Emergent law
Jamie Murray

Bruno Latour
The normativity of networks
Kyle McGee

Žižek and Law
Edited by Laurent de Sutter

Forthcoming titles in the series

Roberto Esposito
Law, community and the political
Peter Langford

Žižek and Law

Edited by
Laurent de Sutter

Routledge
Taylor & Francis Group
a GlassHouse Book

First published 2015
by Routledge
2 Park Square, Milton Park, Abingdon, Oxfordshire OX14 4RN

and by Routledge
711 Third Avenue, New York, NY 10017

First issued in paperback 2016

Routledge is an imprint of the Taylor and Francis Group, an informa business

British Library Cataloguing in Publication Data
A catalogue record for this book is available from the British Library

Library of Congress Cataloging-in-Publication Data
A catalog record has been requested for this book

ISBN 13: 978-1-138-24156-5 (pbk)
ISBN 13: 978-1-138-80184-4 (hbk)

Typeset in Baskerville
by Wearset Ltd, Boldon, Tyne and Wear

Contents

Contributors

Maria Aristodemou is Senior Lecturer in Law, Assistant Dean for International Links, and Director and Admissions Tutor LLM General at Birkbeck College, University of London (United Kingdom). She is the author of *Law and Literature: Journeys from Her to Eternity* (Oxford University Press, 2000) and *Law, Psychoanalysis, Society: Taking the Unconscious Seriously* (Routledge, 2014).

Anne Bottomley is Reader in Law and Property at Kent Law School, Canterbury (United Kingdom). Her articles have appeared in *Law and Critique, Cardozo Law Review,* and *Griffith Law Review.* She is the co-editor (with Simone Wong) of *Changing Contours of Domestic Life, Family and Law: Caring and Sharing* (Hart, 2009).

Dan Hassler-Forest is Assistant Professor of Film and Literature at the University of Amsterdam (The Netherlands). He is the author of *Capitalist Superheroes: Caped Crusaders in the Neoliberal Age* (Zero Books, 2012) and *Transmedia* (Amsterdam University Press, 2013). With Joyce Goggin, he also has edited *The Rise and Reason of Comic and Graphic Literature: Critical Essays on the Form* (McFarland, 2010).

Adrian Johnston is Professor in the Department of Philosophy at the University of New Mexico (Albuquerque, USA) and Assistant Teaching Analyst at the Emory Psychoanalytic Institute (Atlanta, USA). He is the author of *Time Driven: Metapsychology and the Splitting of the Drive* (2005), *Žižek's Ontology: A Transcendental Materialist Theory of Subjectivity* (2008), *Badiou, Žižek, and Political Transformations: The Cadence of Change* (2009), and *Prolegomena to Any Future Materialism, Volume One: The Outcome of Contemporary French Philosophy* (2013), all published by Northwestern University Press, and *Adventures in Transcendental Materialism: Dialogues with Contemporary Thinkers* (Edinburgh University Press, 2014). He is also the co-author, with Catherine Malabou, of *Self and Emotional Life: Philosophy, Psychoanalysis, and Neuroscience* (Columbia Press, 2013).

Adam Kotsko is Assistant Professor of Humanities at Shimer College (Chicago, USA). He is the author of *Žižek and Theology* (Continuum, 2008), *Awkwardness* (Zero Books, 2010), and *Why We Love Sociopaths: A Guide to Late Capitalist Television* (Zero Books, 2011). He also has translated several books by Giorgio Agamben for Stanford University Press.

Chris McMillan is Lecturer in Sociology and Communications at Brunel University (United Kingdom). He is the author of *Žižek and Communist Strategy: On the Disavowed Foundations of Global Capitalism* (Edinburgh University Press, 2012) and *The Blood of Capital: Evoking the Consequences of Our Way of Life* (Zero Books, 2013).

Nathan Moore is Lecturer in Law and Director of QLD Assessment at Birkbeck College, University of London (United Kingdom). His articles have appeared in *Law and Critique*, *Law and Humanities*, *Cardozo Law Review*, *New York Law School Law Review*, etc.

Molly Anne Rothenberg is Professor of English at Tulane University (New Orleans, USA). She is the co-editor of *Perversion and the Social Relation* (Duke University Press, 2003, with Slavoj Žižek and Dennis A. Foster) and *Žižek Now: New Perspectives in Žižek Studies* (Polity, 2013, with Jamil Khader) and the author of *The Excessive Subject: A New Theory of Social Change* (Polity, 2010). She also is a practicing psychoanalyst.

Frank Ruda is a Research Associate at the Collaborative Research Centre on Aesthetic Experience and the Dissolution of Artistic Limits at the Free University of Berlin (Germany). He also is Visiting Lecturer at ECLA Bard, Liberal Arts University Berlin, and at the Institute of Philosophy, Scientific Research Centre, Ljubljana (Slovenia). He is the author of *Hegel's Rabble: An Investigation into Hegel's Philosophy of Right* (Continuum, 2011, preface by Slavoj Žižek).

Jeanne L. Schroeder is Professor of Law at Benjamin N. Cardozo School of Law, Yeshiva University (New York, USA). She is the author of *The Vestal and the Fasces: Hegel, Lacan, Property, and the Feminine* (University of California Press, 1998), *The Triumph of Venus: The Erotics of the Market* (University of California Press, 2004), and *The Four Lacanian Discourses: or Turning Law Inside Out* (Birkbeck Law Press, 2008).

Laurent de Sutter is Professor of Legal Theory at Vrije Universiteit Brussel (Belgium). He has been Visiting Honorary Research Scholar at Benjamin N. Cardozo School of Law, Yeshiva University (New York), and Lecturer in Law at Facultés Universitaires Saint-Louis (Brussels). He is the author of *Deleuze: La pratique du droit* (Michalon, 2009), *Contre l'érotisme* (La Musardine, 2011), *Théorie du trou* (Léo Scheer, 2013) and *Métaphysique de la putain* (Léo Scheer, 2014). He has edited *Deleuze and Law* (Edinburgh University Press, 2012, with K. McGee) and *Althusser* *and Law* (Routledge, 2013). He also is the managing editor of the "Perspectives Critiques" series at Presses Universitaires de France and of the "Theory Redux" series at Polity Press.

Fabio Vighi is Reader at Cardiff University (United Kingdom), where he also is co-Director of the Žižek Centre for Ideology Critique. He is the author of *Critical Theory and Film: Rethinking Ideology through Film Noir* (Continuum, 2012), *On Žižek's Dialectics: Surplus, Subtraction, Sublimation* (Continuum, 2010), and *Žižek: Beyond Foucault* (Palgrave Macmillan, 2007, with H.M. Felder) and the co-editor of *Did Somebody Say Ideology? On Slavoj Žižek and Consequences* (Cambridge Scholars Press, 2007, with H.M. Felder).

Slavoj Žižek is Senior Researcher at the Institute of Sociology, University of Ljubljana (Slovenia), and a Visiting Professor at a number of American Universities (Columbia, Princeton, New School for Social Research, New York University, University of Michigan, etc.). He also is a returning faculty member of the European Graduate School and International Director of the Birkbeck Institute for the Humanities, University of London. He is the author or the editor of more than 50 books, translated into more than 30 languages. In the last 20 years Žižek has participated in over 350 international philosophical, psychoanalytical, and cultural-criticism symposiums around the world. He is the founder and President of the Society for Theoretical Psychoanalysis, Ljubljana.

Introduction

Laurent de Sutter

On the 28 November 2011, in Brussels, the capital of Europe, Slavoj Žižek was supposed to pronounce an address on the topic of "The Struggle for European Legacy." The venue was Bozar, a sumptuous late Art Nouveau building conceived by Victor Horta, which has become one of the most important concert halls of the continent. Weeks before the talk Žižek had sold out the two thousand plus seats of the Henry Le Boeuf room – leaving unsatisfied a waiting list of hundreds of people. The occasion of this talk was the joint publication of a Dutch translation, by Boom, of Žižek's *First as Tragedy, then as Farce*, and of a new edition, at Presses Universitaires de France, of Žižek's very first book, written directly in French, *Le plus sublime des hystériques*. When Žižek started to talk, the heat was already considerable – at the very last moment, to the 2000 seats had been added 100 others, directly put on stage, behind the speaker (they were sold in 20 minutes). As often in his conferences of the time, he began with a discussion of Beethoven's *Ninth Symphony*, a favorite of Nazi Germany before its "Ode to Joy" became the official anthem of the European Union. Beware, said Žižek: don't be fooled by the choirs of the "Ode to Joy," because what matters the most in this symphony is not that; it is what immediately follows. And, with a gesture to the sound engineer, the audience suddenly started to hear the bombast of the third variation on the theme of the "Ode," at the beginning of the fourth movement of the Symphony. Suddenly, at its acme (at bar 331, precisely, as Žižek recalled), a silence irrupted – followed by a long, low note, played by bassoons: "This," commented the speaker, "is the European *fart*." The room burst with laughter. Yet, despite its apparent silliness (and, even, *because* of it), there was a truth in this assumption: with the beginning of the *marcia turca* following the third variation on the "Ode," something like the obscene counterpart to what we heard before made itself visible on the very scene that pretended to foreclose it. As "Ode to Joy" was the official hymn of the European Union, the Turkish march was what the European authorities refused to listen to, even though it was on the very repression of its "Turkish" dimension that contemporary Europe was "grounded." This little exercise, typical of Žižek, could serve as a perfect appetizer for what the present collection is all about: trying to understand the place of law in his system of thought – a place to which he himself has apparently devoted only a few enigmatic propositions. Yet, as the reader will undoubtedly notice, there is a important novelty in Žižek's theory of law, a novelty that precisely consists in the curious game of hide and seek that law plays with its own obscene remainder.

The legal dimension of the obscene, the dimension of the obscene in law, the obscenity of law itself are then the starting points of the different investigations that one will discover in the following pages. In her opening contribution, Maria Aristodemou has decided to start again with a description of Žižek's position apropos law – his position not in intellectual or theoretical terms, but as a subject. More precisely, her chapter takes the form of an analysis of what a legal subject is. It proceeds by identifying some persistent symptoms including the subject's desire for the law, and explores how such symptoms might be addressed and enjoyed if not ultimately resolved. The chief dialectic is between the hysterical subject in search of a would-be master, and a master who turns out to be not masterful enough. The chapter focuses on how a Žižekian (in contrast to, and in addition to, a Freudian or Lacanian) analysis might proceed in excavating the subject's unconscious desires: such desires are glimpsed not only from the subject's dreams and the subject's speech, but from the symbolic order's legal and cultural products and practices. A dream, a short story by Woody Allen, a Supreme Court decision against the Catholic Brotherhood, the killing of Osama bin Laden and the series *Breaking Bad* are some of the vignettes used to illustrate the progress from identifying those desires to assuming responsibility for them and lastly to the difficult task of attaining the status of an ethical subject whose desires the subject herself is the cause. This analytic process, the chapter suggests, holds lessons not only for the unsatisfiable subject of law but also for her would-be legal masters who ultimately turn out not to be that masterful.

Drawing further on the idea that the figure of the subject is the one around which Žižek's understanding of law revolves, Adam Kotsko offers a comparative discussion of Badiou's and Žižek's reading of Saint Paul as a representative of this figure. According to Kotsko, what is distinctive about Žižek's interpretation of Paul on that account is not immediately clear. This is due first of all to the context in which his primary readings of Paul take place. In *The Ticklish Subject*, Žižek discusses Paul in the course of a critique of Alain Badiou's philosophy and particularly his book *Saint Paul: The Foundation of Universalism*, but Paul in himself is not at issue for Žižek at this point, and he leaves his own position on Paul ambiguous. Žižek again turns to Paul in *The Puppet and the Dwarf*, specifically in the midst of a somewhat elliptical critique of Agamben's book *The Time That Remains*, but more broadly in the context of an interpretation of Actual Existing

Christianity, in which Paul serves as the point of Christianity's emergence out of Judaism. Beyond the necessity of discerning Žižek's implicit positive position on Paul from his critique of another reading, there is a further potential for misunderstanding. Given that Žižek is often seen (erroneously) as an advocate or popularizer of Badiou's philosophy, one might assume that Žižek's critique of Agamben amounts to a simple reassertion of Badiou's reading of Paul. This is not the case. In fact, Žižek's reading of Paul in *The Puppet and the Dwarf* is at least implicitly a critique of Badiou's, and more importantly represents a significant advance over Badiou's, particularly on the question of the law in Romans 7. In support of this contention, Kotsko first briefly outlines Badiou's interpretation of Paul's position on the law and then moves on to Žižek's critique of Badiou in *The Ticklish Subject*. Finally, he turns to the task of making sense of Žižek's discussion of Paul in the context of his argument in *The Puppet and the Dwarf*, and tries to answer this question: what is the subject of law, according to Žižek?

Molly Anne Rothenberg then adds another layer of questioning concerning the status of the legal subject in Žižek's thought, shifting focus on the politic consequences of its definition. In the third part of *The Parallax View*, she notices, Žižek wonders whether a revolutionary legal order will necessarily reproduce the same problems as the old order on account of some inherent and irremediable feature of Law itself that would force the repetition of the same old oppressive regime. This question arises from Žižek's engagement with Jacques Lacan's Master's discourse and its transformations as elaborated in *Seminar XVII, The Other Side of Psychoanalysis*. At the same time, Žižek agrees with Lacan that the subject's relationship to the Law has been changed for the worse by the weakening of the Master's discourse, primarily as a consequence of capitalism, a condition Žižek deplores in the vitiation of symbolic efficiency, the crisis of symbolic investiture, and the society of enjoyment. Yet Žižek's continued use of the four discourses of the Master as his analytical tools can create confusion because, as Rothenberg argues, he is describing the structure of social bonds that are better captured by a different set of discourses altogether, a mutation of the Master's discourse under capitalism. Using examples from his work that directly address the question of the Law's revolutionary potential (including his contribution to this volume), she shows how Žižek's ideas about the Law, rights, and revolution correlate to the discourse universe of Capitalism. Understanding the Law under the sign of capitalist discourse allows us to locate the revolutionary subject and, in this way, address his call for a revolutionary "sociopolitical transformation that would entail the entire restructuring of the entire field of relations of the public law and its obscene supplement."

Indeed, politics is at the heart of Žižek's conception of law – since, as Jodi Dean once recalled in a seminal article, he is by no means a legal theorist. In his contribution, Chris McMillan tries to isolate the place of law in his political–theoretical agenda, a place that has something to do with the very idea of "the symbolic." Žižek's evocation for a radical politics of "emancipatory terror" in response to the normative hegemony of the "liberal-democratic horizon" is, he begins by stating, one of the most controversial elements of his political engagement. Žižek argues that the democratic symbolic law (as part of the wider logic of cultural capitalism) acts to mediate against the increasingly disruptive antagonisms of global capitalism by simulating the possibility of political change while simultaneously limiting the horizon for political demands. In doing so the liberal democratic horizon becomes an apolitical form of politics that is unable to accommodate anti-systematic demands yet insists that political struggle must remain within its horizon. In response to the apolitical dominance of liberal democracy, Žižek argues that radical politics requires a return to the (Real) dimension of the political within the symbolic order, a return that can be productively evoked by an insistence upon those demands that are unable to be accounted for within the form of the symbolic law of liberal democracy yet that speak directly to the content of that ideological space. In this chapter, as part of a larger consideration of the possibilities for radical political transformation of the imaginary-symbolic order through the Real, McMillan engages with Žižek's critique of liberal democracy *qua* the symbolic law, suggesting that a truly subversive politics must resist those channels for resistance provided by the democratic order. Here he locates the universality of the "part with no-part" of the increasingly identifiable "surplus humanity" of the developing world as a particularly unaccountable, and thus volatile, moment within the democratic horizon, one that both speaks both to its inadequacy as the horizon for global emancipatory demands and to the possibility of breaching the hegemony of the democratic symbolic law.

Is Žižek successful in his attempt to redefine law in a way that might allow for his general critique of liberal democracy? Fabio Vighi is not fully convinced. Going back to the roots of the question, he starts his chapter by recalling that has been developing his theory of law and its excess since the very beginning of his work, namely his groundbreaking *The Sublime Object of Ideology* (1989). The basic argument behind such theory is that law is anchored in some excessive (strictly speaking, "unlawful") remainder that at the same time embodies the very inconsistency of law itself. While, Vighi acknowledges, the specific issue of law is particularly useful to measure both the Hegelian and the Lacanian inflexion of Žižek's philosophy, it indeed also leaves open a number of questions concerning its political ambition. In order to understand this, he argues, one has to focus on the typical Žižekian injunction to over-identify with the law's own excess as the most effective strategy to undo a given ideological order (or to cause such order to collapse). And, as a matter of fact, it seems to Vighi that over-identifying ("enjoying") with the law's excess ("symptoms") is an intrinsically more ambiguous injunction than it may appear from Žižek's argument. In particular, he argues that political transformation cannot be seamlessly derived from the above strategy and requires additional operations that Žižek omits to formulate properly.

As an intermission, Dan Hassler-Forest's contribution turns towards the images of superheroes. Throughout their long and varied careers in American cultural history, superheroes have always acted as paradoxical embodiments of a "universal law": existing in their diegetic universes as the private enforcers of juridical notions of "order" and "justice," they have simultaneously remained separate from the institutions that define the exact boundaries of these very issues. As such, they are engaged in a perpetual negotiation between notions of immanence and transcendence, their actions both exploring and defining the limits of popular understandings of the law. From this perspective, the superhero clearly provides a convenient embodiment of Lacan's concept of the "big Other": the tangible yet indefinable sense of order that aligns a society along shared norms and coordinates. The superhero's massive popularity in twenty-first-century cinema may therefore derive in part from the anxiety triggered by what Žižek has described as the postmodern dissolution of this symbolic fiction. In the absence of any shared belief in the "big Other" that imparts structure and meaning, superheroes provide useful opportunities to negotiate these fantasies and anxieties. In his chapter, Hassler-Forest then applies these notions to the most popular embodiments of the Law in the superhero genre: Superman, whose dedication to "truth, justice, and the American way" represents an ideal of transcendence, and Batman, whose perpetual state of "becoming" is purely immanent. Using examples from recent films and select comic books, he argues that their enactment of a postmodern "big Other" serves as one of the most vital representations of the contradictions that inform our understanding of the Law under neoliberal capitalism.

Answering Vighi's observation that law can help us understand the importance of Hegel in Žižek's thought – and of which Hegel – Adrian Johnston offers detailed insights on two aspects of Žižek's revivification of Hegel, as, in his recent magnum opus *Less Than Nothing: Hegel and the Shadow of Dialectical Materialism*, they stand out as heterodox vis-à-vis currently prevailing sensibilities among the majority of Hegel scholars: his rejections of both anti-metaphysical readings of Hegel's mature philosophy in general as well as moderate, centrist (as per liberal-democratic standards in the Western world) appropriations of Hegel's political philosophy in particular. Johnston's primary purpose in this intervention is to make explicit what Žižek leaves as a largely implicit link between metaphysically and politically deflationary interpretations of Hegel. Through contextualizing Žižek's Hegelianism in relation to the still-popular deflated version of him (as developed from J.N. Findlay, Klaus Hartmann, and Charles Taylor to Robert Pippin, Robert Brandom, Terry Pinkard, Paul Redding, Jean-Francois Kervegan, and others today), Johnston tries to delineate both the merits and limitations of Žižek's specific version of a "re-inflated" Hegel. In so doing, he also sketches some alternate possibilities for re-inflating Hegel's metaphysics and politics within the parameters of the contemporary conjuncture.

Hegel is not the only figure involved in Žižek's theory of law. As is shown in Frank Ruda's contribution, Kant's role should not be underestimated. In particular, the distinction between positive, negative and infinite judgment offered by Kant has been made famous by numerous elaborations in the work of Žižek. If the positive judgment can be defined by the assertion of a predicate to a subject (X is dead), the definition of a negative judgment implies the negation of such an assignation (X is not dead, which implies another positive judgment, X is alive). The infinite judgment – that in Kant exceeds the ordinary logic of judgments and has its place in the transcendental realm – assigns a non-predicate to a subject by taking up the form of the positive judgment and inscribing the negating power of the negative judgment into the very type of predicative assignation used (X is Non-B). The infinite judgment – in Kant it proves the immortality of the soul – designates a different understanding of the subject of a judgment and what it means to judge (from subsumption to reflection). Ruda argues that Žižek's work demonstrates in what sense one even needs to apply the infinite judgment onto itself generating what Ruda calls an "infinitely infinite judgment." In such a type of judgment, as Ruda shows in a reconstruction of Žižek's discussion of Hegel parallel although contrasting to the one of Johnston, a non-subject is aligned with a non-predicate and through this very structure one enters into a domain which cannot even any longer be said to be transcendental. Infinitely infinite judgments, as Ruda demonstrates, depict the structure proper to what Žižek calls an "act": something that generates a fundamentally different relation to the law, offering a new answer to the question "What is to be judged?" that can only be measured by taking into account its consequences.

Hegel also has a role to play in Jeanne Schroeder's chapter, although her main focus is on H.L.A. Hart – and what Hart can teach us about Žižek's views on the morality of law. Hart, indeed the most influential jurisprudential theorist in the English-speaking legal world, famously claimed to separate law from morality. Although Hart's notion of the relationship of law and morality at first glance might seem antithetical to a speculative account, on further examination he may have unintentional affinities with Žižek. According to Hart, one does not obey law because it is moral or just or for any other substantive reason, but rather just because law is Law. Law is a master signifier that stands for nothing but itself. According to Hart, "officials" identify law through "rules of recognition."

They do not make the law, they are the merely the agents of the law. To put this in Žižek's terminology, when the official speaks, "*it is the law itself which speaks through him*," the official is "spoken" by the law, since his "speech acts are totally regulated" by the symbolic order. This is what Hart calls the internal position with respect to the law. Despite occasional insightful moments, however, Hart's concept of law is inadequate. In order for his positivism to work, he must imagine that law is complete, with no slippage or lacunae. When confronted with the obvious fact that officials confront "hard cases" where the law is not clear and the official must engage in the subjective act of interpretation, he insists that these are infrequent exceptions that prove the rule. What he calls the "open texture" of law is an empirical, rather than an internal, logical limit; if the legislature had sufficient time it could fill the legal universe. In other words, Hart does not recognize the "real" – the symbolic order's own logically necessary limitation. Hart's fantasy of a closed and complete symbolic order is a necessary moment for the functioning of law. Ironically, however, Hart's attempt to separate law and morality has the opposite result, making law dependent on right. By expelling morality from law, morality acts as the law's *object petit a* – its missing object of desire. Nevertheless, Hart intuits correctly that one cannot find morality, or in Hegel's account "right," by looking for it in the law. Right, once again to cite Žižek, is precisely that to which the law simultaneously has no access, as well the as obstacle that prevents such access. As Hegel explains in the *Philosophy of Right*, this is because right does not exist, in the same way as Woman does not exist. Wrong, in contrast, does exist. Wrong is not the violation of right, but its pre-condition. Right only appears in the righting of wrongs.

Hegel is still present in Laurent de Sutter's chapter, as it tries to illuminate the role played by a very specific concept in Žižek's thought: the concept of transgression, as, in particular, it is developed in *The Puppet and the Dwarf*. Despite the fact that Žižek is very discreet on the sources of his understanding of this concept, one cannot help but think of Georges Bataille's famous definition, as offered in *Eroticism* – and as discussed by Michel Foucault in his "Preface to Transgression." Discussing these two texts and their Hegelian and Lacanian harmonics, de Sutter tries to outline the originality of Žižek's take on it, an originality consisting in something like a de-dramatization of transgression, a "deflation" to use Johnston's term, that is at the same time a dramatic recasting of its possible effects. In particular, if, as Bataille and Foucault have argued, transgression has nothing to do with subversion, its relationship to the limit has consequences for the very art of the management of limits that is law. From the position of the guardian of limits, law becomes the very transgression of all limits – a position that Žižek has to some extent adopted. The novelty brought out by Žižek, though, concerns the type of law involved in transgression. Is it not that the difference between transgression and the limit the difference between two types of law? Is it not the difference between the grandiose and oppressive type of law defended by liberalism and criticized by the post-structuralists, and the very concrete, pragmatic, practical, ordinary, banal type of law that one could find in the everyday work of the petty civil servant? This is one of the many paradoxes of law that Žižek's take on transgression illustrates.

Anne Bottomley and Nathan Moore then turn to Schmitt in order to assess the place and importance of decision (and the exception) in Žižek. Indeed, Schmitt's well-worn definition of the sovereign continues to be invoked as a central, some might say "foundational," conceptual model in a great deal of politico-legal scholarship. However, as Bottomley and Moore argue, this scholarship has been characterized by a seemingly uncritical acceptance of the priority of "the exception" over "the decision." The issue of the decision has, within this framing, been reduced to a question of mere (exceptional) authority. Even more problematically, as far as the authors are concerned, such a reduction is only able to produce a thinking of "decision" that is acutely restricted to both *a* time and *a* place. The decision remains a discrete cut, which is then containable as the cause of a series of consequences; however, the latter series is itself decided upon only by reference to the original decision. This results in an inevitably anthropocentric mode, where the decision is assessed, retroactively, in terms of what the deciding-sovereign *intended*. That is, the decision is assessed only as a matter of *liability*. Žižek's response to this has been to assert as fundamental and non-negotiable "a right" to political life. However, in so doing, they suggest, he simply repeats a dialectical move of countering the sovereign decision with the counter-sovereign decision. Consequently, he remains caught within the Schmittian formulation, having to nevertheless argue for what is, according to him, the inarguable right to sustain and preserve human life. To get beyond this impasse, Bottomley and Moore refuse a beginning in Schmitt and, instead, consider the decision as an ecological matter. Utilizing an exploration of music and sound, they argue that decisions reverberate across complex spatio-temporal assemblages. Finally, in a critical engagement with Žižek's writing on opera, framed through the fictional opposition between ear and eye (as an "as if"), they claim that "the decision" is capable of being re-thought when, detached from the question of sovereign authority, it can become, instead, a mode of interacting with the world: that is, a mode of world expressivity.

As the very embodiment of *plus-de-jouir*, the volume closes on the wonderful gift that are Žižek's personal remarks on his own vision of law – remarks that, of course, are of a parallax nature, meeting the topic of law only laterally. The pleasure of reading Žižek also originating in the effect of surprise that, like the half-truth one meets in psychoanalysis, accompanies a theorem, it will be left to the reader to discover how Žižek summarizes and restates for the present his take on law. The only thing left to be done before letting the reader do so, and browse through the different contributions to the present volume, is to thank all the contributors for their brilliant essays, Peter Goodrich and David Seymour for having accepted the volume in their series, Colin Perrin and Rebekah Jenkins at Routledge for having accepted to publish it and having tolerated the usual delays, the anonymous reviewers for having granted one of the most straightforward green lights ever to this project, and to Slavoj Žižek himself for having so generously supported it and so substantially contributed to it.

Part I

Law's obscenity

Chapter 1

The pervert's guide to the law

Clinical vignettes from *Breaking Bad* to breaking free

Maria Aristodemou

Session 1: transference

It is well known that any successful analysis (rare as those occasions are) culminates in a double murder: first the annihilation of the analysand and her re-birth as a new subject; second, and less interesting, the ritual discarding of the analyst. Once the analysand has become her own cause and author of her own desire, the analyst who occupied, temporarily, the place of the patient's cause of desire can be tossed into the nearest bin. At that point, supposedly, the patient has crossed the threshold not only of the analyst's home for the last time, but her own fundamental (and invariably embarrassing, not to mention shameful if not criminal) fantasies. In Lacanese this is called the "pass" and signals the patient's accession to the status of an ethical subject and, should she wish, an analyst.

As a humble lawyer, and an academic lawyer at that, I harbor no such grand ambitions. The purpose of this chapter is much more modest; it aims to remind the legal subject, of some "events" that took place along the way, that is, instances where the patient's relationship to the law was not only severely challenged but was shattered to pieces, requiring a new understanding with the law and its wily ways with her desire. These are events that had the legal subject shuffling awkwardly out of the analyst's house, having barely been able to get to her feet, let alone gather her thoughts, the sessions having been cut unceremoniously short, the price having been deposited on the analyst's desk, and the patient now being left to mull over why she exposed herself to the humiliating journey of encountering herself in the first place.

Slavoj Žižek is a heavy, not to mention loud and colorful weight to toss, but the deed must be done as is the cleaning up after a murder. To be clear, whether Žižek (or anyone else for that matter) positioned himself in the role of the analyst, let alone that of the master, is beside the point here; nor does it exonerate him of the fate of being ritually discarded and dethroned. As any analyst knows, a would-be master's impotence, incompetence, or limitation of any sort never stopped hysterical subjects from transferring their wishful desire for answers, indeed for right answers, to him. The hysteric will transfer her desire for knowledge and ascribe the position of the master to whoever she assumes knows, only to decide shortly afterwards that the master was never that knowledgeable or that masterful in the first place. Along the way of dethroning the master from his position as the subject supposed to know, the analysand picks up a few lessons, not only for herself, but for the master whose position is constantly under challenge. This chapter will report some of these lessons for the patient subject of law as well as for the would-be legal master along the way.

Session 2: law

Like many analyses, this one also starts with a dream: in the dream the legal subject's double is paying her a visit. The visitor relates to our patient that she has discovered a sweet little bookshop near the British Museum, where she picked up lots of great new books. The friend unpacks her backpack and displays her new treasures. The new books are all from a publisher called Chronos. One of the titles is by an author called Slavoj Žižek. The title is *All you Need is Punishment*.

Although Žižek writes faster than many people read, as far as we know he has not (yet) written a book with this title. Why the ascription of this volume to this author, then, by the legal subject's unconscious? Since Freud's "discovery" of the unconscious, it has been common to glamorize it as a seat of unruly instincts unsettling the subject's equanimity and threatening the composure of the ego and its relations to the social order: "From the point of view of instinctual control, of morality" Freud suggested, "it may be said of the id that it is totally non-moral, of the ego that it strives to be moral, and of the super-ego that it can be super-moral."[1] What is less often pointed out is Freud's insistence that the unconscious is made up not only of unruly impulses but of contradictory ones, including the subject's desire for and enjoyment of rules: "the normal man" as Freud put it, "is not only more violent than he believes, he is also more moral than he knows."[2]

One of Žižek's first lessons to legal subjects, one that he has been stressing repeatedly for three decades now, is that the desire to obey is no less repressed and hidden from the subject than the desire to disobey and rebel. Indeed with modernity the unconscious desire to obey has grown: modern man's so-called murder of God has not meant that the subject is blissfully and wildly free but the opposite: without God, far from everything being permitted, Lacan insisted, everything is prohibited.[3] Why is that? On the one hand, if there is one meaning to God, as Lacan made clear, is that he is All-enjoying, that he is jouissance: Christianity, he says, "naturally ended inventing a God so that he is the one who gets off."[4] The problem with killing the All-enjoying being who obeys no one is that the subject is left with no axis around which she can measure her defiance or enjoy her transgression. As I have discussed before, the morning after the death of God is a nasty hangover without us having had the party the night before: our modernist parents had the party and we are left with cleaning up the mess of their enjoyment.

From God's point of view, as Žižek has joked many times, he has become undead, like the cartoon character who continues running long after he has crossed the precipice: he is dead but doesn't know that he has died. From the subject's point of view, the so-called "naturalist liberation of desire," as Lacan says, has also failed historically: "We do not find ourselves in the presence of a man less weighed down with laws and duties than before the great critical experience of so-called libertine thought."[5] What we do find is Michel Houllebecq's desireless atoms who often crave prohibition to resuscitate their sleeping and crushing lack of desire. Their preferred mode of suffering, as one of his characters puts it, is modern society's symptom par excellence, depression. "It's not that I feel tremendously low," he explains; "It's just everyone around me appears high."[6]

With Žižek's work we begin to understand modern man's (and to a lesser extent woman's) paradoxical predicament in the absence of restrictions: when there is no agency issuing commands and prohibitions from above, the subject takes the task unto herself and enacts and enforces them with greater zeal than any outside authority. Since the discourse of modernity dwells on the subject's freedom from constraints, what the subject ends up repressing is not her supposedly illicit desires for transgression but her desires *for* prohibition, for obedience and for punishment. As Žižek puts it, the more everything is permitted, the more our desire for prohibition is displaced onto our unconscious: "We should renounce the usual notion of the unconscious as a reservoir of wild, illicit drives: the unconscious is also (one is even tempted to say: above all) fragments of a traumatic, cruel, capricious, unintelligible and irrational law text."[7] Or, to put it another way, when everything is permitted, desire has no axis around which to circulate, so the only thing left to desire is prohibition.

In a permissive society, therefore, the subject comes to desire rules, prohibitions and punishment. The more the subject proclaims herself not to be bound by any laws, the more she loads prohibitions onto her unconscious. And the less external prohibitions there are, the more internal prohibitions press on her: as Žižek writes, "far from being a mere extension or internalization of the external law, the inner law (the law of conscience) emerges when the external law fails to appear."[8] The subject may no longer subscribe to a religion demanding strict fasting; instead she subscribes to the latest diet fad or health regime. Indeed in the absence of an external authority, the subject finds that she is called upon to wage battle with and is in vain combat with herself. As we will see later, many subjects choose the burden of prohibitions to the greater burden of self-legislation. Those who choose self-legislation (and Žižek readily admits they are more likely to be women) attain what Lacan calls the status of an ethical subject.

Session 3: unconscious

Having paid lip-service to the image of Freud in popular imagination by starting her analysis with a dream, the legal subject soon has to come to terms with the fact that the unconscious is not safely tagged away in nocturnal recesses that she may or may not choose to reveal but will sooner or later, and whether she likes or not, manifest itself in her speech. If for Freud the royal road to the unconscious was dreams, and for Lacan the royal road to the unconscious was speech, we can venture the suggestion that for Žižek the royal road to the unconscious is the products and practices of our culture.

Hard as it is to find an example that Žižek has not already addressed, the following story may serve as an illustration: "I am in love with two women, a not terribly uncommon problem." Woody Allen writes in a short story he penned in 1980. "That they happen to be mother and child? All the more challenging!" he continues. His girlfriend's daughter reciprocates his attraction, as of course does her mother. When he marries the mother, at the wedding party the daughter finds a quiet place where she tries to seduce him: " 'It's a whole new ball game,' " she tells him, "pressing close to me. 'Marrying Mom has made you my father.' She kissed me again and before returning to the festivities said, 'Don't worry, Dad, there'll be plenty of opportunities.' "[9]

What can this short story tell us that all the legal, media, and social circus surrounding the recent furore about Woody Allen's alleged sexual crimes and misdemeanours neglected? News and social networking sites were abrim with analyses and opinions, debates and reflections on the participants' credibility, motives, likelihood to commit crimes or, respectively, to lie about uncommitted crimes. From a psychoanalytic perspective, however, what is most interesting about the case is observers' feigned shock and surprise at the revelations. For psychoanalysis, truth, that is, the truth of the subject's desire, is already out there and it will come as no surprise that for Lacan the place we should be searching is not far from the place where the subject's enjoyment resides: truth, he says, is "the sister of that forbidden jouissance."[10] It is not, as Edgar Allen Poe put it, at the bottom of a well, nor hidden and supposedly hard to excavate, but on the surface of our words and practices.[11] If only we dared to read and look; a big "if" of course.

The subject herself already knows that truth, even if she doesn't know that she knows it: we can be sure, however, that she will do everything possible to prevent us, and herself, from finding it. What is the royal road to this place then? For psychoanalysis the royal road to this place is speech:

truth appears not in facts, or thoughts, or feelings, but in words. Signifiers, we can say, have all the luck. As Lacan insisted, "It is because that which is known can only be known in words that that which is unknown offers itself as having a linguistic structure."[12] As Kafka illustrates with his grim tale *In The Penal Colony*, the unconscious is above all a form of writing, exteriorizing the subject's hidden desire and inscribing it, indeed branding it on the subject's body with its wounds. The chief concern of psychoanalysis therefore is not that of judging but of reading: the unconscious leaves traces in the subject's speech just as it leaves wounds on the convict's body, making itself into a text, out there, for us to read.

How does fiction, including Woody Allen's fiction, enable us to get to the truth? Far from lying being the opposite of truth, analysts and poets have always appreciated that lies can lead us to the truth. For psychoanalysis the castration wrought by language is so central that our ability to lie is what constitutes us as subjects. Indeed for Lacan the human being becomes a subject not when she starts to speak but when she starts to lie. Beginning to lie means the subject has recognized the arbitrariness of the signifier, in other words, has worked out how to manipulate language. The subject's statement may be false, it may be a lie, but the act of enunciation can reveal the truth of the subject's desire, behind and despite the lie; as Shakespeare knew, truth, sooner or later, will hitch a ride with the lies.[13]

As Peter Serafinowicz quipped about another celebrity accused of child molesting, "Jimmy Savile was a child molester who hid behind the disguise of a child molester." The more it was advertised in fiction, the more its basis in reality could be protested and protected. Woody Allen did indeed advertise his attraction to underage girls in his films, in interviews, and, as the extract from his short story above shows, in his fiction. Of course the fact that Woody Allen may have dreamt or written or fantasized about sex with his partner's daughter does not mean that he "did it," nor that, from a legal point of view, he was guilty. What it does mean is that the legal question doesn't exhaust, let alone determine, the ambit of guilt and punishment in psychoanalysis. For psychoanalysis guilt is another matter altogether, leaving legal notions of guilt trailing miserably and pathetically behind.

As far as criminal law was concerned, evidence relating to Mr Allen's alleged crime was inconclusive. Although an arrest warrant had been issued, it was never enforced, and the civil judgment on custody addressed but of course could not determine the alleged criminal offence:

> Mr Allen's relationship with Dylan remains unresolved. The evidence suggests that it is unlikely he could be successfully prosecuted for sexual abuse. I am less certain, however, than is the Yale–New Haven team that evidence proves conclusively that there was no sexual

> abuse.... I agree that we will probably never know what happened on 4 August 1992. Credible evidence does suggest, however, that Mr Allen's behavior toward Dylan was grossly inappropriate and that measures must be taken to protect her.[14] If for the legal system the inconclusiveness of evidence is a defense, however, for psychoanalysis matters are not that simple.

The theme of guilt has been at the heart of psychoanalysis from its inception and, as we can already guess, psychoanalysis is much less forgiving than law. As Freud discusses in *Dostoevsky and Parricide* when it comes to the brothers Karamazov, "it is a matter of indifference [which brother] actually committed the crime; psychology is only concerned to know who desired it emotionally and who welcomed it when it was done."[15] In that sense, the subject who actually commits the crime serves as a redeemer for those who desired but did not dare commit it: "Dostoevsky's sympathy for the criminal is in fact boundless" continues Freud. "A criminal is to him almost a Redeemer, who has taken on himself the guilt which must have been born by others."[16]

In psychoanalysis therefore it's not the deed, not even the thought, but the desire that counts: and we cannot cheat the unconscious when it comes to our desire. If this sounds harsh then it is worth remembering that analysis is not about judging or sentencing or punishing. The analyst is not there to judge, or to understand, or to explain, or to produce right answers, or to exert power, or even to sympathize or empathize with the patient. It is about something much worse: ultimately psychoanalysis aims at the destitution of the subject and her rebirth as a new subject, a very painful and rare event.

Session 4: fathers

If there is one character in the annals of psychoanalysis who attracts the attribution of guilt like a moth to a flame, it is the figure of the father. I will focus again on an example that I have (yet) to encounter in Žižek's myriad illustrations of sinful fathers in popular culture. In HBO's series *True Detective* Rustin Cohle is relating his daughter's death at the age of two in a car accident. There is no doubt this invasion of the real will never be understood, let alone assimilated, by the subject. Only one bitter truth can be rescued from the unabating tragedy and that is that his daughter's death "spared me the sin of being a father."

What is it that Detective Rust appreciates that his partner Marty, also a father, is unable, or unwilling, to acknowledge? Žižek's work helps us see through the father's many guises and disguises, in particular of the obscene father of Freud's *Totem and Taboo* who doesn't acknowledge limits to his enjoyment in contrast to the supposedly benign figure of the father in modernity. The first is the Father of pure jouissance, the father in the Real as Lacan would have it, while the second is the father in the symbolic, the father whose prohibitions enable the subject to negotiate the dictates of the social order by setting limits to enjoyment and turning it into desire in the name of the Law.

While Detective Rust has escaped the sin of being a father, that sin has not escaped Walt White in *Breaking Bad*; the series charts Walt's transformation from the benign father helping to immerse his son in the symbolic order, to the obscene father of pure will ruling over the Eisenberg criminal empire. For Walt Junior a weak and impotent father is not only the norm but the preferred role; the shock is when his father not only breaks the rules but makes them anew. Although at times such transgressions are welcome (as when Walt disposes of the youths bullying his son in the store changing room), Walt's gradual ascent to the father of pure will terrifies his son. When Walt Junior arrives on his birthday to find his father beaten, broken and bruised after a fight with another surrogate son (Jesse Pinkman), Walt Junior is relieved: "Remembering you that way wouldn't be so bad," he tells Walt. "The bad way would be remembering you the way you've been last year. At least last night you were real."

The father Walt Junior wants to remember is the Walt White we encounter at the start of the series, that is, the symbolic father whose function is not to prohibit desire but instead to set limits to enjoyment and thus incite desire within the law. Appreciating that unlimited freedom often horrifies and paralyses the subject, Lacan insisted that the function of Law is not to forbid enjoyment but to act as a defence against unlimited enjoyment and thus give birth to desire within the law. Access to unbridled enjoyment would be unbearable for the subject so the father acts as a limit, not to freedom, but to limitless, and therefore unbearable, enjoyment.[17] "It is not the Law," Lacan explains, "that bars the subject's access to jouissance – it simply makes a barred subject out of an almost natural barrier.... The true function of the Father is fundamentally to unite (and not to oppose) a desire to the Law."[18] The subject gives up the dream of unlimited enjoyment and in return gets desire within the pleasure principle. For the pleasure principle, paradoxically, does not seek unlimited pleasure but manageable pleasure: in effect what the pleasure principle demands is that "pleasure should cease."[19]

Law (and morality as we'll see in the next session) functions as a defence, and indeed as an excuse, against the risk of unlimited enjoyment and of exercising real freedom: against the prospect of becoming, in other words, an ethical subject. As Lacan explains, Law as an external prohibition frustrating the subject's desire compensates for the fact that desire cannot be satisfied anyway; that is, law's prohibitions are reassuring, making it look as though what we cannot attain due to our inherent lack is instead prohibited. The "limit-loving classes" that Nathaniel Hawthorne refers to is not just one class but all of us.

Walt Senior performed the function of the symbolic father unthinkingly and mostly without protest for half a century (we meet him on his 50th birthday) but that performance came at a cost: as he confesses to his family, and most importantly to himself, "I never had any choices my entire life. I never had any say, about any of it." The series starts with a catalyst that transforms him into a new subject but the process is not automatic. Even after the life sentence of inoperable lung cancer has been pronounced on him, and even though he appreciates that "the only choice I have left is how to die," he soon gives in to his family's, and in particular his wife's, demands that he should undergo treatment. It is a few seasons yet before Walt attains the status of an ethical subject and becomes author of his own desire: before he can respond, to his family, to law-enforcers, and to fellow-accomplices alike, with "I'm done explaining myself."

Before Walt becomes one with his desire, before the subject of the enunciation and the subject of the statement, as linguists put it, coincide, what we witness is his transformation from the gentle father of the symbolic to the obscene father in the real. The process is gradual but we know it is complete when Skyler enquires apprehensively "What happened?" and Walt's response is a simple, "I won." From then on Walt's word is the law: "How do we know it's OK?" his supposed partners (now better described as his "assistants") Jesse and Mike ask at one point; "Because I say so" is the simple response. Even the criminals' "criminal" lawyer Saul Goodman is not allowed to get in Walt's way: "we're done when I say we're done," Walt reminds him when Saul tries to halt his advances. He has become, in the space of a year, the father embodying obscene, radical evil. Marie thinks she is joking when she tells him "You are the devil," but Hunk is more apprehensive: "I don't know who you are," he admits to his brother in law; to which Walt warns, "So tread lightly." It is at this point in the narrative, when Walt has ceased to be *in* danger, but has *become* the danger, that the audience's identification with their hero starts giving way to apprehension and horrified awe.

Session 5: excess

What is it that horrifies and at once fascinates us about Walt's metamorphosis? In Freud's mythology, the primordial crime that establishes a community of legal subjects is the son's murder of the father in *Totem and Taboo*. Once the real father is dead he returns as the *symbolic* father: the all-enjoying, all-prohibitive primal father is domesticated and transformed into the "Name of the Father," presiding over the symbolic order in the form of public rules and principles. The transformation, however, is not seamless. A surplus remains from the primal father haunting the symbolic and what remains, Žižek has been telling us, is the obscene underside: the remainder of the dead father of *Totem and Taboo* is the excess that has not been absorbed by the symbolic order.

What does Žižek mean by the "obscene excess"? For Žižek, the social law of neutral rules which deprives us of enjoyment is penetrated by an obscene dimension of private enjoyment and draws its energy from the enjoyment it deprives the subject when it acts as an agent of prohibition.[20] This obscene underside to the public law, as Žižek has been insisting, is intrinsic to the functioning of the system and indeed supports and guarantees it.[21] Modern theories of law starting with Kant's insistence on pure form did not count on the fact that the very renunciation of the Good and adherence to pure form can generate its own libidinal enjoyment. Žižek calls this the obscene surplus, referring to the all-too familiar scenario we observe of subjects deriving libidinal satisfaction from the supposedly neutral activity of performing their duty: whether it is following the rules, filling in the forms, or tidying up their files. Alenka Zupančič explains this alliance between obscene pleasure and duty: it's as if "the pathological," she writes, "takes revenge and imposes its law by planting a certain kind of pleasure on the path along which we follow the categorical imperative."[22]

Take the example of Osama bin Laden's killing by the Navy Seals in Pakistan in 2011. The Special Operations Forces Situation Report tells how "operator after operator took turns dumping magazines-worth of ammunition into Bin Laden's body." The Report acknowledges that the Navy Seals may have felt it was "morally, legally, and ethically appropriate to shoot the body a few times to ensure that he is really dead and no longer a threat," but doubt that this can justify the extent of the damage. "What happened on the Bin Laden raid is beyond excessive," author Jack Murphy writes. "The level of excess shown was not about making sure that Bin Laden was no longer a threat. The excess was pure self-indulgence."[23] At "the most conservative estimate," the report says, "more than one hundred bullets" were fired into his body *after* killing him. That excess is the surplus enjoyment derived from adhering to the strict letter of the law.

Like the abuses at Abu Ghraib, far from being isolated "bad apples" in an otherwise functioning system, such excess is part and parcel of the machinery of prohibition. Žižek goes further to suggest that one becomes a "full" member of a community not when one identifies with the community's explicit rules, but when one participates in its hidden rules and its excesses.[24] So it is not only the abuses themselves that we can imagine the perpetrators "enjoying" but the fact that they are sharing an illicit secret. While prisoners' interrogation is meant to respect the universal prohibition of torture, the practice of torture is the system's dirty little secret which also keeps the officials bound to each other. Racism in the police, sexism in colleges and in the workplace, paedophilia in the Catholic

Church are all examples of such an obscene underside to the official rhetoric, an institutional dirty secret running alongside and underneath the official line of the rule of law, equality between the sexes, and protection of children in one's care. It is to this last example that we turn to in the next session, and we find a surprising, albeit late-in-coming, coalescence between psychoanalysis and legal doctrine.

Session 6: obscenity

Common law has long recognized that an employer can be vicariously liable for torts committed by her employee in the course of her employment. While the concept has expanded over the years to include not only the employee's authorized acts but also unauthorized, and even at times illegal, acts, common law has always insisted that if the employee goes off on a "frolic of her own," indulging in behavior that has nothing to do with her duties and indeed is antithetical to them, the employer bears no responsibility for the wayward employee. What is novel about the Supreme Court's judgment in *The Catholic Child Welfare Society v The Institute of the Brothers of the Christian Schools* is its recognition, for perhaps the first time in English common law, of what Žižek has been describing and exposing as the obscene core of every institution, and of the Catholic Church in particular.

The case was a group action brought by 170 men in respect of physical and sexual abuse they were subjected to at St William's School in England from 1958 to 1992 by Brothers of the Christian School, an Institute founded in France in 1680.[25] The Institute was an unincorporated association whose members, found all over the world, were lay brothers of the Catholic Church; its rules, approved by Papal Bull in 1724, stated that the brothers "should make it their chief care to teach children, especially poor children, those things which pertain to a good and Christian life." The liability of the school's management was not at issue in the appeal: both the court of first instance and the Court of Appeal judgments found the school liable, and the plaintiffs in the group action were content to recover compensation from the first defendants and therefore played no part in the appeal proceedings.

What was novel about the case, and contested in the Supreme Court, was the ascription of liability not only to the School, but to the Institute whose members the brothers were. How did the Supreme Court find the necessary connection between the individual brothers who committed the abuse and an Institute founded in another country in another century? The Court of Appeal had dismissed the case against the Institute on the grounds that "the relationship of the individual brothers to the Institute, was insufficiently close to give rise, of itself, to vicarious liability on the part of the Institute for sexual abuse by brother teachers."[26] The Supreme

Court reversed the Court of Appeal's decision, and their reasoning recalls Žižek's long-standing insistence on the necessary connection between law's explicit command and its superegoic supplement, between adherence to the form of law and its obscene underside.

Before looking at the Supreme Court's reasoning, a reminder of its precursors in law and in literature: St Paul had already appreciated the intimate link between conscious command and its unconscious supplement: "What shall we say?" he asks in a famous passage in *The Romans*: "That the law is sin? By no means! Yet if it had not been for the law, I should not have known sin. I should not have known what it is to covet if the law had not said, 'You shall not covet.' "[27] We find the same appreciation in Dostoyevsky's discussion of "A Little Demon" in *Brothers Karamazov*; even saintly Alyosha admits that "there are moments when people love crime" to which Liza retorts enthusiastically,

> Yes! Yes! They love it, they all love it, they love it always and not just at "moments." You know, it's as if at some point they all agreed to lie about it, and have been lying about it ever since. They all say they hate what's bad but secretly they love it.[28]

Poe called this ineradicable radical, primitive, elementary, and unconquerable force to do wrong *because* we know it to be wrong the "Imp of Perversity":

> Of this spirit philosophy takes no account. Yet I am not more sure that my soul lives than I am that perverseness is one of the primitive impulses of the human heart – one of the indivisible primary faculties or sentiments, which give direction to the character of Man. Who has not, a hundred times, found himself committing a vile or a stupid action for no other reason than because he knows he should *not*? Have we not a perpetual inclination, in the teeth of our best judgment, to violate that which is *Law*, merely because we understand it to be such?[29]

Žižek discusses both St Paul and Poe to illustrate the conflict between the explicit injunction of the law and its unconscious superegoic supplement; his own discussion, however, comes in the beautiful book *The Fright of Real Tears*, an extended analysis of Krzysztof Kieślowski's *Decalogue*, a series of short films staging each of the 10 commandments with shocking results. As Žižek describes it, Kieślowski pushes each commandment to its extreme until its obscene truth becomes visible: one by one the ten commandments are revealed to undermine their own premises and demand the exact opposite from the subject.[30] So the conscious law that commands "Do not kill" becomes, in the unconscious that knows no negation, "Kill!'[31]

The same paradox is acknowledged by the Supreme Court when ascribing liability to the Institute for the acts of the brothers: "the risk of sexual abuse was recognized, as demonstrated by the prohibition on touching the children in the chapter in the Rule dealing with chastity."[32] Once again, the incidence of abuse was intimately connected with, indeed part and parcel of the brothers' duties:

> The brother teachers were placed in the school to care for the educational and religious needs of these pupils. Abusing the boys in their care was diametrically opposed to those objectives but, paradoxically, that very fact was one of the factors that provided the necessary close connection between the abuse and the relationship between the brothers and the Institute that gives rise to vicarious liability on the part of the latter.[33]

As a Canadian case had held before, and the Supreme Court confirmed here: "the necessary connection between the employer-created or enhanced risk and the wrong complained of" was established because "The Bishop provided the priest with the opportunity to abuse his power, this opportunity being incidental to the functions of a parish priest. The priest's wrongful acts were strongly related to the psychological intimacy inherent in his role as priest."[34] This is a theme and an intimate connection that Žižek revisits and underlines again in this volume.

Session 7: morality

If, as the patient learned in previous sessions, law is a defence against, rather than a prohibition of, enjoyment, then how might the subject settle her own idiosyncratic relationship with the law and accede to the status of an ethical subject? As I discussed before, that is only possible when the subject has come to terms with her own limits, as well as those of the Big Other, including Law, God, and any and all masters and mistresses she has put in His place. It means coming to terms with the limits of language and the symbolic order, with the impotence and non-existence of the Big Other (including its varied guises as judge, master, teacher), and finally with her own mortality. The hallmark of the ethical subject is one who has dissolved her existing identifications, come to terms with her own mortality and is reborn as a new subject. In José Saramago's novel *Blindness*, the real of the epidemic of blindness leads to the victims to accept that "Anyone who is going to die is already dead and does not know it, That we are going to die is something we know from the moment we are born, That's why, in some ways, it's as if we were born dead."[35] It is the same ethical understanding Walter White comes to in *Breaking Bad* and shares with a fellow cancer patient: it's not only our life, but *every* life that is a death sentence, he reminds the other patient.

The transition from being a subject acted upon to one acting, and from a subject who is spoken to one doing the speaking in Walt's case, can be summed up by his declaration to Jesse early on in the series: "I am awake." The catalyst that awakened him is the death sentence delivered to him by the diagnosis of inoperable lung cancer: the death sentence liberates him from his symbolic links to the law of his society. Like Sophocles' Antigone, he now dwells in a space between two deaths: while awaiting real death, he is already symbolically dead and has no qualms about violating the law. He has lost his fear and takes on the town bullies as well as the psychotic drug lord with the minimum of fuss. Significantly, however, again like Antigone, one law he does not violate and continues to subscribe to is the sanctity of the family: indeed his violation of other laws is subjugated to his continued reverence for the higher law of the family.

Throughout the series, like Antigone, Walter White proclaims and maintains the illusion that he is doing it all for his all-important and sacred "family." The good of the "family" is put forward as the rationale and justification for increasingly extreme measures: since the "family" is sacred, everything can be done in its name, including killing. Walt White is not the only character in the series to use the Family as his excuse: for the group's executive "executioner" Mike, again "there is no better reason than family," in his case his granddaughter Kaylee. Businessman Ted Beneke also invokes the ethics of the "family firm" and the security of his employees as the excuse for falsifying his tax accounts. Of course when Skyler offers Ted a way to pay his debts to the tax office, Ted's first move is not to protect his "family" but to buy himself a flash new car. Skyler of course can see through the pretensions of both men who invoke the family as their excuse: to Walt's "Everything I do, I do to protect this family," she replies sternly, "Someone has to protect the family from the man who protects his family."

Even worse, by convincing themselves that they are adhering to the so-called higher moral law of the sanctity of the family, subjects like Ted Beneke use the notion of duty as an excuse to absolve themselves from exercising free will and for refusing to acknowledge that they have a choice. Indeed the family becomes the phallus for these men: protecting the family translates to having the phallus, that is to *being*, a man. Forgetting, of course, not only that the phallus is a "paper tiger" which no one *has* or *is* it, but that morality, including the claim of "protecting the family," is a common excuse for compromising one's desire.[36] Žižek is fond of repeating G.K. Chesterton's aphorism that "morality is the darkest and most daring of conspiracies"; it conspires, in other words, to absolve us from the task of *ethics*. Or, as Žižek might say, in the same way that reality is for those who can't handle the real of their desire, morality is for those who can't handle the real of ethics. As we see in the next session, however, it is ethics, not impersonal legal or moral rules, that hold the promise of genuine transformation: of the subject, as well as of the system.

Session 8: ethics

While Ted Beneke and Walt White compromise their desire and lie to themselves and to everyone around them about doing everything for their all-important family, psychoanalysis reminds us that lying to oneself is the easy option; it is far easier to find comfort and assurances from existing rules and moral principles than to confront one's own limits. For Lacan and Žižek, however, it is not when the subject compromises her desire (for the good of the family or for any other excuse) but when she identifies with it, at the subject's confrontation with her own limits, that ethics can begin. Ethics, in short, is not, or not just, about one's relation to the other but about one's relation to oneself; before the subject can act ethically she must first come face to face with the Real, that is, with her own limits and her own death drive.[37] Although this step is terrifying and fraught with risks, there is no way round it: as my colleague Michael Rosen put it in a justly famous and wise book charting a family's efforts to hunt down the terrifying bear, the only way to encounter the bear is not by endlessly circling around it but by facing it head on: "We can't go over it, we can't go under it, we've got to go *through* it," the refrain reminds us.[38]

So what is the nature of an ethical act? First, as Alenka Zupančič argues, the ethical act cannot look for guarantees within ethics itself: ethics by definition cannot define what is ethical because what is ethical is what breaks and remakes the parameters of ethics.[39] The ethical act is the "excess," the *miracle* that makes the law anew. As such, the ethical act is not only illegal but *beyond* legality: it redefines the parameters of what is legal and what is illegal. It is beyond obeying or disobeying the law, as it *redefines* the law. Similarly, it does not presuppose any notion of the Good but *determines* what is Good. So an Act does not simply disobey, or break, the rules but changes the nature of the rules and redefines the game itself. It does not just tinker with the boundaries of what is forbidden and what is permitted, but changes the parameters of what is possible. As such, the Act, as Žižek says, is revolutionary in Lenin's sense: it is an act authorized not by a fictional Big Other but by the subject herself.[40] Not surprisingly, as we see in the next and last session, this is a difficult and rare act indeed.

Session 9: freedom

In her reading of Kant, Alenka Zupančič points out that the subject's experience of freedom is one that is often accompanied not with jubilation but with anxiety and guilt. Indeed guilt, she says, "is the way in which the subject participates in freedom."[41] Why should the subject feel guilt at the prospect of freedom? Not only because human beings, as Freud had discovered and as Zupančič reminds us, are more moral than they know, but also because "man is not only much more unfree than he believes but also much freer than he knows.... One could even say that, for the subject, the most difficult thing to accept is not our slavery but our freedom: that, in a certain sense, she is 'God,' that she has a choice."[42]

Since the exercise of freedom is such a frightful and fraught step, it is no wonder that Ted Beneke is not alone in using the notion of duty as an excuse to absolve himself from exercising free will and for refusing to acknowledge that he has a choice. Walt White too, and the patient in this, like most patients in many analyses, is also desperate to hold on to the illusion of a God, a master, a teacher, and persists in appealing to Him because such slavery is preferable to the experience of encountering herself. Human beings are terrified, in other words, of experiencing themselves without the support of comforting illusions and imaginary limits, that is, of being *free:* being weighed down by the responsibility of being one's own master and legislator is more oppressive than being someone's slave. Houellebecq describes many subjects when expressing his doubts about the wisdom of self-rule and the "dignity" of the free will: "According to Immanuel Kant," one of his characters says, "human dignity consists in not accepting to be subject to laws except inasmuch as one can simultaneously consider oneself a legislator. Never had such a bizarre fantasy crossed my mind. I was quite happy to delegate whatever powers I had."[43]

One of the few people who recognize the intolerable burden of freedom unsupported by consoling fantasies is the Portuguese poet Fernando Pessoa. Lacan is clear that such freedom is the price, and the prize, of an analysis and Pessoa describes it in similar terms: "Creeds, ideals, a woman, a profession – all are prisons and shackles. To be is to be free.'[44] Freedom is the capacity to detach oneself from comforting illusions, from other people and from cults: "freedom is the possibility of isolation. You are free if you can withdraw from people, not having to seek them out for the sake of money, company, love, curiosity.... If you can't live alone, you were born a slave."[45] Pessoa recognizes, moreover, that man's so-called murder of God in an effort to become "free" was neither all that successful nor all that difficult. Killing God, he suggests, was the easy, if not pathetic, step: our parents were able to cast religious belief aside, he reminds us, *because* they had the strength of belief behind them. Once that belief has been undermined, it is not only belief, but also *lack* of belief that becomes difficult. In the first stage, Pessoa explains, like Socrates, we come to doubt ourselves: "all I know is I know nothing," we can proclaim. More radically, however, in the second stage, even our doubt loses the strength to doubt: we don't even know that we know nothing.[46] In other words, even our doubt becomes doubtful. So what has died in the modern subject is not only the capacity to believe, but further the capacity *not* to believe: "For people without beliefs, even doubt is impossible, even their scepticism will lack the strength to question."[47]

What happens if and when we do accede to such radical disbelief? In a short passage in *The Book of Disquiet*, Pessoa describes the experience of letting go of his fantasies and of his fantasies letting go of him:

> All of a sudden, as if a surgical hand of destiny had operated on a long-standing blindness with immediate and sensational results, I lift my gaze from my anonymous life to the clear recognition of how I live. And I see that everything I've done, thought or been is a species of delusion or madness.... I noted with metaphysical astonishment how my most deliberate acts, my clearest ideas and most logical intentions were after all no more than congenital drunkenness, inherent madness and huge ignorance. I didn't act anything out. I was the role that got acted. At most, I was the actor's motions.[48]

Such an experience of freedom, he discovers, is shattering. It is the experience of dis-being that Lacan describes as accompanying the end of analysis, and it is not pretty. When Pessoa experiences this state he recognizes its significance and is in a hurry to chase it away; being free from the fictions making up his reality also means being lost: "The sudden awareness of my true being, weighs on me like an untold sentence to serve ... and so, I wait for the truth to go away and let me return to being fictitious and non-existent, intelligent and natural."[49] As the discourse of Law, like the discourse of God, of morality, or, nowadays, of humanity and human rights, are some of those comforting fictions, we can assume Pessoa returns, like all of us, to those fictions to avoid the much more terrible state of experiencing true freedom.

Walt White, by contrast, rises, I suggest, to the status of an ethical subject. Towards the end of the series his wife challenges him again about his feeble excuse that he is doing everything for his all-important and sacred family. This time and for the first time Walt doesn't lie: "I did it for me," he admits. "I enjoyed it. I was good at it. I was alive." Here at last Walt ceases to be what we all are most of our lives, that is a divided subject; finally there is no distance between the subject of the saying and the subject of the said. This anagnorisis is one redeeming moment back from Walt's inexorable descent into not only illegality but, for psychoanalysis, the greater crime of inauthenticity: the subject lying to himself. I suggest Walt's ethical act, in line with his goddess chemistry, is transformative: "Chemistry is the study of change," he told his students in the first lesson in the first episode: "It is growth, then decay, then transformation." In the final episode, Walt White is united with the object cause of his desire, the invention that bears his name and in that sense he has *transformed* himself. Even though he is about to die, he is also reborn as an ethical subject; as Apollo Sunshine sung it earlier in the series, "we are born when we die."[50]

Unless the patient in this as in any analysis arrives at this ethical status, a state that we can call "freedom," when the subject becomes her own, rather than the Other's cause, she will, to paraphrase Pessoa, keep arriving at new masters and new mistresses, at new gods and new goddesses, but not at a conclusion.

Notes

1 Sigmund Freud, The Ego and the Id, The Standard Edition of the Complete Psychological Works of Sigmund Freud, Volume XIX (1923–1925), ed. James Strachey (Vintage, 2001), 54.
2 Ibid., 52.
3 "'Fat chance,' he protests, the death of the father liberates us from the law. 'The good news, [that God is dead] does not liberate us from the law, far from it. If God is dead, nothing at all is permitted'." Jacques Lacan, *The Other Side of Psychoanalysis, 1968–1969, Book XVII* (W.W. Norton, 2008), 119–120.
4 Ibid., 66, and Jacques Lacan, *Encore: On Feminine Sexuality: The Limits of Love and Knowledge 1972–1973, Book XX* (W.W. Norton, 1998), 76.
5 Jacques Lacan, *Ethics of Psychoanalysis, Book VII (1959–1960)*, ed. Jacques-Alain Miller (Routledge, 1992), 4.
6 Michel Houllebecq, *Whatever* (Serpent's Tail, 1998), 135.
7 Slavoj Žižek, *Looking Awry: An Introduction to Jacques Lacan Through Popular Culture* (MIT Press, 1992), 152; see also Žižek, "The Three Fathers," in *For They Know Not What They Do: Enjoyment As A Political Factor* (Verso, 2002), 366: "The basic lesson of psychoanalysis is that the unconscious is, at its most radical, not wealth of illicit desires but the fundamental law itself."
8 Slavoj Žižek, *The Ticklish Subject* (London: Verso, 2000), 280.
9 Woody Allen, "Retribution," *The Kenyon Review*, 1(3), Summer 1980.
10 Lacan, *The Other Side of Psychoanalysis*, 61.
11 Edgar Allan Poe, *The Murders in the Rue Morgue*, in *Selected Writings* (Penguin, 1967), 204: "there is such a thing as being too profound. Truth is not always in a well. In fact, as regards the most important knowledge, I do believe she is invariably superficial."
12 Lacan, *Ethics of Psychoanalysis, Book VII*, 32.
13 "Your bait of falsehood takes this carp of truth." William Shakespeare, *Hamlet*, Polonius, Act 2, Scene 1.
14 Judge Elliott Wilk, 7 June 1993, Supreme Court, New York County.
15 Freud, "Dostoyevsky and Parricide," in *Standard Edition Volume XXI (1927–1931)*, 189.
16 Ibid., 190.
17 Jacques Lacan, "The Subversion of the Subject and the Dialectic of Desire," in *Écrits* (W.W. Norton, 2006), 700: "Castration means that jouissance must be refused in order to be attained on the inverse scale of the law of desire."
18 Ibid., 696–698.
19 Jacques Lacan, *The Ego in Freud's Theory and in the Technique of Psychoanalysis, Book II (1954–1955)* (W.W. Norton, 1991), 84.
20 Slavoj Žižek, *Looking Awry: An Introduction to Jacques Lacan Through Popular Culture* (MIT Press, 1992), 158.
21 Slavoj Žižek, *In Defense of Lost Causes* (Verso, 2008), 29.

22 Joan Copjec, ed., *Radical Evil* (Verso, 1996), 120.
23 http://sofrep.com/33599/why-us-govt-hasnt-released-photos-ubl-corpse/.
24 Žižek, *For They Know Not What They Do*, iv.
25 *The Catholic Child Welfare Society and others (Appellants) v Various Claimants (FC) and The Institute of the Brothers of the Christian Schools and others (Respondents)*, Supreme Court, 21 November 2012.
26 Para 23.
27 *Romans*, 7.7–23.
28 Fyodor Dostoevsky, *The Brothers Karamazov* (Vintage, 1992), 482.
29 "Black Cat," in Edgar Allan Poe, *Selected Writings* (Penguin, 1967), 322.
30 Slavoj Žižek, *The Fright of Real Tears: Krzysztof Kieślowski Between Theory and Post-Theory* (British Film Institute, 2001), 111–113.
31 As Freud notes in relation to dreams, "'No' seems not to exist as far as dreams are concerned." *The Interpretation of Dreams*, in *The Standard Edition Volume IV (1900)*, 318.
32 *The Catholic Child Welfare Society and others (Appellants) v Various Claimants*, Para 93.
33 Ibid., Para 92.
34 Ibid., Para 66.
35 José Saramago, *Blindness* (Vintage, 2005), 191.
36 Lacan describes the phallus variously as a "paper tiger," a "ghost" which enters when signification fails, an impostor used to cover up lack, and "the signifier for which there is no signified," *Encore*, 80.
37 Lacan, *Ethics*, 21–22: "Moral action is, in effect, grafted onto the real ... [The practice of psychoanalysis] is only a preliminary to moral action as such – the so-called action being the one through which we enter the real."
38 Michael Rosen, *We're Going On a Bear Hunt* (Walker Books, 1997).
39 At the heart of ethics, as Alenka Zupančič beautifully shows, "is not ethics but the Real": *Ethics of the Real* (Verso, 2000), 253.
40 As Žižek, following Lenin, explains the concept of the revolutionary, she is someone who "ne s'autorisé que de lui-même." Glyn Daly, *Conversations with Žižek* (Polity, 2003), 164.
41 *Ethics of The Real*, 27.
42 Ibid., 28, 97.
43 Michel Houellebecq, *Platform* (Vintage, 2003), 329–330.
44 Fernando Pessoa, *The Book of Disquiet* (Penguin, 2001), §236.
45 Ibid., §283.
46 Quoting Sanchez, ibid., §149.
47 Ibid., §263.
48 Ibid.
49 Ibid., §39.
50 Apollo Sunshine, *Shall Noise Upon* (Headless Heroes, 2008).

Chapter 2

Politics and perversion

Situating Žižek's Paul

Adam Kotsko

What is distinctive about Slavoj Žižek's interpretation of Paul is not immediately clear. This is due first of all to the context in which his primary readings of Paul take place. In *The Ticklish Subject*, Žižek discusses Paul in the course of a critique of Alain Badiou's philosophy and particularly his book *Saint Paul: The Foundation of Universalism*, but Paul in himself is not at issue for Žižek at this point, leaving his own position on Paul ambiguous. Žižek again turns to Paul in *The Puppet and the Dwarf*, specifically in the midst of a somewhat elliptical critique of Agamben's book *The Time That Remains*, but more broadly in the context of an interpretation of Actual Existing Christianity, in which Paul serves as the point of Christianity's emergence out of Judaism.[1] Beyond the necessity of discerning Žižek's implicit positive position on Paul from his critique of another reading, there is a further potential for misunderstanding. Given that Žižek is often seen (erroneously) as an advocate or popularizer of Badiou's philosophy, one might assume that Žižek's critique of Agamben amounts to a simple reassertion of Badiou's reading of Paul. This is not the case. In fact, Žižek's reading of Paul in *The Puppet and the Dwarf* is at least implicitly a critique of Badiou's, and more importantly represents a significant advance over Badiou's, particularly on the question of the law in Romans 7. In support of this contention, I will first briefly outline Badiou's interpretation of Paul's position on the law, then move on to Žižek's critique of Badiou in *The Ticklish Subject*. Finally, I will turn to the task of making sense of Žižek's discussion of Paul in the context of his argument in *The Puppet and the Dwarf*.

In *Saint Paul: The Foundation of Universalism*,[2] Badiou organizes his chapter "Paul Against the Law" around five parallel oppositions: faith vs. works, grace vs. law, spirit vs. flesh, life vs. death, and universality vs. particularity. The first member of each pair is what Paul is supposed to be advocating, and in Badiou's argument any of the terms on one side can be substituted for any of the other ones on that same side – so law is opposed to grace first of all because grace is necessarily universal. This is because grace would only be truly gratuitous if it applied to all. Yet "for Paul, the law always designates a particularity, hence a difference."[3] In fact, it is only in the context of the opposition between universality and particularity that Badiou treats *directly* of the opposition between grace and law. Law deals with the sphere of rights, of wages, of the state – grace, by contrast, "comes *without being due*" and is "communist."[4] Insofar as grace is in excess of law, it is also in excess of sin, which depends on the desire generated by the law: "The law is what gives life to desire. But in so doing, it constrains the subject so that he wants to follow only the path of death."[5] Sin colonizes the life of the subject, turning it into a living death – the goal of redemption is to reverse this, so that sin as repetitive desire "would occupy the place of the death."[6]

Sin errs not in breaking the law, but precisely in not breaking *with* the law – it gets sucked into the automatism of desire, hovering around the same particularity, tracing the limit of the law. This is a living death insofar as death *is* the limit, whereas what Badiou wants is the unlimited, the universal, the sheer gratuity that is unlimited by qualification or desert. The subject is a sinner insofar as he stands in relation to the law – because for Badiou sin denotes *the only possible relationship to law*: sin "is that of which the law, and the law alone, is capable."[7] Badiou wishes to distinguish the subject of salvation from the pre-legal subject insofar as the latter was undivided. The legal subject is constituted by the division between life and death, which is always and only brought about by the law: "The law distributes life on the side of the path of death, and death on the side of the path of life."[8] The subject's power is separated from life and given over to death, separated from spirit (thought) and given over to flesh (for which "sin" as a subjective position seems to be the name throughout this chapter). The law as power of death is the coercive force of the commandment, which renders thought powerless through its automatic application of the prescribed letter.

Sin is the subjective position of the subject of law; it can only be overcome by breaking from that subjection to become the subject of life. Thought, being initially powerless under the condition of law, "cannot *wholly* account for the brutal starting over on the path of life in the subject, which is to say, for the rediscovered conjunction between thinking and doing"[9] – some contingent event that "exceeds the order of thought," what Badiou calls a Truth-Event, is necessary precisely in order to reinstate the power of "an active thought." Paul's word for this reinstatement of the power of thought is "resurrection," which "redistributes death and life to their places, by showing that life does not necessarily occupy the place of the dead."[10] The law – the law of the particularity – is always and everywhere what killed the subject who stands in need of resurrection, because the law was the sole agency capable of putting death in the place of life and life in the place of death.

In the subsequent chapter on "Love as Universal Power," Badiou emphatically raises the stakes: "the Christ-event is essentially the abolition of the law, which was nothing but the empire of death," and so continued observation of the law is tantamount to denying the Resurrection (86). Badiou explains those statements in which Paul seems favorably disposed toward the law by proposing the existence of "a transliteral law, a law of the spirit,"[11] that is, the law of love. The subject who is saved from the law that kills "recovers the living unity of thinking and doing. This recovery turns life itself into a universal law."[12] While Badiou is implicitly arguing that Paul's statements would hold for every culture's legal code, he clearly believes that Paul's primary target is the law of his own people and excludes the possibility that Paul could, on principle, say anything positive about the Jewish law – for instance, Badiou seems to regard the inclusion of the love commandment in the Old Testament as a fortunate accident that Paul exploits for political purposes,[13] rather than taking seriously the idea that "love is the fulfillment of the law." Overall, Badiou envisions a break with the law that allows for an overcoming of the division of the subject.

In *The Ticklish Subject*,[14] Žižek undertakes a broad critique of Badiou's philosophical project as a whole. The point on which Žižek finds Badiou to be most questionable is on the question of the law in Romans 7, and as is usually the case, he poses the problem with Badiou's reading by reference to his distance from Žižek's two primary authorities: Hegel and Lacan. The distance from Hegel is found in Badiou's one-sided insistence on the Resurrection as opposed to the cross; for Žižek, Badiou "*radically dissociates Death and Resurrection:* they are not the same, they are not even dialectically interconnected.... Here Badiou is openly anti-Hegelian: there is no dialectics of Life and Death.... The Truth-Event is simply a radically New Beginning."[15]

In terms of Lacanian psychoanalysis, this can be expressed as a radical dissociation of the death drive and the Truth-Event. This is a natural connection not simply because Badiou lays out parallel oppositions between law vs. grace and death vs. life, but more significantly because of the way Badiou describes the relationship of the sinful subject to the law – all his references to a continual circling around the law, to an automatism of desire, etc., are clearly intended to evoke the Lacanian death drive.

Thus one could say that for Badiou, the problem in Romans 7 is how to escape the law and thereby the death drive. Žižek, drawing on Lacan's own reading of Romans 7 in his seminar on *The Ethics of Psychoanalysis*, argues that the situation is more complex than that – the question is not that of escaping the law as such, but rather of escaping a particular relationship to the law. Specifically, for Žižek, "the problem St Paul struggles with is how to avoid the trap of *perversion*, that is, of a Law that generates its transgression, since it needs it in order to assert itself as Law."[16] As should be clear from this quotation, "perversion" here is not meant in the usual sense of unusual sexual practices. Rather, it refers to the system of psychoanalytic diagnoses, which Lacan formalizes into a series of subject positions that are "detachable" from their metaphoric ground (a homosexual is not necessarily a psychoanalytic "pervert," a "hysteric" does not have to be a biological woman, etc.). Throughout Žižek's work, the term "perversion" has a negative valence, whereas the "hysterical" (or "feminine") position is highly valorized. The hysteric's relationship to the Other (the symbolic order, the law) is one of perpetual questioning, attempting to discover what it is that the Other wants. By contrast, the pervert believes he immediately *knows* what the Other wants and directly delivers it. Thus, the hysterical position opens up the possibility for change, whereas the pervert is essentially locked in place.

The opposition between perversion and hysteria is tied in with the problem of what Žižek calls the "obscene superego supplement." In contrast to the popular notion of the superego as something analogous to the guilty conscience, Žižek follows Lacan in arguing that the superego actually incites the subject to *enjoy*. Behind every moral prohibition there stands an incitement to violate it, precisely to reinforce its power as law – that is, to increase the law's hold over the subject's enjoyment (*jouissance*). The classic example of this effect is found in the dynamics of ascetic renunciation: the ascetic performs various rituals of renunciation in order to free himself or herself from sexual desire, but those very rituals become libidinally charged. Hence the apparent paradox that the most fastidious individuals feel most guilty isn't really a paradox at all – the feeling of guilt is a form of libidinal satisfaction, by which the law binds the subject to itself. The subject of Romans 7 is essentially a hysterical subject who has become conscious of this mechanism. The temptation, then, is to take up the perverse position by skipping over the tortured ambiguity and cutting straight to the violations that the law so obviously desires; or in the words of Paul's opponents, to say, "Let us do evil that good may result" (Romans 3:8).[17] Accordingly, Žižek can say:

> St Paul's problem is thus not the standard morbid moralistic one (how to crush transgressive impulses, how finally to purify myself of sinful urges), but its exact opposite: how can I break out of his vicious cycle of the Law and desire, of the Prohibition and its transgression, within which I can assert my living passions only in the guise of their opposite, as a morbid death drive?[18]

In other words: How can I reach the point of "a fully subjectivized, positive 'Yes!' to my Life?"[19]

Thus, while he disagrees with Badiou about the problem at issue in Romans 7, Žižek agrees with Badiou about the final goal. The question that arises is whether Lacan can get us to that point or whether Lacan stops at the analysis of the problem without giving any positive replacement. This hinges on the definition of the term that Badiou cites as the core of the problem: namely, the death drive. For Žižek, Badiou has not simply used the term "death drive" where he should have used the term "perversion," but, beyond that, Badiou has misidentified "death drive" as a problem when it is precisely the *solution*. That is, in Lacanian theory, "death drive" indicates a radically negative gesture of "unplugging" from the symbolic order. The hysteric's incessant questioning of the Other's desire, which can end in capitulation to the trap of perversion, can also lead to the acknowledgment of the "nonexistence of the Other" or of the Other's constitutive incompleteness – that is to say, the fact that *the Other doesn't know* what it wants from the subject, that there is no positive and fully consistent "content" that the subject is failing to live up to. When this position is reached, the problem of the "obscene superego supplement," grounded as it is in the question of the Other's (law's) desire, dissolves as a matter of course. Thus it appears that Lacan simply "wipes the slate clean," opening up the space for the kind of Truth-Event that Badiou (and Badiou's Paul) are calling for. Žižek argues that this negativity of the death drive is constitutive of the faithful subject and that only the Lacanian death drive can allow one to discern a genuine Truth-Event:

> Lacan is not a postmodernist cultural relativist: there definitely *is* a difference between an authentic Truth-Event and its semblance, and this difference lies in the fact that in a Truth-Event the void of the death drive, of radical negativity, a gap that momentarily suspends the Order of Being, continues to resonate.[20]

Badiou wants to deny the necessity of this gap and proceed as if the response to the Truth-Event is obvious and straightforward – this places him in fundamental opposition to Žižek's philosophical position, even if Žižek will come to find in Badiou an increasingly indispensable point of reference.

While Žižek's critique of Badiou in *The Ticklish Subject* is relatively clear, his position on Paul is ambiguous – on the one hand, he correlates Romans 7 with Lacan, but on the other hand, he does not clarify whether Paul should be understood to be calling for a Truth-Event of a Žižekian rather than a Badiouian type. Before Žižek explicitly turns to this question in *The Puppet and the Dwarf* (2003), two books intervene that appear to change the terms of debate for him, specifically by adding greater complexity on the question of law. The most important is Eric Santner's *The Psychotheology of Everyday Life: Reflections on Freud and Rosenzweig*.[21] Santner is himself highly influenced by Žižek's work, and this appears to have made Žižek understandably more open to this reading of Rosenzweig, a thinker in whom he otherwise would seem to have had little interest. While Santner is one of the most-cited figures in *The Puppet and the Dwarf* (and not only for *Psychotheology*), the insights Žižek gleans from his work that are most relevant for our purposes are the broadly Rosenzweigian idea that Judaism and Christianity need each other and the claim that the devout Jew typifies a relationship to the law that avoids perversion or "the obscene superego supplement"[22] – that is to say, in contrast to "normal" or "pagan" law, Jewish law does not generate its own inherent transgression. Santner's understanding of Judaism and of its relationship with Christianity serves as the lens through which Žižek proposes to "read Paul from within the Jewish tradition."[23]

The second book that intervenes is Agamben's *The Time That Remains*.[24] What Žižek takes from Agamben's text is the division of the law into its meaning and its force and the ways that those two aspects can be separated. In the Schmittian "state of exception," the law's force remains active, while its meaning is suspended, producing an emergency situation in which literally any act could be punished as a violation of the law. Agamben argues that in Paul's understanding of the messianic event, Schmitt is done one better: the force of the law is suspended as well, leaving the law inoperative – yet somehow fulfilled insofar as it is pure potential. Žižek seems to accept this basic schema, but he translates the difference between the meaning and the force of law (or the way law operates under the state of exception) into psychoanalytic terms as the difference between the law itself and its "obscene superego supplement." Žižek's parallel for Agamben's second suspension, the suspension of the force of law, is the "excess of mercy without proportion to what I deserve for my acts."[25] For Žižek, this excess of mercy is eventually reinscribed back into the domain of law, such that Christians eventually do end up falling into the temptation of perversion ("Let us sin more that grace may abound").

This reference forward to Christianity in its present form indicates what is distinctive about Žižek's approach to Paul – whereas both Badiou and Agamben are only interested in Paul "in himself," Žižek tries to understand Paul as the moment where we see Christianity "in its becoming," more specifically in its emergence from Judaism. Žižek begins his analysis in *The Puppet and the Dwarf* by citing certain "perverse" (in the Lacanian sense) features of Christianity: the fall of humanity and the betrayal of Judas. In both cases, God appears to be following the logic of the "obscene superego supplement," giving a positive command, but actually desiring its transgression – that is, God seems to need the fall to happen in order to allow him to save humanity, and Jesus needs Judas's "officially" despicable act of betrayal in order to carry out his sacrifice. These are not isolated incidents in Žižek's mind. In fact, the entire chapter on Chesterton, despite Žižek's obvious love of Chesterton as a writer and thinker, stands as an indictment of the perverse character of Christianity, which puts on an act of renunciation, but only to provide a safe context for the enjoyment of pagan pleasures. Thus, vis-à-vis Judas's betrayal, Žižek says that "the entire fate of Christianity, its innermost kernel, hinges on the possibility of interpreting this act in a nonperverse way."[26]

What makes this question so urgent is not a concern for Christianity as such, but rather his search for a way out of the deadlock of perversion. For Žižek, modern society as a whole is "perverse" insofar as the dominant ideological stance requires subjects to *enjoy* – but to do so in a completely non-dangerous way. Similarly, the project of revolutionary communism ends in the disaster of Stalinism, which serves for Žižek as *the* privileged example of perversion. Eastern religions, harshly critiqued in the first chapter of *The Puppet and the Dwarf*, seem to Žižek only to reinforce the logic of perversion. Thus while one would be tempted to understand the subtitle "The Perverse Core of Christianity" as referring to the "subversive" element that Žižek is hoping to retrieve, the "perverse core" is instead precisely what needs to be jettisoned if one is to reactivate the revolutionary potential of Christianity.

This revolutionary potential is encapsulated in the founding gesture of St. Paul – a gesture that Žižek argues is only possible within the Jewish context. As noted above, Žižek gets from Santner the idea that the Jewish law already operates without the obscene superego supplement, but he specifies this idea in terms of a rereading of the Book of Job. For Žižek, God's appearance to Job at the end of that book is, for all God's boasting, a tacit confession of God's own impotence. Job's silence, then, has to be reinterpreted: "he remained silent neither because he was crushed by God's overwhelming presence, nor because he wanted thereby to indicate his continuous resistance ..., but because, in a gesture of solidarity, he perceived the divine impotence."[27] The Jewish subject, then, always lives in the wake of the acknowledgment of the non-existence of the Other (i.e., the powerlessness of God). The Jewish community's relationship to the law is thus free of the superego supplement; instead of being stuck in the cycle of the prohibition generating the transgression, they follow God's law in order to hide God's powerlessness: "The paradox of Judaism is that it maintains fidelity to the founding violent Event [of confronting the impotence of God] precisely by *not* confessing, symbolizing it: this "repressed" status of the Event is what gives Judaism its unprecedented vitality."[28] At the same time, despite the "unplugged" character of the Jewish experience of law, precisely this shared, disavowed secret binds the Jewish nation together in a form of "pagan love" directed toward one's in-group.[29]

Based on this reading of Job, Žižek develops what amounts to an entire Christology, which he then appears to tacitly attribute to Paul. Where Job, symbolizing here the Jewish community as a whole, expresses his solidarity with the divine impotence by remaining silent about it, Christ as God-become-man directly reveals the divine impotence through his death on the cross and particularly in his cry of dereliction, meaning that Christianity is essentially "the religion of atheism."[30] For this reason, Žižek argues (against Badiou) that cross and resurrection are dialectically identical, insofar as Christ's death immediately is the foundation for the new community, which Žižek calls the "Holy Spirit." This is because the public disclosure of what Judaism kept secret makes the Jewish "unplugged" stance toward the law available to everyone, resulting in a new, universal form of love to go along with the Jews' "new" (from the pagan perspective) experience of law. This combination is illustrated by Paul's logic of the "as if not" in 1 Corinthians 7, in which the subject does not simply maintain a vague distance toward symbolic obligations – which for Žižek is how the symbolic order *normally* works – but enacts "the disavowal of the symbolic realm itself: I use symbolic obligations, but I am not performatively *bound* by them."[31] That is to say, I am freed from the logic of the "obscene superego supplement" that binds me to the law through enjoyment. Referring to Agamben's idea of the messianic law as a further state of emergency above and beyond the "normal" Schmittian state of exception, Žižek argues that

> what the Pauline emergency suspends is not so much the explicit Law regulating our daily life, but, precisely, its obscene unwritten underside: when, in his series of *as if* prescriptions, Paul basically says: "obey the law as if you are not obeying them," this means precisely that *we should suspend the obscene libidinal investment in the Law, the investment on account of which the Law generates/solicits its own transgression.*[32]

Thus Paul radicalizes the Jewish tradition by "betraying" it – that is, revealing its secret through his reference to the cross – and universalizing it precisely by forming *particular* communities founded in this new experience of law and love.

Unfortunately, Žižek's point here is obscured by what seems to me to be a surface-level error. It is clear, on the one hand, that Žižek views the law confronted in Romans 7 as being the normal or "pagan" law that generates its own transgression through the obscene superego supplement. Strangely, Žižek simultaneously claims that the Jewish law "is already a law deprived of its superego supplement, not relying on any obscene support," i.e., the Jewish stance toward the law is fundamentally what Paul is after, yet he also follows the long-standing tradition of claiming that, nonetheless, the Jewish law is "the main target of Paul's critique."[33] The problem with this contradiction is obvious: it presupposes that Žižek understands the Jewish law better than Paul does. If asked, Žižek (it seems to me) would almost certainly give up the idea that Paul's main target is the Jewish law, simply because he hangs no further interpretative weight on it whatsoever. In these terms, he could easily argue that later Christian interpreters got Paul wrong on this point precisely because they reject the anxiety of rootlessness that is introduced by "unplugging" pagans and giving them the Jewish "rootless" stance toward the law.[34] In fact, Žižek effectively argues precisely that: for him, Christianity needs the "reference to the Jewish Law" because only that reference can "sustain the specific Christian notion of Love that needs a distance, that thrives on differences, that has nothing to do with any kind of erasure of borders and immersion in Oneness."[35] It is the rejection of the Jewish stance toward law and the reintroduction of the pagan experience of law that forms the "perverse core" of Actual Existing Christianity.

That being said, one can state the inner logic of Žižek's reading of Paul in a fairly straightforward schematic form. Judaism represents an "unplugged" stance toward the law that Žižek valorizes, but it is combined with a "pagan" form of love that is bound to one's own in-group. Actual Existing Christianity represents a universal love that cuts across differences, but it is combined with a "pagan" form of law that generates its own transgression through the obscene superego supplement. What the letters of Paul present to us is a fragile moment of emergence, where pagans are inducted directly into the Jewish "unplugged" stance toward the law, not through adherence to the positive law of the Jewish community, but rather through participation in the love beyond the law. Yet tragically, it is precisely that "love beyond the law" that necessarily collapses back into the obscene superego supplement, generating a return to the perverse pagan stance toward law.

To my mind, this reading has much to recommend it over Badiou's. First and foremost, it takes seriously Paul's self-understanding as apostle to the Gentiles, but precisely *from the Jews*, whereas for Badiou Paul's reference to Judaism is a superficial and instrumental one. Second, although on the surface he follows the broad consensus of biblical scholars in supposing that Paul only ever uses the term "law" to refer to the Torah,[36] the inner logic of his argument points toward the fact that this univocality of the term "law" cannot possibly be sustained in light of what Paul is actually saying in Romans 7 – that is, Paul must be referring to pagan law and describing the plight of a pagan subject. Although he arrives at this position "dishonestly," through an anachronistic application of Santner's psychoanalytic reading of Rosenzweig, without very much in the way of detailed readings of particular texts, and in the midst of some logical inconsistencies and general *faux pas*, it seems to me that at a very basic level, Žižek's fragmentary argument gets Paul *right* and opens up promising paths for future work on Paul, Judaism, and Christianity – some of which Žižek himself actually follows up on in later works, most notably *The Parallax View*. Beyond that, Žižek's approach of reading Paul in relation to later Christianity has the benefit of insisting that every philosophical interpretation of Paul and of Christianity must necessarily also be an interpretation of Judaism, not as a dispensable historical preface, but as that which Christianity constitutively betrays.

Notes

1 Paul also makes a few appearances in *The Parallax View* (Cambridge: MIT Press, 2006), but these references do not represent a qualitative development beyond the position arrived at in *The Puppet and the Dwarf.* For a summary and brief analysis of these references, see Adam Kotsko, "Žižek's Flawed 'Magnum Opus'" (Review of Slavoj Žižek, *The Parallax View*), *Journal for Cultural and Religious Theory*, 8(1) (2006): 111–12, www.jcrt.org/archives/08.1/kotsko.pdf.
2 Alain Badiou, *St. Paul: The Foundation of Universalism*, trans. Ray Brassier (Stanford: Stanford University Press, 2003).
3 Ibid., 76.
4 Ibid., 77.
5 Ibid., 79.
6 Ibid., 81.
7 Ibid., 83.
8 Ibid., 82.
9 Ibid., 84.
10 Ibid., 85.
11 Ibid., 87.
12 Ibid., 88.
13 Ibid., 89.
14 Slavoj Žižek, "The Politics of Truth, or, Alain Badiou as a Reader of St. Paul," in *The Ticklish Subject: The Absent Core of Political Ontology* (New York: Verso, 1999). I commend his chapter on Badiou to anyone who is looking for a clear and straightforward introduction to the latter's thought that does not require knowledge of set theory.
15 Ibid., 146.
16 Ibid., 148.
17 I would remark that the very fact that Paul's opponents apparently draw this conclusion from Paul's teaching indicates that Žižek is correct in citing it as a "temptation" for the Pauline subject.
18 Ibid., 149. Here he is summarizing Badiou's argument and thus uses the term "death drive" in Badiou's sense.
19 Ibid., 150.
20 Ibid., 162–3.
21 Eric Santner, *The Psychotheology of Everyday Life: Reflections on Freud and Rosenzweig* (Chicago: University of Chicago Press, 2001).
22 This contention is repeated in *The Parallax View*, 427, note 55.
23 Slavoj Žižek, *The Puppet and the Dwarf: The Perverse Core of Christianity* (Cambridge: MIT Press, 2003), 10.
24 Giorgio Agamben, *The Time That Remains: A Commentary On The Letter To The Romans*, trans. Patricia Dailey (Stanford: Stanford University Press, 2005). Due to the vagaries of academic publishing, the English translation of this work was delayed until 2005, meaning that Žižek was once again able to introduce English-speaking readers to a major European thinker's book on Paul significantly before it was available in English, as he did with Badiou.

Žižek's reading of Agamben does not appear to have been as careful as his reading of Badiou, producing at least two major errors: namely the claims that Agamben is trying to argue that "Benjamin 'repeats' Paul" and that he (Žižek) is the first one to ask why both Paul and Benjamin are readable in the current political situation (*Puppet and the Dwarf*, 108). In point of fact, the latter is precisely Agamben's argument, and Agamben does not go beyond arguing that Benjamin includes several distinctly Pauline echoes in his Theses on the

Philosophy of History. While this mistake does not, in my view, affect the overall structure of Žižek's argument, it still seems worth pointing out.

25 Žižek, *Puppet and the Dwarf*, 110.
26 Ibid., 16.
27 Ibid., 126.
28 Ibid., 128.
29 Ibid., 120.
30 Ibid., 171. For this reason, one could argue that Žižek is essentially a "death of God" theologian.
31 Ibid., 112.
32 Ibid., 113.
33 Ibid., 113.
34 Ibid., 119.
35 Ibid., 120.
36 See, for instance, Stanley Stowers, *A Re-Reading of Romans: Justice, Jews, and Gentiles* (New Haven: Yale, 1994).

Chapter 3

Changing the subject

Rights, revolution, and capitalist discourse

Molly Anne Rothenberg

In the third part of *The Parallax View* (hereafter TPV), Slavoj Žižek wonders whether we can have a "*sociopolitical transformation that would entail the restructuring of the entire field of the relations between the public law and its obscene supplement*" (TPV 308, italics in original). While one might expect a theorist of revolutionary politics to concern himself with the Law – its range of application, its enforceability, its capacity to sustain justice, the mechanisms of power it enables, and so on – it is perhaps surprising to those unfamiliar with his work that Žižek focuses on the question of the Law's *structure*. He wonders whether a revolutionary legal order will necessarily reproduce the same problems as the old order on account of some inherent and irremediable feature of Law itself that functions as a permanent obstacle to justice.

Žižek's question arises from his engagement with Jacques Lacan's four discourses (social bonds), elaborated in *Seminar XVII, The Other Side of Psychoanalysis*. Anyone familiar with his work knows that Žižek has been tracing the effects of the weakening of the Master's discourse in numerous essays on the vitiation of symbolic efficiency, the crisis of symbolic investiture, and the society of enjoyment inaugurated by capitalism. Žižek is not an anarchist; he never proposes abandoning the Law, even though he is well aware that the Law is inconsistent, has an unsavory side, and produces some pernicious effects. He agrees with Lacan that the inanition of the Master's discourse is adversely affecting the subject of the unconscious. His focus on the retreat of the Master's discourse under capitalism has led some readers to argue that Žižek is an authoritarian: it can sometimes be unclear whether Žižek is attacking the Master's discourse (a time-honored revolutionary strategy) or lamenting its demise.[1]

I argue that this kind of confusion stems from Žižek's continued use of the four discourses as his analytical tool when in fact he is describing the structure of social bonds that are better captured by a different set of discourses altogether.[2] We can recall that Lacan initially proposed that Capitalist discourse was structured like University discourse. Žižek follows this insight, which means that he expresses his ideas in terms of the four mathemes in the discourse universe of the Master. However, in the Milan address, *Television*, and elsewhere in his final seminars, Lacan postulates a *mutation* in the Master's discourse that he designates as Capitalist discourse. By taking this mutation as setting the order of the terms for its transformations, an entirely new discourse universe opens up – the discourse universe of the Capitalist.[3] Not only do the mathemes of Capitalist discourse and its transformations serve Žižek's purposes better, but they also clarify his view of the significance of rights for revolutionary politics.

The divided law in the Master's discourse universe

I assume that readers are familiar with Lacan's four discourses, but a review of some germane features will be useful for understanding the nature of the Law in Žižek's revolutionary thought. Lacan begins with the Master's discourse because it represents the process of subjectification, by means of the falling of the subject under the signifier, and its aftermath, the structure of the unconscious. The subject so produced is a *split* subject, divided from itself. All of the discourses, the elements of which appear in a fixed order set by the Master's discourse, represent, at one level, unconscious internal relations to the Other, Imaginary relations on which social bonds are formed and which exist to deny the underlying split (inconsistency, self-division, non-self-coincidence) of the subject – and the Law.

The subject's relation to the Law as a matter of its own divided psychic constitution can be explained as follows. The subject experiences the signifier that brings it into being as prohibiting its return to its undivided state of pure enjoyment or *jouissance*. The subject, to remediate that division, fantasizes that it could actually return to its prior (mythological) state of wholeness and still remain a subject. Of course, no such return is possible: the subject did not and could not exist in that state. Nothing is *prohibiting* the subject from accessing enjoyment directly, because such access is in fact impossible. The fantasy that there is a Law prohibiting enjoyment also involves the correlative fantasy of the subject's wholeness and autonomy, a masterful ego that could overcome this prohibition. That is, the subject fantasies a strong prohibiting Law in order to avoid realizing the impossibility of enjoyment, but at the same time this fantasy involves a view of the Law as somehow providing an entrypoint to enjoyment, an entry it bars from the subject but which nonetheless inheres in the Law and which an autonomous masterful ego should be able, so the fantasy goes, to access.

This Law, then, is a product: it comes into being in a "knot" simultaneously with the subject and with the fantasy of full enjoyment, deriving from the initial activity of the signifier. As such, the Law is founded *extra-legally*. There is always an aspect of the Law that is non-Law, what the subject imagines is full enjoyment. The unfounded condition of the Law, its internal non-self-coincidence, persists as a feature of the public Law, as debates about constituent power and popular sovereignty attest.

There is also a law that governs the subject's unconscious, the law of the death drive, which operates at the most fundamental level. The subject tries to return to its pre-subjectivated state – a state which would spell the death of the subject but which the subject nonetheless would like to enter (fantasying that it could still remain a subject) as much as it would like to avoid, since that state spells its death. In order to keep the subject alive while it is pushing toward death, the death drive has a built-in brake: it affords the subject some partial access to enjoyment (surplus enjoyment), that is, sufficient enjoyment through some form of sublimation so that the subject will seek the activities leading to that partial enjoyment instead of pressing ever onward to its own death. The death drive, in other words, has a way to keep the subject alive by means of its search for death.[4] So even at this most fundamental, non-fantasmatic level of the subject's "exsistence," the Law, like the subject, is divided.

This division cannot be made whole: the fantasies designed to disguise its split will always invoke the division somehow. In the case of the Law as superego, self-division appears in the form of a Law that is simultaneously prohibiting the subject and enjoining the subject to transgress the Law in order to access enjoyment. The subject experiences the Law as saying something like "If you enjoy, you will be punished. The only way to enjoy is to do your duty. Of course, if you enjoy doing your duty, you will be punished." This contradictory imperative reproduces the dynamics of the death drive. It keeps the subject attached to the Law while providing some surplus enjoyment for a subject that is necessarily both law-abiding and transgressive.

Because the evidence that it is irremediably divided from itself haunts the subject, a defense is mounted in the form of an ego fantasied to be autonomous, omnipotent, unconditioned. The ego develops *as though* it were an undivided subject by identifying with a particular signifier (S1), the unary trait. In this way, the Symbolic world of signification into which the subject has been precipitated by the signifier is made to seem stable: although actual language depends upon the loose and arbitrary linkage of signifier to signified, the unary trait functions to make it seem as though signifiers line up with signifieds, to halt the sliding of signifiers. When the subject identifies with S1 as the (fantasied) force stabilizing the Symbolic "once and for all," it has a tremendous stake in maintaining its connection to that force which serves as the foundation for the mirage of the masterful ego, a mirage that could disappear since it is merely a veneer covering the split in the subject.

S1, however, has no power on its own: it is just a contingent signifier – like the timbre of the father's voice or a characteristic paternal gesture – taken from the sea of signifiers, S2, and as such always in danger of sinking back into that sea. What transforms that contingent signifier into the quilting S1 (unary trait) is the subject's investment in it: the subject invests S1 with authority, although the subject imagines and must imagine that this power comes from outside the subject. The subject's identification with the unary trait constitutes that trait as the basis of the superego. In this way, the subject aligns itself with the force that appears to guarantee the ego's autonomy and wholeness, as though that force dictates the conditions under which the ego can survive. As such, S1 takes on the character of a Law to which the subject attaches via the paradoxical contingent/universal unary trait. The very ferocity with which people cling to their choice of relationship to the Law, be it sociopathy or neurosis, is a marker of the irremediably non-all nature of that relationship which, after all, founds the subject *qua* subject. In other words, Lacan's account explains how the Law's paradoxical structure attaches the subject to the Law at the point each is self-divided.

Every one of the four discourses contains this irremediable self-division as its motor (Figure 1). The top level of each matheme can be understood as a command to create a wholeness out of that division represented by the bar between the top left and bottom left elements. This command operates at the level of the Imaginary, since it is in actuality impossible. As a result of this impossibility, the discourse produces a by-product, the element at the bottom right, which registers as a loss to the system, what the system does not have, even though this "missing" element has actual effects. This element can be regarded as a scapegoat, the reason why the system fails to cohere. So long as the discourse operates at the level of the Imaginary, this element will seem prohibited, which is to say accessible in principle as a remedy for the split, rather than (as it is in actuality) necessarily non-accessible. It is the function of the discourse to account for this inaccessibility.

Positions and relations of the discursive elements

agent → (impossible demand)	Other
truth ←// (impotent)	product/loss

(Figure 1)

The Master's discourse is the matheme of the subject's self-division, production of the ego and superego, and relationship among the Law, enjoyment, and subject. However, this discourse presents these divisions Imaginarily, as flaws that can be overcome by a (fantasied) access to enjoyment (*a*). Because enjoyment is impossible, except as surplus enjoyment, *a* represents both the fantasied whole enjoyment and the actual surplus enjoyment. No matter how much surplus enjoyment is created, however, it is never enjoyment per se, and it never heals the division in the subject. At the same time, the bottom of the structure delineates the separation between the two elements, their insurmountable disconnection. The subject ex-sists as non-self-coincident and enjoyment ex-sists as surplus: the two do not make a whole. They have a relation of *non-relation.*

Insofar as the Master's discourse represents the *external* Law for the subject, we can read it in the following way: as self-divided, the subject necessarily escapes total superintendence of the Law (Figure 2). The Law (S1 as superego) does not "know" that the subject's division is the flaw that corresponds to *its own* divided character: it does not know that it is castrated. Instead, the Law "imagines" that it could superintend the whole field if some unspecified flaw were eliminated. It commands S2, the universe of signifiers or sets of regulations, to eradicate this flaw, to cover all cases, but because it is impossible to eradicate the subject (site of the Law's own fundamental division) from the Symbolic, which is after all the register within which the Law operates, this command can never succeed. The by-product of the command's impossibility is object *a*, both the unspecified something that the Law imagines could be resolved and the surplus enjoyment that attends the operation of the Law, the extra-legal dimension of its founding. The powerlessness of this element to undo the division in the subject (that is, from the Law's point of view, to make the subject fall wholly under its sway) is registered in the bottom of the matheme. This impotence corresponds precisely with the failure of the subject to completely obey the Law's injunctions as a matter of structural necessity, thereby providing the motor for the entire discourse. It also provides the impetus for the transformation to another discourse.

Master's Discourse

<u>Master Signifier (S1)</u>	→	<u>knowledge (S2)</u>
Subject (*$*)	←//	enjoyment (*a*)

(Figure 2)

The inability of any given discourse to produce the wholeness at which it aims creates the sense that another discourse might do a better job: in fact, any of the four discourses can only address one aspect of the fundamental antagonism of the entire structure. For example, the University discourse pushes S1 under the bar in an effort to indemnify the Law against the Hysteric's complaint that the Law is internally inconsistent, that it is castrated and so fails to live up to an ideal of an all-encompassing Law, a demand that produces nothing but more and more rules and regulations (Figure 3).

University discourse

<u>S2</u>	→	<u>*a*</u>
S1	←//	*$*

Hysteric's discourse

<u>*$*</u>	→	<u>S1</u>
a	←//	S2

(Figure 3)

At the same time, S1 under the bar distances the subject from the Law of its own founding, its constitutive split experienced as prohibition. S2 "covers" for the Law's castration. Regarded in this way, the purpose of the Analyst's discourse is not to heal the subject's self-division but to help the subject discover the unique ways in which it organizes its psyche fantasmatically in relation to the Law and so neutralize the pathological superegoic injunction to obey/transgress the Law (Figure 4). Although it cannot heal the subject's self-division, it permits the subject to re-locate the source of the Law within itself.

Analyst's Discourse

$$\begin{array}{ccc} \underline{a} & \rightarrow & \underline{\$} \\ S2 & \leftarrow // & S1 \end{array}$$

(Figure 4)

For this reason, the Analyst's discourse seems to offer Žižek the tool he needs for changing the relationship of the subject to the Law. As we will see, this tool is insufficient, even though the subject, as he surmises, does indeed have to change.

Žižek's predicament

Žižek repeatedly argues that the problem with the Law is that it has an *obscene* underside, equivalent to the superego that demands/punishes transgression as a condition of obedience. In other words, from his perspective, this extra-legal dimension of the Law has to be acknowledged and addressed rather than swept under the rug. So long as we understand this obscenity to reside in the superego, it is possible to imagine that analysis would neutralize it, bringing about a new relationship to the Law.

Although, as we will see, Žižek promotes the Analyst's discourse as a remedy for the unsatisfactory dodges of the other three discourses, it does seem strange to think that changing an individual analysand's relationship to its internalized Law will affect the domain of the *public* Law. Yet perhaps it is even stranger that Žižek offers the Law as the target of revolutionary activity in the first place, given that he devotes so much attention to the predations of capitalism. In what way does attacking the Law's obscene, superegoic underside lead to an emancipatory politics against capitalism? These efforts to collectivize the Analyst's discourse or to make it apply to the public Law might be useful so long as we are living in a discourse universe structured by the Master. But what if the Master's discourse no longer holds sway?

In *Seminar XVII: The Other Side of Psychoanalysis*, Lacan suggests that the Master's discourse has largely disappeared, although, at that time, he seemed unclear about whether it had been eclipsed by a capitalist version of University discourse or whether a new discourse had emerged (Lacan 2007, 24). Then in his address at the University of Milan, he introduces an entirely new discourse, the discourse of the Capitalist, with a mutation in the order of the elements (as I will discuss in the next section) that he argues has *replaced* the discourse of the Master (Lacan 1972, 6, 10–11).

This new discourse particularly alarms Lacan because he believes that it attacks the very subject of the unconscious. Žižek takes up this suggestion when he asks "what if, in the constellation in which the Unconscious itself, in its strict Freudian sense, is disappearing?" (TPV 307). We hear echoes here of other Žižekian analyses concerning the weakening of the Master's discourse, the vitiation of symbolic efficiency, the crisis of investiture, the disappearance of totalizing politics and the politics of protest, among other signs of capitalism's incursions. The entire last section of *The Parallax View* is a discussion that the problem of a collapsing Master's discourse poses for revolutionary thought. He asks

> Should we then … take seriously (not merely as cynical wisdom) Lacan's claim that the discourse of the Analyst prepares the way for a new Master, and heroically assume the need to pass from the negative gesture of "traversing the fantasy" to the formation of a New Order, including a new Master and its obscene superego underside? Was Lacan himself, in his very last seminars, not pointing in this direction with his theme "toward a new signifier/ *vers un signficant nouveau*"? The question remains: how, *structurally*, does this new Master differ from the previous, overthrown one (and its new fantasmatic support from the old one)?
>
> (TPV 307)

We can note that Žižek assumes throughout this passage that we are in the Master's discourse, but to make his argument work, he no longer respects the terms of the four discourses: for example, he says that attacking the Master using the Analyst's discourse will lead to a new Master, when in fact Lacan attributes this result to the Hysteric's discourse.

Žižek himself points out that if capitalism is the reason for the weakening of the Master's discourse, then attacking the Law will not achieve revolutionary results, a predicament he ascribes to Badiou:

> After defining the task of emancipatory politics as undermining the state of representation from the standpoint of its constitutive excess … and after taking note of how such a permanent undermining of every state is already the central feature of capitalist dynamics (which is why capitalism is properly "worldless"), he suddenly discovers the new task of forming a new world, of proposing signifiers that would allow a new Naming of the situation.
>
> (TPV 308)

Once we are in the orbit of Capitalist discourse, our first task, it seems, is to re-enter the Master's discourse, not subvert it.

We can see other signs that Žižek finds himself in Badiou's situation. For example, he describes the efficacy of the Analyst's discourse as follows:

> the analyst's discourse stands for the emergence of revolutionary–emancipatory subjectivity that resolves the split of university and hysteria. In it, the revolutionary agent – *a* – addresses the subject from the position of knowledge that occupies the place of truth (i.e., which intervenes at the "symptomal torsion" of the subject's constellation), and the goal is to isolate, get rid of, the master signifier that structured the subject's (ideologico-political) unconscious.
>
> (Žižek "Four Discourses," unpaginated)

As Levi Bryant points out, however, this description is not consistent with the Analyst's discourse (Bryant 36). In that discourse, the Master-Signifier is not excluded but produced. Neither does the analyst speak from the position of knowledge: the analyst's *lack* of knowledge situates her as the subject-supposed-to-know for the analysand; the knowledge in this discourse resides only within the analysand, albeit in an unconscious way. Because Žižek never explicitly explores the possibility that we have shifted from the discourse universe of the Master to an entirely new discourse universe, he finds himself applying the Analyst's discourse even when he is trying to cope with the effects of capitalism.[5]

But Lacan's conjecture that we are no longer in the Master's discourse universe means that this particular meditation may be irrelevant. The question then would become, as Žižek indicates in Badiou's case, how could an attack on the Law/Master's discourse have any revolutionary impact if the discourse universe of the Master has collapsed? Must we strengthen the Master's discourse before we can deal with capitalism in a revolutionary way, or is there some other resource available? If the aim of revolution is to overthrow the Master, then the shift into the discourse universe of the Capitalist that has displaced the Master should have led to an emancipated society. But obviously, capitalism's effects are insupportable: radical politics must target capitalism. It is imperative, then, that we look at the possibilities for revolutionary politics that might inhere in the discourse universe of the Capitalist.

Law in the discourse universe of the Capitalist

Even though he does not make use of the mutated discourse of Capitalism, Žižek has described the operation of the Law under capitalist discourse as a transformation of the subject's relationship to its superego, a shift from the Master's superegoic prohibition of enjoyment to the superego command to enjoy. Of course, for subjects, full enjoyment is impossible:

that is the condition of their subjectivization. In the Master's discourse this impossibility is re-figured as prohibition to enable an Imaginary psychic organization, while in Capitalist discourse, enjoyment is no longer prohibited but fantasied to be directly accessible. When the subject necessarily fails to enjoy, this discourse attributes that failure to the subject.[6] It is as if the superego were saying "Go ahead and enjoy! Nothing is stopping you! If you don't enjoy, you have only yourself to blame." This discourse, then, attaches the subject to the superego by means of a failure, and it offers the subject a way to succeed by participating in the system as (alienated) labor and the purchase of commodities. If you fail to enjoy, it is because you have not worked hard enough, consumed enough, produced yourself as a commodity. As in the Master's discourse, the subject aims for enjoyment, but here, as each failure re-commits the subject to the search for enjoyment, the subject generates a surplus value elsewhere and for someone else.

The command to enjoy treats the barrier to enjoyment (the brake inherent to the death drive) as though it does not exist. This is tantamount to saying that the Law ceases to function as prohibition, even though that prohibition brings the subject its only freedom and its only access to enjoyment. Capitalist discourse's command to enjoy is a command to be free, to choose one's enjoyment for oneself, a command that cannot be fulfilled but which transforms the subject into the source of capitalism's surplus value. In Capitalism, no one is free but everyone imagines that freedom, in the form of full enjoyment, is readily to hand, if only we enslave ourselves.

One consequence is that certain psychodynamics predominate that foster aggression. Why? In the society of enjoyment everyone seems to be enjoying except the subject. We cannot get away from the spectacle of other people enjoying, intruding on our own enjoyment. Not only are others enjoying when I am not, but these others seem to stand in the way of my enjoyment. Experiencing one's own inability to enjoy becomes intolerable, since it marks the subject as lesser than others, as defective – *castrated* – in some way. In order to defend against castration, the Imaginary ego inflates its sense of omnipotence. In effect, the subject of the unconscious is parasitized by primitive narcissistic ego functions, and because the Law no longer embodies the brake inherent to the death drive, the system can then harness the death drive directly as its engine. This is what Lacan means when he indicates that Capitalist discourse works to change the subject of the unconscious.

We also lose the public space secured by the Law of prohibition. Encounters with others become occasions for proving one's noncastration: aggressive contestations become the norm and society takes on an increasingly uncivil, even violent, character. The narcissistic ego no longer experiences the social *order*, the Law, as standing in the way of its enjoyment. Rather, it experiences others more or less like itself as encroaching on its enjoyment. When others stand in one's way without the mediation of the "transcendental," disinterested Other, the public sphere collapses. (The fantasy of) the transcendence of the Law – its universal applicability, its disinterested status – is necessary for civil society. With the loss of that illusion, the glue holding civil society together dissipates. The society of enjoyment tends toward what Hobbes called the state of nature, aggressive encounters among narcissistically invested individuals who regard each other as threats and obstacles to their "property." In the psychoanalytic account, we don't *start* in a state of nature, we enter it via Capitalist discourse.

Žižek takes seriously that we are living in a society of enjoyment, as his analyses of politics and films demonstrate. But because he regards the predations of capitalism from within the discourse universe of the Master, he never closes the gap between a transformed individual subjectivity and a collectivized revolutionary subject. Nor does he resolve the question as to whether the Law is the problem or whether the Law's inanition is the problem. However, if we turn to the mutation Lacan posits as Capitalist discourse, it is possible to find a path to resolution.

In Capitalist discourse, the terms on the left side of the Master's discourse are flipped, so that S1 falls under the bar with the split subject on top. If this new discourse sets a new order of the elements within the matheme, an entire discourse universe opens up. Capitalist discourse positions the split subject as the "agent" of Capital (S1): the subject commands S2 to provide its direct access to enjoyment, but because this is impossible, enjoyment is produced as a remainder that cannot be accessed by the subject (Figure 5).

Capitalist Discourse

$$\begin{array}{lll} \underline{\$} & \rightarrow & \underline{S2} \\ S1 & \leftarrow // & a \end{array}$$

(Figure 5)

This remainder is re-configured as accumulable surplus-value by the system, which is good from the point of view of the system but generates perpetual irritation for the subject, who is severed from the little bit of surplus enjoyment it used to access through the prohibiting Law. Now, the superego of a subject under capitalism treats that irritation as "evidence" that the subject is failing to enjoy, which galvanizes the subject to ever greater efforts to acquire enjoyment via consumption, for example, and ever more alienation from enjoyment. This discourse encourages the subject to believe that it is in control (position of the agent), when in fact capital pulls the strings behind the scenes (its invisible hand). The subject addresses itself to S2, knowledge (economics, for example), and commodities that are supposed to supplement its agency and provide it with the enjoyment of total control. That fantasy, as the matheme demonstrates, hooks the subject to the system so that it generates enjoyment/surplus value (*a*) for the benefit of the system's continued operation.

How does it stand with the Law in this discourse? Despite its flaws, the discourse universe of the Master is organized as a Law that, while laced with the Imaginary, has positive functions: sustaining a civil society, serving as a point of universal identification (as in citizenship), and supporting the subject of the unconscious in its symbolic identity. But in Capitalist discourse, the Law loses its Imaginary consistency, and so loses its claims to universality: only temporarily stabilized signifiers (S2) are available. Laws proposed on behalf of capitalism will not have even the appearance of universality (that is why Žižek continues to point out the counterproductive nature of multiculturalist politics).

The flaw in capitalist discourse that must be papered over is the waste generated by the system, *object a*, which, of course, is a function of the subject's self-division. Capitalist discourse uses the split in the subject to squeeze out a surplus, aiming for increasing efficiency, the elimination of waste. But since the subject cannot be completely harmonized with the system, since the subject as split always escapes in some way, more and more knowledge has to be produced or put to work to *condition* the subject, to make it more productive and less wasteful. These efforts belong to the discourse of Bio-Power, generated by rotating the elements one quarter-turn from the Capitalist discourse (Figure 6).

Discourse of Bio-Power

$$\frac{S1}{a} \quad \begin{matrix} \rightarrow \\ \leftarrow // \end{matrix} \quad \frac{\$}{S2}$$

(Figure 6)

In this discourse, the "social relation aims at mastery of the bodies it acts upon":

> The dream of bio-power is a completely regulated body that could function as a gear in the machine of production without friction, waste, or remainder ... aimed at producing knowledge of the various techniques through which humans can be effectively regulated and controlled, thereby maximizing production and efficiency.
>
> (Bryant 27)

This discourse has *object a* as its "truth" because the pursuit of surplus-value is the engine of the system and because waste cannot be eliminated.

Bryant points out that the discourse of Bio-Power is underrepresented in Žižek's analyses: Žižek prefers to focus on what Bryant calls the discourse of Immaterial Production, because this is the field in which ideology's effects are felt:

> the discourse of immaterial labor is a privileged site of political engagement ... because [it] is today what maintains social relations after the decline of symbolic efficiency by continuously weaving and unweaving the social field, creating temporary fields of social ties and opening new commodity markets, while perpetually recapturing or reterritorializing new subjectivities that do not fit with existing social codes.
>
> (Bryant 29–30)

In this discourse, S2 commands *object a*, as "that which is not yet named or integrated into the system of capital" (Bryant 32) (Figure 7).

Discourse of Immaterial Production

S2 → *a*
$ ←// S1

(Figure 7)

It produces S1s that (attempt to) name a unified identity, to generate a "One People" out of a heterogeneous multiplicity. The new names function not only as temporary points of identification but also as the names of new markets. These identities are supposed to serve as the (Imaginary) totality of the subject as well as the society, which means that they are also supposed to provide access to complete enjoyment. Of course, S2 can never make the subject whole, but because the naming always fails (S1 is impotent to adequately symbolize the subject), it generates the necessity for more names, more ideology.

The knowledge generated by the discourse of Bio-Power and the constant churning of Master-Signifiers with which we are supposed to identify in the discourse of Immaterial Production are two ways that Capital seeks to turn the waste that it produces into surplus value.[7] But the discourse universe of the Capitalist contains one discourse – Critical Theory – that changes the nature of the relationship among its terms (Figure 8). Like the Analyst's discourse, *object a* is located in the place of the agent, with S2 in the place of truth. Thanks, however, to the mutation in the order of the elements, the agent in Capitalist discourse addresses S1 and produces the divided subject on the right side (the old left side of the Master's discourse).

Discourse of Critical Theory

a → S1
S2 ←// $

(Figure 8)

Bryant comments that the position of the Master-Signifier in this Critical Theory discourse should come as no surprise, given that the object of a revolutionary politics is not to uncover the Master-Signifier organizing an individual subject's unconscious but to challenge ideological hegemony. In other words, this discourse, unlike the Analyst's, is not addressed to an individual analysand but to the system of hegemony itself. On this count, the discourse of Critical Theory has the advantage of the Analyst's discourse for revolutionary politics.

We should note that this discourse of Critical Theory "produces" the fundamental matheme of the subject of the unconscious, the seminal element of the Master's discourse, and so redresses the weakening of the Master's discourse. Just like the Analyst's discourse, the discourse of Critical Theory alters the subject's relationship to the Law, but in this case the relationship concerns the subject's attachment to (identification with) the social order rather than to its own psychic order. In this discourse, the subject discovers how its alienation supports the very ideology, the Master-Signifier, that alienates it. The resistance to hegemony of the Imaginary social order on offer in Critical Theory discourse concerns the *public* function of the Master-Signifiers. And because capitalism deprives *all* subjects of the security of social order, making the Imaginary status and true function of these signifiers visible offers a possible route to collectivization.

Locating the revolutionary object

We can see now why Žižek sometimes appears to occupy the position of the Hysteric, demanding that S1 fulfill its function efficaciously, in a consistent way (that is, without its obscene underside). No matter what problems the Master's discourse brings, not least of which is its obscene enjoyment of punishment, it nonetheless supports the subject of the unconscious. And it also provides a tidy target for revolutionary activity. So, in recurring to the discourse universe of the Master, in his efforts to bring about a masterful Master-Signifier, Žižek may be less nostalgic for authoritarianism, and less of an Hysteric, than he is registering the difficulties of re-politicization in a sphere where responsibility for the powerful effects of capitalism cannot be easily located. Let me turn now to an example of his work that demonstrates the importance of understanding the discourse universe of Capitalism, in particular because it helps us see how Žižek's view of rights has revolutionary potential.

In his essay in this volume, Žižek offers two contradictory "revolutionary" positions vis-à-vis the Law. In the first section of the essay, he explains that "radical emancipatory politics ... should not focus on the overthrowing of the existing legal order," yet in the conclusion to the essay, he advocates "open rebellion against the established legal order." In the former, his target is the obscene underside of the Law; in the latter, he locates an "uncanny legal principle" that authorizes, by way of the Law itself, rebellion against the existing legal order: the extra-legal dimension of the Law serves as the warrant for revolution. That is, at first he seems bent on the subversion of the Law (without an attack on the Law) while later he argues for the importance of the Law (with an attack on the Law).

For Žižek, the warrant for revolution based on Law's non-law dimension comes into view when the sphere of rights is threatened with depoliticization, when people are reduced to bare life, deprived of the right to have rights. As he argues in "Against Human Rights,"

> [p]aradoxically, I am deprived of human rights at the very moment at which I am reduced to a human being "in general," and thus become the ideal bearer of those "universal human rights" which belong to me independently of my profession, sex, citizenship, religion, ethnic identity, etc ... "universal human rights" designate the precise space of politicization proper; what they amount to is the right to universality as such – the right of a political agent to assert its radical non-coincidence with itself (in its particular identity), to posit itself as the "supernumerary," the one with no proper place in the social edifice; and thus as an agent of universality of the social itself.
>
> (127, 131)

The right to have rights is key to the Law, since this right serves to include the subject in "the domain of social recognition" of the Symbolic (Žižek in this volume).

So, in "Against Human Rights," Žižek places his bets on a revolutionary act that he calls "subjective destitution": when the subject renounces or refuses its Symbolic determinants as the essence of its identity ("profession, sex, citizenship, religion, ethnic identity, etc."), all signifiers of the Imaginary narcissistic ego, it accesses the singularity of the organization of its own self-division, which is the basis for its universality. Since every subject is constitutively split, the community of humans is also split: referring to Rancière, Žižek argues that "[t]he gap between the universality of human rights and the political rights of citizens is thus not a gap between the universality of man and a specific political sphere. Rather, it "separates the whole of the community from itself'" ("Against Human Rights," 131). Asserting one's "radical non-coincidence" with oneself allows one to embody the split in the community, the split that is the community's point of universality (131).

In the conclusion to *The Parallax View*, Žižek proposes Bartleby to us as an example of a subject that has undergone the process of subjective destitution, renouncing his symbolic determinants as the essence of his identity, refusing all of the Imaginary identifications attaching him to the Law, in a way that has revolutionary effects. Bartleby, Žižek explains, is revolutionary not because he attacks the Law (he doesn't) but because his "gesture is what remains of the supplement to the Law when its place it [*sic*] emptied of all its obscene superego content" (TPV 382). Bartleby derives his surplus enjoyment, on the one hand, from admitting the force of the Law and, on the other, by choosing to speak from the position of the Law's inconsistency, that is, from the point at which the Law's failure to cover all cases is visible. In this way, Bartleby fits the bill of a revolutionary subject insofar as he occupies the position of universality, the universal alternative to all particular symbolic identities.

Still, as I have argued elsewhere, it is unclear how Bartleby achieves any revolutionary effects from this position since, for one thing, Bartleby doesn't change anything in the public sphere, and his suicide by starvation is no martyrdom.[8] What is more, Žižek approaches Bartleby from the standpoint of the Analyst's discourse as the figure who, like the analyst, renounces his positive determinants: in fact, thanks to his reliance on the Analyst's discourse rather than the discourse of Crtical Theory, Žižek has to position Bartlebey as both analyst and analysand and in this way obscures the mechanism by which Bartleby achieves subjective destitution. In any case, as we have seen, the Analyst's discourse is insufficient to produce a collective subject.

It is perhaps the unsatisfactory nature of Bartleby's candidacy as revolutionary subject that leads Žižek to propose the collectivizing of the situation of subjects objected by capitalism in the concluding section of "The Rule of Law." Both Bartleby and those deprived of the right to rights are subjectively destituted: in both cases, their symbolic identities are refused. But of course the difference between them makes all the difference, given that Bartleby *chooses* destitution while these other object-ified subjects *suffer* destitution. And unlike Bartleby, these objects are not held up as examples for us to emulate. In other words, within the parameters of the Analyst's discourse, it is impossible to make a distinction between destituted subjects who function as revolutionaries and those who are victims of capitalism.

In the discourse universe of Capitalism, we find destituted subjects, subjects reduced to waste, objects, or obstacles. In Capitalist discourse, the subject in the position of agent addresses itself to S2 (commodities, "objective" knowledge, regulations) to make it whole (access full enjoyment), but the product of this address is the increasing alienation of the subject from enjoyment and the accumulation of the surplus elsewhere. We have already seen how this discourse de-subjectivates the subject by harnessing it to the death drive as an agent of S1, Capital. In this discourse universe, then, *object a* stands for the alienation of all subjects from surplus enjoyment: the subject is reduced to an *abject*.

To find the revolutionary potential of the discourse of Critical Theory, then, I think we must look to the location of the *abject*, the subject transformed by capitalist discourse, not the location of the divided subject, which fantasies its freedom even as it is enslaved. Abjects are the *truth* of the discourse of Bio-Power, the ineliminable remainder of waste/surplus enjoyment that drives the system and secures all subjects to it. The discourse of Immaterial Production addresses every abject as the remnant spoiling the unity of the People, that is, as targets for elimination. These "obscenities" are not products of the Law; they are not the Law's obscene underside. They are the consequence of Law's inanition and the engines of capitalism.

The discourse of Critical Theory affords the only opportunity for the abject to address S1 as the source of its abjection. Once we find ourselves in the discourse universe of Capitalism, within the society of enjoyment, there is no other choice. As Žižek says, one becomes a revolutionary because one must: there is simply nothing else one can do if one wishes to be a subject at all. With the help of Critical Theory, we see how capitalism positions the obviously destituted members of our world within these discourses. Consequently, we can and must see that Capitalist discourse positions all of us in the same way as the universally unassimilable excess to the system. By focusing on this universality, Critical Theory discourse collectivizes.

From within the discourse of Critical Theory, we might read the "right to rights/right of rebellion" conclusion to "The Rule of Law" as follows. The discourse of Immaterial Production has to constantly produce new Master-Signifiers, although unmasking them as temporary and insufficient has no revolutionary effect: it actually serves the interests of Capital by returning them to their status as ordinary signifiers and making them available again for ideological re-formulation. But the Law does have a special status as Master-Signifier for subjects of Capitalism insofar as it is both internal (a formal operator crucial for subjectivization) and external (the Imaginary public Law). Unlike all the other purported Master-Signifiers of Capitalism, to which subjects attach solely by way of the Imaginary, the Law has a special status for subjects, because they can attach to the Law by way of their own self-division at the very point of the Law's self-division: recall that the self-division of the Law and the of the subject are two sides of the same coin. For the zero-degree of the Law – the right to have rights – is equivalent to the self-founding of the Law, the "uncanny legal principle" that marks the Law's failure to coincide with itself. What the discourse of Critical Theory makes visible is that the abjects of capital *are* "the gap that separates something from nothing, from the void of its own place … the 'pure' difference between the set of social regulations and the void of their absence" (TPV 382). The abjects of Capital can attach to the Law *as* its zero degree, as what is in the Law more than the Law, as the extra-legal foundation of the Law. Addressing the Law from the embodied point of the Law's own inconsistency, that is, from the position of *object a* as the necessary supplement to the Law, can produce subjects collectively attached to the public Law at its "structural minimum."

The fact that the "Law" is self-divided must be accepted and deployed. The incompleteness of the Law is the source of both its subjectivizing effects and its production of a social order that sustains subjectivity. *We*, as divided subjects attached to the Law at the point of universality, can provide the dimension of the Real that is required to keep the Law from collapsing; *we* can make the Law's minimal difference from itself available for symbolization. We can't recommend subjective destitution: we don't want to create *more* abjects, *more* Bartlebys, *more* destitutes. Abjection is the universal effect of capitalism. We have too many actually destituted people, and we are in immediate danger of destituting everyone. Rather, we want to create subjects – we want to change the subject of capitalism. So, when we decide to speak collectively from the position of the abjection that capital demands, we speak *as the Law* – because we must: this is the only way that we can be subjects, divided and partially enjoying. Structurally speaking, which is to say, regarded from the vantage of the discourse universe of the Capitalist, we are already in a position to answer Žižek's call for a sociopolitical transformation of the entire field of relations to the Law.

Notes

1 Jeanne L. Schroeder's *The Four Lacanian Discourses: or Turning Law Inside-Out* (2008) provides an excellent analysis of the Law in Lacan's four discourses.
2 Throughout I follow Levi Bryant's (2008) terminology and discussion of the discourse universe of Capitalism, "Žižek's New Universe of Discourse: Politics and the Discourse of the Capitalist."
3 Levi Bryant has proposed that Žižek's work can serve as a map for this new discourse universe of the Capitalist, even though Žižek may not be aware that this is what he is doing (Bryant 2008: 6).
4 Joan Copjec's "The Tomb of Perseverance: On *Antigone*" (1999) explains the operation of the death drive's brake in terms that link it to the function of the Law. See also Paul Verhaege's "Enjoyment and Impossibility" (2006), 37.
5 For example, in an argument with Miller, Žižek points out that the unconscious subject itself is under attack from capitalism and then proposes the production of new Master signifiers via the Analyst's discourse, as he does in the passage just cited (TPV 307).
6 In this section, I am indebted to Todd McGowan's brilliant exposition of the society of enjoyment in *The End of Dissatisfaction? Jacques Lacan and the Emerging Society of Enjoyment* (2004).
7 Hylton White (2013) describes the situation of de-subjectivated subjects under capitalism in this way:

> [T]hey find the material world already appropriated as capital (Marx, *Capital* 927–30). In order to act materially, they are forced to act as the producers of commodities (or marginally, or not at all). As producers of commodities, however they interact as extensions of the impersonal dynamics of valorization. Where they could be subjects, then, they cannot act materially. But where they act materially – as in their relations of labor – they do so non-subjectively.
>
> [p. 679]

8 I have discussed the problems with Žižek's Bartleby in *The Excessive Subject* (2010), 187–94, 211–15.

References

Bryant, Levi. "Žižek's New Universe of Discourse: Politics and the Discourse of the Capitalist," *International Journal of Žižek Studies* 2.4 (2008): 1–48.

Clemens, Justin, and Russell Grigg, eds. *Reflections on Seminar XVII: Jacques Lacan and the Other Side of Psychoanalysis*, SIC 6. Durham and London: Duke University Press, 2006.

Copjec, Joan. "The Tomb of Perseverance: On *Antigone*," in Joan Copjec and Michael Sorkin, eds. *Giving Ground: The Politics of Propinquity*. London and New York: Verso, 1999, 233–66.

Lacan, Jacques. "Discourse of Jacques Lacan at the University of Milan on May 12, 1972," trans. J. W. Stone. http://web.missouri.edu/~stonej/Milan_Discourse2.pdf. Accessed 20 February 2014. Unpaginated.

Lacan, Jacques. *Television*. Trans. Denis Hollier, Rosalind Krauss, and Annette Michelson. New York and London: W. W. Norton, 1990.

Lacan, Jacques. *Seminar XVII: The Other Side of Psychoanalysis*. Trans. Russell Grigg. New York: W. W. Norton, 2007.

McGowan, Todd. *The End of Dissatisfaction? Jacques Lacan and the Emerging Society of Enjoyment*. Albany, NY: SUNY Press, 2004.

Miller, Jacques-Alain. "On Shame," in Justin Clemens and Russell Grigg, eds. *Reflections on Seminar XVII: Jacques Lacan and the Other Side of Psychoanalysis*. SIC 6. Durham and London: Duke University Press, 2006, 11–28.

Rothenberg, Molly Anne. *The Excessive Subject: A New Theory of Social Change*. Cambridge: Polity Press, 2010.

Schroeder, Jeanne L. *The Four Lacanian Discourses: or Turning Law Inside-Out*. Abingdon: Birkbeck Law Press, 2008.

Verhaege, Paul. "Enjoyment and Impossibility," in Justin Clemens and Russell Grigg, eds. *Reflections on Seminar XVII: Jacques Lacan and the Other Side of Psychoanalysis*. SIC 6. Durham and London: Duke University Press, 2006.

White, Hylton. "Materiality, Form, and Context: Marx contra Latour," *Victorian Studies* 55.4 (Summer 2013): 667–82.

Žižek, Slavoj. "Postscript: The rule of law between obscenity and the right to distress" [in this volume].

Žižek, Slavoj. *The Parallax View*. Cambridge, MA, and London: MIT Press, 2006.

Žižek, Slavoj. "Jacques Lacan's Four Discourses," www.lacan.com/zizfour.htm. Accessed August 2014.

Žižek, Slavoj. "Against Human Rights," *New Left Review* 34 (July/August 2005): 115–31.

Chapter 4

Changing fantasies

Žižek and the limits of democracy

Chris McMillan

Late in 2013, a debate over the continued relevance of democratic participation emerged between two prominent British comedians. During his world tour for *The Messiah Complex*, Russell Brand (2013) had guest-edited an edition of the Labour-orientated magazine *the New Statesman*, in which he argued that young people and the disenfranchised should eschew voting and withdraw from democratic participation rather than offering their "tacit compliance." Young people, Brand asserted, are right to feel apathetic and powerless when the democratic system of governance offers no effective choice. Moreover, Brand highlighted the multitude of symptoms of the democratic-capitalist order, from global inequality to climate change and the influence of financial capital.

These symptoms of the "market economy" were not a prominent feature of the critique of Brand's very public intervention. While several commentators sanctioned (Carswell, 2013; Reed, 2013) Brand's description of the contemporary state of democracy, most rounded on his call to relinquish democratic mechanisms (Dawson, 2013; Perkins, 2013; Slinger, 2013). To withdraw from the system, it was argued, would only serve to lose all influence over its functioning. While it might not hold the excitement of revolutionary vigour, we need to re-engage with the democratic process others have fought for us to enjoy rather than discarding it altogether in the name of an undefined revolutionary path. Here, Robert Webb (2013), star of the TV comedy *Peep Show*, directly rebuffed Brand by insisting that " 'They're all the same' is what reactionaries love to hear. It leaves the status quo serenely untroubled." Democracy, Webb argued, may not be perfect but we should count our blessings for living in a twenty-first century liberal democracy and remember that politicians serve at our liberty. The alternative would not appear so enticing if Brand were to "read some fucking Orwell."

This pop-culture skirmish is symptomatic of one of the basic political issues of our time: is democracy the ultimate horizon for political organization and participation? Moreover, is democratic discourse the most effective language for mobilizing resistance to the global economic symptoms identified by Brand? My contribution to this text engages with this debate, not by providing a decisive answer to how our societies should be governed, but by utilizing Žižekian theory of law, ideological fantasy, and the Real to open up space to question the mobilization of democratic discourse in pursuit of radical causes.

Democracy is the master signifier of politics in the "developed world" and beyond, the nodal point that holds together the symbolic order such that social and political practice only makes sense in relation to democracy. In this way democracy – as a signifier, rather than as a form of governing institution[1] – acts as the symbolic law through which social life is orientated. By occupying the place of law, democracy is not just a symbolic order of prohibitions and injunctions but is imbued with an underlying surplus enjoyment and unspeakable symptomatic points cohered within a fantasmatic narrative.

Žižek's earliest writings can be located within a broad post-Marxism/radical democratic territory, albeit with a supplementary Lacanian focus on enjoyment, fantasy, and the Real. From the late 1990s, however, Žižek began to engage in the critique of democracy, moving within a more totalitarian language, a shift that has piqued critics (Boucher, 2010; Boucher and Sharpe, 2010; Laclau, 2000; Sharpe and Boucher, 2010; Stavrakakis, 2010) and invigorated more supportive theorists (Daly, 2010; Dean, 2005; 2006; McGowan, 2013, pp. 38–46; Vighi and Feldner, 2006). In this chapter I will argue that Žižek's reading of democracy is not based on any normative claims about the way we should live (Žižek has remarkably little to say on these matters[2]) but is a response to contemporary conditions for political action. Žižek (1993, p. 221; 2002, p. 168) suggests that democracy has become *the* undisputed political horizon that determines symbolic practice, the master signifier that structures the hegemonic terrain of political engagement, and yet is an inadequate means for disruptively evoking the antagonisms that currently threaten capitalism, stating that "What, today, prevents the radical questioning of capitalism itself is precisely *the belief in the democratic form of the struggle against capitalism*" (2008, pp. 183, original emphasis).

This institutional and ideological inadequacy is not because democratic ideology rejects resistance, but because it courts it through a fantasmatic subsumption of political antagonism and dislocation into electoral desire. Here the democratic symbolic order that overdetermines the political horizon within developed capitalist economies is able to practice "politics without the political" (Daly, 2009) by hosting a form of engagement that embeds subversive activity within the law but displaces anti-systematic claims and acts.

What is required is a return to the Real dimension of the political so as to, in Glyn Daly's (2009) terms, "subvert the existing logic of subversion" within democracy. To do so means to break from the loop of democratic fantasy by evoking the impossibility of eliminating the symptoms of contemporary capitalism through contemporary democratic politics. To do so is not to forego democracy as a form of governance but to abandon democratic language in order to forge new ways of speaking, if not to propel the hope of forging new ways of being.

The democratic law

For Claude Levi-Strauss (1951), from whom much of Lacan's work on law is attributable (Evans, 2003, p. 98), the law should not be reduced to its institutional and codified instantiation, but acts as an inter-subjective guide for social action. In governing social existence, law can be considered in both form, whereby law is a signifying system – the symbolic order[3] – and in the hegemonic content of the law in any given field. Moreover, these two modes cannot be separated in practice, as the hegemonic occupation of the symbolic order and its ideological suturing mediate our unconscious perception of the grammar of law that governs the structuring patterns of its exclusions and nodal points. Most importantly for my discussion in this chapter, the law determines both what is excluded from hegemonic conceptions of shared social life (as well as the way we experience this exclusion) and the underlying modes of enjoyment that maintain its stability.

The primary Lacanian contribution to law is that law *qua* the symbolic order is not rationally constructed but is forged through the entry of the body into a pre-established symbolic realm, a "forced choice" that separates enjoyment and instinct from the body. This "symbolic castration" acts to over-ride the "natural" enjoyment of the body. The law is thus not a naturally given entity (human nature) according to which human relations are propelled, nor a purely discursive (moral) practice of legality used to regulate human behaviour. Instead, law acts as a mediating order that both separates and entwines enjoying bodies and organizing ideas (Elliott, 2009, p. 98), restricting the terrain of bodily expression while establishing the possibilities for human enjoyment. We may be born as biologically driven animals, but we enter into the existing law of the symbolic order – what Lacan called "the Big Other" – that not only symbolically defines the possibilities for enjoyment but inscribes upon the body a different mode of attachment and pleasure: the Lacanian *jouissance*.

In this regard law both enforces normative social obligations, prohibitions, and roles and enacts the terrain through which we can approach enjoyment, hosting the fantasmatic narratives that stage our desires in a symbolic-imaginary form. This form holds its grip upon the human body by way of *jouissance* generated through transgressive activity which is at the same time proscribed and permitted by the law. Consequently, in transforming biological need to symbolic desire supported by ideological fantasy, law regulates the social of bodily enjoyment in both its normative and transgressive forms.

The ultimate agency of this regulation is the super-ego. Freud (1960) positioned the super-ego as the internal agency of social authority, suggesting that societal law does not need to be externally enforced, as obedience (and deviance) is internally regulated by the guilt enacted through the super-ego. Thus, against our tendencies towards aggression and sexuality, the civilizing processes inherent within the law socialise us into patterns of being that disavow these instincts (Freud, 2002).

While Žižek endorses the basic psychoanalytic dynamic of the super-ego in the internalization of the law into the body, he goes further by suggesting that the super-ego also lays the foundation for its own transgression. Here the law provides unconsciously accepted modes of transgression to the public law. If law presses for our compliance to the symbolic order, the particular formation of the necessarily incomplete law (language being unable to completely encapture the body) also propels our desire. As a consequence, law acts as both a form of proscription, enforcing forms of prohibition, and deviance. We might believe in sexual equality in public, but enjoy a laugh at sexist jokes in private. The latter may not over-ride the former in public practice, but allows a socially-acceptable form of release of the desire to go beyond the law. Consequently, the dominant law of a discourse does not function through repression but is infused with *jouissance* produced through the unconscious acknowledgement of sanctioned violations of the law.[4]

Thus the symbolic order does not specifically prohibit enjoyment through the civilizing process, as Freud had suggested. Original, primordial enjoyment of the body does not exist, but enjoyment is experienced in other ways, ways that are produced with the law. Law may indicate which forms of enjoyment *are* proscribed – perhaps the public performance of sexual acts – but allows space for both pleasure (the private performance of these acts) and their quasi-permitted transgression, such as the *jouissance* of private sex that risks becoming public. In this way the law, as Žižek suggests, is always infused with an underlying enjoyment that is, according to Jodi Dean (2004, p. 2), "fundamentally split between the public letter and its obscene super-ego supplement."

The other side of the incomplete "non-all" symbolic law is the anxiety that exists around its points of failure and impossibility. These points, those that Lacan identifies as the Real, may be what is impossible to say within the symbolic order, but they are also constructed by the symbolic order. Every ideological discourse both produces its own specific co-ordinates of failure and seeks to integrate these points of anxiety and impossibility, which provide an unacceptable transgression to law in that they cannot be accounted for within the law. Here, in confronting a point previously unaccounted for within the symbolic-imaginary order, the cohering mechanisms of the law (narratives of ideological fantasy) seek to explain and disarm the presence of this disruption (Daly, 1999).

Ideological fantasy is thus primarily an unconscious narrative defence against the cut of the symbolic law and the breaks within it. This narrative functions not by excluding the Real but by implicitly explaining its threatening presence in a way that sustains the *jouissance* of desire (Stavrakakis, 1999, p. 46). Here, as Stavrakakis contends, "the lack of the symbolic is covered by imaginary constructions which take the form of delusions" (ibid., p. 32), delusions that are not determined by their form, although they are propelled by this non-all form. Instead, the occupation of the law produces particular modes of fantasy that construct our relationship to enjoyment and exclusion. These modes can be productively divided into three categories: utopian, encircled, and disruptive (this latter category will be discussed in the final section).

Stavrakakis (2003, p. 58) argues that within utopian forms of fantasy,

> discourses localize the cause of negativity in one particular social group or political actor. Thus, the essential by-product of the utopian operation is invariably the stigmatization and even the elimination of the social group presented as incarnating negativity (qua Evil).

This elementary operation of fantasy can be seen most clearly in the figure of the Jew in Nazi Germany and in the contemporary location of the immigrant, who is often positioned as a threat to the very fabric of the law (Gye, 2013). In an everyday sense, we see a similar logic in the process of consumer desire in the fantasy that one more product will complete our *jouissance*, perhaps in the circumstance in which we are attending an event where we will likely feel anxious but hypothesise (on a largely unconscious level) that buying more appropriate clothing will diminish this anxiety.[5]

Stavrakakis (1999, pp. 71–98) clearly contrasts this form of fantasmatic *jouissance* with democratic modes that encircle, rather than exclude, the Real. Here democracy is able to respond to the traumatic dimension of negativity by positioning this negativity as the organizing center of the symbolic law: an institutionalized lack (both in terms of symbolic and governing law) around which different fantasmatic conceptions compete without attempting to achieve closure. This symbolic institutionalization of lack within the law is the basis of radical democracy.

Žižek the (radical) democrat or Žižek the totalitarian?

The critique of democracy itself (as opposed to the particularities of its mechanisms) is problematic across the political spectrum. Democracy stands not only as the "natural" and most enlightened method for organizing political affairs, such that a legitimate rebuke of the decision-making process of any small group is that it is not democratic, but as the only alternative to the much-hyped horrors of totalitarianism (Laclau, 2000, pp. 289–290). Democracy acts as the outward public law of enlightened societies: the protestors of the Arab Spring do not call for the arrival of capitalism but of democracy, just as the fall of communism did not (ideologically) bring in an era of capitalism but of democracy. As a consequence, to stand against democracy is like taking a stand against chocolate or freedom of speech – it casts immediate suspicion against both your character and your sanity.

Indeed, the broad post-Marxist field within which Žižek's work emerged sought to renew rather than reject democracy, such that, as Chantal Mouffe suggested, "the objective of the Left should be the extension and deepening of the democratic revolution initiated two hundred years ago" (Mouffe, 1992, p. 1).[6] Mouffe, along with Ernesto Laclau (Laclau and Mouffe, 1985; Mouffe, 1992; 1993; 2005), built upon the work of Claude Lefort (1988) in association with a range of post-Marxist theorists within Laclau's Essex School of Discourse Analysis,[7] in order to develop a new democratic imaginary beyond the confines of economically determined socialism that "renewed the democratic invention" by elevating the inherent negativity in social life to the center of political practice.

For these radical democrats, the ethical promise of democratic revolution lies in the direct engagement with this negativity. In place of utopian attempts to exclude negativity from social life through ideological disavowals and displacements, radical democracy positions the failure of the social at the core of democracy through an agonistic politics where the place of power is formally empty and no position can achieve ideological closure. Instead of seeking consensus, radical democracy is dependent upon the acceptance of a state of dissensus that does not seek to eliminate antagonism but, rather, develops agonistic relationships base on a shared acknowledgement that, in Lacanian terms, "the Other doesn't exist."

Žižek's initial theoretical and political works had much in common with Laclauian radical democracy and the acknowledgement of the primacy of antagonism (1989, p. 6) although, as Dean (2005, p. 156) suggests, this thread has always had a degree of scepticism, notwithstanding Žižek's run for the presidency of Slovenia on a liberal democratic ticket in 1990. Moreover, despite the sustained and often tense debate between Laclau and Žižek during the early years of the twenty-first century (Butler et al., 2000; Laclau, 2006; Žižek, 2006) they share similar territory in the identification of the ontological negativity of social life within which political demands struggle for hegemony around structuring nodal "empty" or master signifiers (Laclau and Mouffe, 1990; Žižek, 1990). To this Žižek, supplemented by a field of theorists seeking into Lacanian theory with Laclau's work (Glynos and Stavrakakis, 2003; Stavrakakis, 2007), initially supplied

Laclau's "discourse theory" with a "level of enjoyment" (Žižek, 1989, pp. 95–144) that enabled it to explain why otherwise free-floating signifiers held such a grip on the body politic. This addition, and Žižek's (1990) insistence that antagonisms are internally rather than externally located (discourse being always already dislocated), have been largely integrated into Laclau's work (Laclau, 2003; 2004).

Conversely, Žižek has rejected attempts, both in Laclau's notion of populism (2006) and Stavrakakis' democratic (feminine) *jouissance* (2007, pp. 304–329), to formalise a politics that attempts to utilize Lacanian psychoanalysis as the basis for political organization. More pertinently, Žižek also rejects radical democracy on account of its eminent compatibility with the excesses and exclusions of global capitalism (2000b, p. 325). Here, contra Laclau, democracy is not simply a matter of particular contents battling for the place of the empty universal (Žižek, 2000a, p. 110), but this field is overdetermined by capital (ibid., pp. 108–109) and made possible by the discursive exclusion of the material presence of surplus population expanding within capitalism (Jameson, 2011; McMillan, 2012; Žižek, 2008, pp. 423–429). Democracy thus becomes, as Dean (2005, p. 155) states, "the form our attachment to Capital takes" and part of the series of "cultural capitalism" that includes human rights (Dean, 2006; Žižek, 2005), multi-cultural tolerance (Žižek, 1997), permissive enjoyment (McGowan, 2004), ethical consumption (Daly, 2009), and employability (Cremin, 2011) as its primary signifiers.

Žižek's critique of democracy and subsequent shift into an increasingly totalitarian language with ill-defined political outcomes has been the point of considerable critical debate. Emblematic of this critique is Boucher and Sharpe's (2010, p. 5) contention that something happened to Žižek towards the end of the twentieth century. Arguing that Žižek's synthesis of Lacan and Hegel was initially aligned with post-Marxist extension of democracy "grounded in a more realistic account of desire and subjectivity" (ibid., p. 26), they posit that this Žižek$_1$ has been replaced by Žižek$_2$, a totalitarian terror intent on opposing liberal democracy with nothing but misplaced ideas (ibid., pp. 24–27)[8] based on a desire for provocative and unpopular positions.

Yet Žižek is not directly endorsing a totalitarian alternative to democratic societies nor proposing an alternative ethic of being, despite his recent dalliance with the "communist hypothesis" (Žižek, 2009). Instead, as Žižek states in *In Defense of Lost Causes*, "the true aim of 'the defense of lost causes' is not to defend Stalinist terror, and so on, but to render problematic the all-too-easy liberal-democratic alternative" (2008, p. 6), a process that requires the break within what Žižek considers the "liberal blackmail" of liberal democracy or fundamentalist terror. As a consequence, "democracy is more and more a false issue, a notion so discredited by its predominant use that, perhaps, one should take the risk of abandoning it to the enemy" (2001, p. 123).[9] To do so, as Fabio Vighi and Heiko Feldner (2006, p. 54) note in regards to *The Ticklish Subject* (1999, p. 205) requires "rethinking the leftist project" to go beyond simply "questioning capitalism" to "questioning liberal democracy."

Thus, although Žižek has shifted away from democratic discourse, his point is not that totalitarian governance would be a "better" solution to the inequities of global capitalism. Instead, he suggests, contra Laclau as well as the likes of Hardt and Negri (2000; 2004), that democracy no longer holds a strategic edge as a radical signifier because it has been co-opted into capitalism in much the same way as counter-cultural identities and human rights discourse. In acting as a mediating "shield" for capitalism, democracy becomes "an empty signifier which any and all can attach their dreams and hopes" (Brown, 2013, p. 44)[10] yet "remains the dominant emblem of contemporary political society" (Badiou, 2013, p. 6). Whether radical democracy provides a political instantiation of Lacanian ethics is not the issue – and neither is whether these politics are either possible or desirable – it is how democracy functions as a signifier and as an ideological fantasy in regards to capitalism that matters.

We could well imagine, as Hardt and Negri do, political circumstances in which democracy acts as a radical signifier. Indeed, Žižek (2008, p. 415) had previously argued that democracy "at its most elementary" stood for those with no proper place in the established order who asserted themselves as the embodiment of the whole. Here we could envisage a political movement that rearticulates democratic language to stand for this point of exclusion. More prosaically, democratic chains of understanding could be expanded to include aspects of the market, such that financial mechanisms come under popular control away from their "technical" management by the state. In post-revolutionary circumstances, radical democracy might also come to fore as a competing vision for the renewed organization of society, one that avoids the horrors and deadlocks of the past. None of these articulations of democracy should be immediately dismissed and all contain emancipatory potential. The question is not, however, of the abstract value of democratic practice but of the capacity of democratic language within contemporary capitalism. Given the previously documented limitations of this language, we must engage in a different struggle, the first battle of which is to shift the terms under which we fight. The initial step in this shift is to understand how democracy is able to maintain its grip on the political horizon.

Fantasies of change

The function of fantasy is not to fulfil desire or to eliminate lack but to provide a framework within which to stage desire in relation to the constituent negativity of the ontic order. So it is with the fantasmatic mechanisms of the democratic symbolic law. Within the injunctions and prohibitions of democratic law, the implicit narrative is that society can be changed if the available processes are employed. Here, desire in democracy exists as a response to the inescapable antagonisms and dislocations that threaten the coherence of our identification and attachments, producing an anxiety we are driven to overcome. Democracy acts to avoid a disturbing confrontation with this negativity by enabling us to approach the Real of the enemy (those democratic opponents or demands that prevent the realization of *our* society) without being overrun by it. That is, as the radical democrats suggest, the democratic law operates most effectively by holding the enemy at a bearable distance without having to eliminate them. Yet, contra Stavrakakis, we can tolerant the presence of the (democratic) enemy not because of some reconfigured *jouissance* but because democracy holds the promise that these obstacles can be removed within the law.

To regulate dislocation in democratic law, we are not prohibited from politics but are permitted to engage in politically confined transgressive activity. As Žižek regularly argues of postmodern law in relation to enjoyment, the super-ego demand of politics has shifted from "you may" to "you must." In being expressly allowed to choose (both in politics and in social life) and thus to follow our desires beyond the public law, we are at the same time being caught up in that law. The law sets the rules through which we can follow and break from the law, each with their own economy of enjoyment. The ultimate effect of this activity, however, is to enforce compliance, which is more effectively secured through the positivity of choosing than through external proscription.

Here, like capitalism, the democratic ethos encourage compliance through constant activity. To take a liberal-democratic example, democratic mechanisms for enabling political and social participation are clearly evident: unions, political parties, freedom of speech, and the right to assemble and demonstrate. We have an overtly open public sphere where new and transgressive ideas are able to receive a hearing. From protest to public debate and voting booths, the democratic law holds open the possibility of change and resistance. As a consequence, if there is a pressing lack within the democratic law – say unemployment or restrictions on lifestyles – the narrative of its fantasy suggests that this lack can be overcome through the democratic Other of governing institutions.

Of course, this ideological face of agential democracy does not necessary reflect political practice in which politicians are able to maintain power whatever the level of political participation. The problem is that not only do politicians know this, but so do the people. Here a super-ego supplement of contemporary democracy is that we know democracy does not work to offer the choice and power that the public law promises, but the continued belief in the efficacy of democracy enables a cynical resignation to the troubles of our times. We may continue to state privately that politicians are useless, or self-interested, or just plain corrupt, but we continue to believe in democracy itself. We know that the emperor has no clothes, but to take that seriously is to take responsibility for the consequent rupture of the law. What matters is not whether we believe, but whether the big (democratic) Other continues to believe in itself by continuing to hold elections, to organize committees, and to preach the lines of the public law. Through this cynicism we can maintain the *jouissance* of our private knowledge, making jokes at politicians' expense and shaking our heads at the latest news story, while continuing to act in practice as if the public law is in effect.

This split logic of choice and compliance is evident in current workplace dynamics, which often borrow from both a democratic ethos and permissive enjoyment (Cremin, 2011). To reorganize a major organization, an employee-centered management will no longer simply tell you what is being done: you are an important part of the process. Instead, committees are formed, consultations are held and feedback is solicited. Views are taken seriously because, after all, it is *our* organization. Of course, as anyone who has experienced this kind of "transformational change" will know, all this consultation is likely to ever achieve is a few tweaks to a predetermined path. We all know that this is the case – that the changes are not being made for our benefit and that the process will follow through with or without our input – but participation ensues. Those that refuse to participate are accused of wasting the opportunity to have their voice heard.

The contemporary dynamics of political protest provides a more troubling example. In Britain, as in many "developed" democracies, one of the key democratic rights is the right to demonstrate. To organize a protest march, however, the Metropolitan Police (2013) of London advise that

> Organisers of public processions are required by law to notify police AT LEAST 6 DAYS BEFORE the event occurs, of the date, time, proposed route and the name and address of an organiser.
>
> Completion of the form 3175 (to be found in the "Related publications" box on this page) satisfies the legal requirement to notify police of a public procession under sections 11(1) and 11(3) of the Public Order Act 1986.

Leaving aside the peculiarly English *jouissance* achieved through bureaucratic procedure, we see a circumstance in which the public law officially allows for resistance, but only if those resisting request permission from the (governing) law. The result is inevitable: the people can have their say, so long as nothing is disturbed. This is not, of course, the official view of the demonstration, which appears to earnestly believe in the possibility of change, as the protest signs distributed by the Union (or whichever organization holds the position of the Other) clearly state. For many, however, the *jouissance* of participation might be far more cynical: we know that nothing is going to change but it is important to go through the ritual to maintain belief in the democratic law.

This dynamic of resistance-participation does not break the prescriptions of democratic law but is an injunction embedded within the law. Democracy does not dismiss the hope of *jouissance* but allows for the possibility through political struggle. Just as consumerist capitalism stimulates desire for unattainable objects (say a gadget well beyond our price range), it opens up the possibility of attaining the product. Formally, there is always the possibility of making the purchase, just as the democratic process (at its most effective) allows (almost) any demand to be submitted to the Other.

The clearest example of this logic is the emergence of "e-Petitions" (as part of the larger fantasmatic logic of "clictivism," in which users lend their support for a cause without actually having to do anything about it) whereby citizens can electronically submit their grievances to the state who will, like any effective Other (God being the most effective example) listen to their demands.[11] Like holding an inquiry or forming a committee, submitting the petition is all that needs to happen for democracy to work. Such a process circumscribes the domain of politics by co-opting public enjoyment, allowing a cynicism in which the Other acts for us: if our cause was truly popular, it would be able to be enacted.

The dynamic of prohibition and transgression in the democracy fantasy can be seen in both the "Occupy" movement and conservative responses to it. One of Occupy's primary demands is for democracy, both in "direct democracy" (Graeber, 2011) within the movement and the ideological demand to rehabilitate "real" democracy (Hardt and Negri, 2011). In this regard, writing in www.occupy.com, Andy Smith (2012) explained that

> The General Assembly is the decision-making model for the Occupy Movement, employing consensus decision-making, a process that demands a high level of agreement on a proposal and is extremely participatory. Members of the movement attend the assembly to ask questions and decide on the proposals on that night's agenda. This high level of participation in the assembly makes Occupy a directly democratic movement. Participation is the key to political empowerment.

Occupy is often (perhaps rightly) positioned as an anti-capitalist movement, but it is also passionately democratic, seeking to redirect and restore both democratic language and practices. Moreover, it is interesting that the message of radical democracy, that antagonism and dissensus is key to democracy, is missing from this vision of direct democracy. In this case the internal operation of Occupy exists as a fantasy within which a just and united community can be achieved through participation and communicative reason.

Nonetheless, Occupy does provide an exemplary example of the limits to transgression within democracy. Immediate public responses to the movement were muted, even if police operations were not so forgiving. The protestors were positioned as an example of the continued functioning of the democratic system: peaceful protest and the free exchange of ideas. As it became clear, however, that they would not simply disappear once their point was publically acknowledged and "awareness" was raised, then the occupiers had violated the officially permitted level of transgression within the law. Now they had to go. Police violence became more prominent and minor laws and complaints were invoked to legalise evictions. The movement was no longer "democratic" and had to be shut down as the demands of the protestors could no longer be addressed through the means of the public law and instead provoked a threatening anxiety.

The violent evictions of the occupiers reveals the limit of the democratic law. In these circumstances in which Occupy was posting demands that could not be simply filed within the narrative of electoral desire, the efficacy of the democratic law becomes threatened. If the defenders of the law were to acknowledge that the demands were unable to be submitted to the democratic law and thus were undemocratic – "what do you want *us* to do about unemployment or living wages? That is not within our power" – then the fantasy of the law of participation, choice, and power begins to unravel as it is revealed that the lack in the social cannot be overcome through the law. If, however, the law recommits itself to itself through the promise of "working through the democratic" process, then the status of the Other is restored.

Conversely, although the methods of the movement transgress the modes of resistance permitted with the public law, the radicalism of Occupy does not extend to the democratic horizon itself. As a consequence, the most overt location of the struggle between the movement and reactionary ideology is over the meaning of "real" democracy. Consequently, the greatest risk faced by Occupy is that instead of holding onto the radicality of the antagonistic demands the movement evokes, it becomes entangled in a hegemonic struggle to occupy the place of the democratic master signifier.

We see this struggle in the rebukes often made against the "Occupy" movement (as well as Russell Brand), that the activists should utilise the electoral democratic political process. Here, if the people really believed in their cause – if they were really the 99 percent – then their political party would be elected to power (*The Economist*, 2011). In this regard Anne Applebaum (2011, also cited in Žižek, 2012, pp. 84–85) states

> In New York, marchers chanted, "This is what democracy looks like," but actually, this isn't what democracy looks like. This is what freedom of speech looks like. Democracy looks a lot more boring. Democracy requires institutions, elections, political parties, rules, laws, a judiciary and many unglamorous, time-consuming activities, none of which are nearly as much fun as camping out in front of St. Paul's Cathedral or chanting slogans on the Rue Saint-Martin in Paris.

These responses reveal the problematic faced by Occupy in relation to the democratic law. The symbolic framework of this law cannot be simply redirected through the advent of new knowledge – say in the circumstances that people become aware of the grip of capital over elections and immediately stop believing in democracy – but remains attached to a fantasmatic *jouissance* that holds a strong grip upon the demos. In engaging positively within the democratic terrain, Occupy (itself a floating master signifier without a settled chain of equivalences) has to confront not only the nationalist *jouissance* (Dean, 2005; Žižek, 1991) that often coheres identities within democracy, such that a threat to the law is a threat to nationalistic identity, but the fantasy of the democratic law. What is required is a strategic practice that evokes the political moment that is sedimented within the law.

Subverting the democratic law

The political, as distinct from the everyday operation of politics (Lefort, 1988; Mouffe, 1993; 2005; Stavrakakis, 1999), is the constitutive moment of undecidability (Daly, 2004, p. 3) within the organization of social life or the "moment(s) of rupture and contestation in which the very organizing principles of the social whole are drawn into question" (Daly, 2009, p. 280). It is this moment of the political, of rupture (Eisenstein and McGowan, 2013) or what Nassim Nicholas Taleb (2007) calls the "Black Swan" of the unknown entering into the known, which propels the narratives of ideology. Ideology, however, does not function most effectively when it ignores or entirely displaces its inherent dislocation but when it is able to reproduce this absence in a more palatable form (Daly, 1999). Consequently,

> [a] totality is not defined simply in relation to what it excludes as threat-negativity but rather through symbolizing, and making sense of, this very division within itself ... a totality is at its strongest when it is able to circumscribe the very terms of its own subversion. It becomes an anonymous horizon that defines our responsibilities and the limits of our action.
>
> (Ibid., pp. 291–292)

It is this comforting reproduction that is the strength of the democratic law which is able to, in Daly's terms, "harness and direct its own failures" (ibid., p. 288). The democratic fantasy is effective because it simulates the possibility of social change (of the radical will of the people being integrated into politics, perhaps to regulate banking activities against the interests of international finance) while foreclosing upon those political moments within the public law. Consequently, democracy is able to maintain its ideological hegemony and, more importantly, keep the symptoms of global capitalism at bay by maintaining a (cynical) distance from the political and reproducing it in more palatable forms.

It is this illusion that we must puncture within contemporary politics. What is needed is a negation of the negation to, again in Daly's terms (2009; 2010), subvert the very logic of subversion. Where capitalism has been the subject of democratic critique, we must go one step further to critique democracy itself as the final barrier against the constitutive contradictions of global capitalism. Here Žižek follows Badiou in evoking the "democratic illusion" of "the acceptance of democratic procedures as the sole framework for any possible change, that blocks any radical transformation of capitalist relations" (Žižek, 2012, p. 87). Thus, while capitalism has come under increasingly explicit examination, democracy "remains the sacred cow that even the most radical of these forms of 'ethical anti-capitalism' ... do not dare challenge" (ibid., p. 86).

In my earlier discussion of Stavrakakis and fantasy, I identified three relationships between fantasy and the Real: utopian, encircled, and disruptive. I would like to finally return to this disruptive dimension. Disrupting the fantasy of the law is not a pre-decided process that can be deployed and replicated in any given circumstances. Instead it relies on a concrete analysis of the way fantasmatic narratives and the *jouissance* that holds them together maintain a distance towards the Real. In regards to democracy, disrupting the fantasy of the law cannot rely upon an expansion or rearticulation of hegemonic chains of equivalence but needs to insist on the points at which democracy fails by asking questions that cannot be answered within the official law. More specifically, we need to begin to discuss the contradictions of capitalism within democratic discourse such that the inadequacy of this language becomes apparent.[12]

The point of this political exercise is not only to reveal the failure of the democratic terrain to people who are already privately cynical but also to force a rupture within the public law such that the agents of the law no longer speak as if these issues were under democratic control. If we are insisting upon the unjust influence of the 1 percent, the game is not to suggest that democracy and the economy need to be reworked to remove this influence (even if this is the case) but to show how the demand to change these circumstances cannot be accommodated by the democratic law. As a consequence, the disruption caused by injustice, by anger, and by transgressive desire would be unable to be as effectively subsumed within the democratic narrative of change, forcing direct exposure to the impossibilities within the law, an exposure which, it is hoped, will open up new space for radical thought.

Perhaps ironically, the freedom of speech and of protest necessary to enact this disruptive strategy are those established within the democratic framework. Consequently, we are not abandoning established democratic practices but rejecting democracy's injunctions to transgress within the territory it prescribes (as Occupy has already done). Moreover, rather than seeking to provide new answers within democracy, such that in protesting about low wages we follow the expectation to provide new answers, answers which necessarily fail within current parameters (suggestions to raise the minimum wage being met by derisive replies that higher wages will actually supress employment), we question the efficacy of democracy by getting defenders of the law to admit their own impotency in controlling wages.

As a consequence, the subtitle to Russell Brand's article, "before we change the world, we need to change the way we think," is particularly apt. However, instead of Brand's (2013) call for a "total revolution of consciousness," what we need is a change in the consciousness of the Other. We all *know* that democracy does not offer any control over the things that affect our lives, but we continue to comply with and commit to the democratic law. Instead, we must produce an acknowledgement within democracy of the deadlock between the governing mechanisms of our societies and the hold of global capitalism. Such an acknowledgement is likely to disrupt the coherence of the gripping fantasmatic hold on the democratic law. What happens after this rupture, however, becomes the new terrain for political engagement and confirms the fundamental undecidability of our shared and social lives, rather than guaranteeing any more just form of political practice. Here, as Barret Weber (2011, p. 7, original emphasis) states, the idea is not "to *reject democracy* as such (elections, for example, can be an important component of political struggle) but rather to challenge the false perspective that *democracy is all that there is.*"

Notes

1 In positioning democracy as law, within this chapter I do not seek to discuss the multitude of democratic forms and practices. Instead I am interested in democracy as a signifier, as an ideological fantasy, and as a mode of the law. The purpose of this line of inquiry is not to consider whether we should abandon the democratic project as a means of governance, but whether those evoking the underside of capitalism should abandon democratic language.

2 Although Žižek does often show sympathy for liberal causes: *of course* we should support sexual equality, anti-racism etc.; this support is not the point of Žižekian theory. It is not how we should live, but how our ideas about how we do live structure our actions that is of primary concern.

3 The law being, according to Lacan (1977, p. 73), "revealed clearly enough as identical with an order of language."
4 Equally, there exists prohibitions that, if broken, cause a disruption to the law that is punished at both legal and social levels. This grammar can be confusing for outsiders not inculcated into the symbolic order. In Britain, for instance, immigrant cultures can be reduced to nicknames that break from officialdom (they would not be used by public figures, unless they were attempting to appeal to these groups). The Antipodean cultures of Australians, New Zealanders and South Africans can be Aussies, Kiwis and Saffers. Conversely, Pakistanis cannot be Pakis because of the historical use of the term. The distinction is difficult for those outside of that history. Nevertheless, violating this law outside of the public order can provide subjects with a private transgressive *jouissance*.
5 Extending this example, a similar logic may operate once we attend and feel that our anxiety would go away if only these shoes were more comfortable, or *that* person was not here.
6 Moreover, as Anna Marie Smith (1998, p. 7) suggests, for Laclau and Mouffe, "a discourse of resistance only becomes politicised insofar as the democratic revolution is reappropriated and redefined in specific historical conditions and transferred to the political site in question."
7 Glyn Daly, Mark Devenney, Jason Glynos, David Howarth, Oliver Marchart, Aletta Norval, Jacob Torfing and Yannis Stavrakakis being the most prominent members.
8 Likewise, Stavrakakis has noted the shift in Žižek's work from democracy to anti-capitalism (2003, p. 64).
9 Further, in his 2002 Foreword to the second edition of *For They Know Not What They Do*, Žižek had proposed to remove the "remnants of the liberal-democratic stance" of his previous work (2002b, p. xviii), despite, as Boucher and Sharpe (2010, p. 111) suggest, the first edition of this text being his most radically democratic.
10 Likewise, Nancy (2013, p. 88) states that "In short, democracy means everything – politics, ethics, law, civilisation – and nothing."
11 See http://epetitions.direct.gov.uk/. At the time of writing, the "trending" e-petitions included a criminal prosecution on British citizens who have fought in the Israeli army and mandatory CCTV for all slaughterhouses.
12 Most specifically the surpluses of humanity exist on the edge of capitalism such as in the slums of Dhaka, the camps of Lampudesa and Christmas Island, the military forces and prisons of the United States, as well as the "NEETS" of Britain – and the overdetermination of politics by financial markets.

References

Applebaum, A., 2011. "What the Occupy Protests Tell us about the Limits of Democracy." *Washington Post*. [Online] Available at: www.washingtonpost.com/opinions/what-the-occupy-protests-tell-us-about-the-limits-of-democracy/2011/10/17/gIQAay5YsL_story.html [Accessed 13 October 2013].

Badiou, A., 2013. "The Democratic Emblem." In: G. Agamben, ed. *Democracy, In What State?* New York: Colombia University Press, pp. 6–15.

Boucher, G., 2010. "An Inversion of Radical Democracy: The Republic of Virtue in Žižek's Revolutionary Politics." *International Journal of Žižek Studies*, 4(2).

Boucher, G. and Sharpe, M., 2010. "Introduction: 'Žižek's Communism' and In Defense of Lost Causes." *International Journal of Žižek Studies*, 4(2).

Brand, R., 2013. "Russell Brand on Revolution: 'We No Longer Have the Luxury of Tradition'." *New Statesman.* [Online] Available at: www.newstatesman.com/politics/2013/10/russell-brand-on-revolution [Accessed 1 December 2013].

Brown, W., 2013. "We are All Democrats Now." In: G. Agamben, ed. *Democracy, in What State?* New York: Colombia University Press, pp. 44–57.

Butler, J., Laclau, E., and Žižek, S., 2000. *Contingency, Hegemony, Universality.* London: Verso.

Carswell, D., 2013. "As a Tory MP, I think Russell Brand has a Point: Democracy is in Retreat." *The Telegraph.* [Online] Available at: http://blogs.telegraph.co.uk/news/douglascarswellmp/100244448/as-a-tory-mp-i-think-russell-brand-has-a-point-democracy-is-in-retreat/ [Accessed 10 December 2013].

Cremin, C., 2011. *Capitalism's New Clothes.* London: Pluto Press.

Daly, G., 1999. "Ideology and its Paradoxes: Dimensions of Fantasy and Enjoyment." *Journal of Political Ideologies,* 4(2).

Daly, G., 2004. "Radical(ly) Political Economy: Luhmann, Postmarxism and Globalization." *Review of International Political Economy,* 11(1).

Daly, G., 2009. "Politics of the Political: 'Psychoanalytic Theory and the Left(s)'." *Journal of Political Ideologies,* 14(3), pp. 279–300.

Daly, G., 2010. "Causes for Concern: Žižek's Politics of Loving Terror." *International Journal of Žižek Studies,* 4(2).

Dawson, A., 2013. "Why Russell Brand IS a 'trivial man' with his apathy-fuelled revolution." *The Mirror.* [Online] Available at: www.mirror.co.uk/news/uk-news/russell-brand-newsnight-paxman-right-2487661 [Accessed 2 December 2013].

Dean, J., 2004. "Žižek on Law." *Law and Critique,* 15, pp. 1–24.

Dean, J., 2005. "Žižek against Democracy." *Law, Culture and the Humanities,* 1, pp. 154–177.

Dean, J., 2006. *Žižek's Politics.* London: Routledge.

Eisenstein, P. and McGowan, T., 2013. *Rupture: On the Emergence of the Political.* Evanston, IL: Northwestern University Press.

Elliott, A., 2009. *Contemporary Social Theory: An Introduction.* London: Routledge.

Evans, D., 2003. *An Introductory Dictionary of Lacanian Psychoanalysis.* London: Routledge.

Evans, R., 2013. "Miliband's Energy Price Cap Hits Centrica and SSE Shares." *The Telegraph.* [Online] Available at: www.telegraph.co.uk/finance/personalfinance/investing/shares/10332705/Milibands-energy-price-cap-hits-Centrica-and-SSE-shares.html [Accessed 30 December 2013].

Freud, S., 1960. *The Ego and the Id.* New York: W.W. Norton and Company.

Freud, S., 2002. *Civilization and its Discontents.* London: Penguin.

Glynos, J. and Stavrakakis, Y., 2003. "Encounters of the Real Kind." *Journal for Lacanian Studies,* 1(1), pp. 110–128.

Gosden, E., 2013. "Miliband Energy Price Freeze: Industry Reaction." *The Telegraph.* [Online] Available at: www.telegraph.co.uk/finance/newsbysector/energy/10331410/Miliband-energy-price-freeze-industry-reaction.html [Accessed 30 December 2013].

Graeber, D., 2011. "Occupy and Anarchism's Gift of Democracy." *The Telegraph.* [Online] Available at: www.theguardian.com/commentisfree/cifamerica/2011/nov/15/occupy-anarchism-gift-democracy [Accessed 5 January 2014].

Gye, H., 2013. "Tory Phillipa Roe warns of Burden Romanian and Bulgarian

Immigrants will Place on Public Services." *Daily Mail.* [Online] Available at: www.dailymail.co.uk/news/article-2531793/Roma-Britain-defecating-peoples-doorsteps-says-Tory-council-leader-warns-burden-Romanian-Bulgarian-immigrants-place-public-services.html [Accessed 4 January 2014].
Hardt, M. and Negri, A., 2000. *Empire.* Cambridge, MA: Harvard University Press.
Hardt, M. and Negri, A., 2004. *Multitude.* New York: Penguin.
Hardt, M. and Negri, A., 2011. "The Fight for 'Real Democracy' at the Heart of Occupy Wall Street." *Foreign Affairs.* [Online] Available at: www.foreignaffairs.com/articles/136399/michael-hardt-and-antonio-negri/the-fight-for-real-democracy-at-the-heart-of-occupy-wall-street [Accessed 20 October 2014].
Jameson, F., 2011. *Representing Capital.* London: Verso.
Lacan, J., 1977. *Ecrits: A Selection.* London: Routledge.
Laclau, E., 1987. "Psychoanalysis and Marxism." *Critical Inquiry,* 13(2), pp. 330–333.
Laclau, E., 2000. "Constructuring Universality." In: J. Butler, E. Laclau, and S. Žižek, eds. *Contingency, Hegemony, Universality.* London: Verso, pp. 281–307.
Laclau, E., 2003. "Discourse and Jouissance: A Reply to Glynos and Stavrakakis." *Journal for Lacanian Studies,* 278–285, p. 1.
Laclau, E., 2004. "Glimpsing the Future." In: S. Critchley and O. Marchart, eds. *Laclau: A Critical Reader.* Oxford: Routledge.
Laclau, E., 2006. "Why Constructing a People is the Main Task of Radical Politics." *Critical Inquiry,* 32, pp. 646–680.
Laclau, E. and Mouffe, C., 1985. *Hegemony and Socialist Strategy.* London: Verso.
Laclau, E. and Mouffe, C., 1990. "Post-Marxism without Apologies." In: *New Reflections on the Revolutions of Our Time.* London: Verso.
Lefort, C., 1988. *The Political Forms of Modern Society.* Cambridge: Polity Press.
Levi-Strauss, 1951. "Language and the Analysis of Social Laws." In: *Structural Anthropology.* New York: Basic Books, pp. 55–66.
McGowan, T., 2004. *The End of Dissatisfaction?* Albany, NY: SUNY Press.
McGowan, T., 2013. "Hegel as Marxist: Žižek's Revision of German Idealism." In: J. Khader and M. A. Rothenberg, eds. *Žižek Now.* Cambridge: Polity Press, pp. 31–53.
McMillan, C., 2012. *Žižek and Communist Strategy.* Edinburgh: Edinburgh University Press.
Metropolitan Police, 2013. *Organising a Protest March or Static Demonstration.* [Online] Available at: http://content.met.police.uk/Article/Organising-a-protest-march-or-static-demonstration/1400002380711/1400002380711 [Accessed 13 December 2013].
Mouffe, C., 1992. *Dimensions of Radical Democracy: Pluralism, Citizenship, Community.* London: Verso.
Mouffe, C., 1993. *The Return of the Political.* London: Verso.
Mouffe, C., 2005. *On the Political.* London: Routledge.
Mouffe, C., 2013a. "'A Vibrant Democracy Needs Agonistic Confrontation' – An Interview with Chantal Mouffe." [Online] Available at: www.citsee.eu/interview/vibrant-democracy-needs-agonistic-confrontation-interview-chantal-mouffe [Accessed 12 December 2013].
Mouffe, C., 2013b. "Five Minutes with Chantal Mouffe: 'Most countries in Europe are in a post-political situation'." [Online] Available at: http://blogs.lse.ac.uk/europpblog/2013/09/16/five-minutes-with-chantal-mouffe-most-countries-in-europe-are-in-a-post-political-situation/ [Accessed 12 December 2013].

Nancy, J.-L., 2013. "Finite and Infinite Democracy." In: G. Agamben, ed. *Democracy, in What State?* New York: Colombia University Press, pp. 58–75.

Perkins, A., 2013. "Russell Brand: Mad, Bad and Dangerous for Democracy?" *Guardian.* [Online] Available at: www.theguardian.com/commentisfree/2013/nov/06/russell-brand-democracy-radical-hero [Accessed 12 December 2013].

Reed, J., 2013. "Russell Brand's Revolution – Let's Think About It?" *Huffington Post.* [Online] Available at: www.huffingtonpost.co.uk/jason-reed/russell-brands-revolution_b_4175692.html [Accessed 30 November 2013].

Sharpe, M. and Boucher, G., 2010. *Žižek and Politics.* Edinburgh: Edinburgh University Press.

Slinger, J., 2013. Letters: "An Open Letter to Russell Brand." *Independent.* [Online] Available at: www.independent.co.uk/voices/letters/letters-an-open-letter-to-russell-brand-8927316.html [Accessed 1 December 2013].

Smith, A., 2012. "Only Occupy can Restore Direct Democracy to America." [Online] Available at: www.occupy.com/article/only-occupy-can-restore-direct-democracy-america [Accessed 5 January 2014].

Smith, A. M., 1998. *Laclau and Mouffe: The Radical Democratic Imaginary.* London: Routledge.

Stavrakakis, Y., 1999. *Lacan and the Political.* London: Routledge.

Stavrakakis, Y., 2003. "Re-Activating the Democratic Revolution: The Politics of Transformation Beyond Reoccupation and Conformism." *Parallax*, 2, p. 9.

Stavrakakis, Y., 2007. *The Lacanian Left: Psychoanalysis, Theory, Politics.* Albany, NY: SUNY Press.

Stavrakakis, Y., 2010. "On Acts, Pure and Impure." *International Journal of Žižek Studies*, 4(2).

Taleb, N. N., 2007. *The Black Swan.* New York: Random House.

The Economist, 2011. "Time to Participate in Democracy." *The Economist.* [Online] Available at: www.economist.com/blogs/democracyinamerica/2011/11/occupy-wall-street-0 [Accessed 7 December 2011].

Vighi, F. and Feldner, H., 2006. "Beyond Liberal Democracy: Slavoj Žižek and the Politics of Ideology Critique." *New Formations*, 58(Summer), pp. 53–61.

Webb, R., 2013. "Dear Russell, Choosing to Vote is the Most British Kind of Revolution there Is." *New Statesman.* [Online] Available at: www.newstatesman.com/2013/10/russell-brand-robert-webb-choosing-vote-most-british-kind-revolution-there [Accessed 1 December 2013].

Weber, B., 2011. "Laclau and Žižek on Democracy and Populist Reason." *International Journal of Žižek Studies*, 5(1).

Žižek, S., 1989. *The Sublime Object of Ideology.* London: Verso.

Žižek, S., 1990. "Beyond Discourse Analysis." In: *New Reflections on the Revolutions of our Time.* London: Verso, pp. 249–260.

Žižek, S., 1991. *Looking Awry: An Introduction to Jacques Lacan through Popular Culture.* Cambridge, MA: MIT Press.

Žižek, S., 1993. *Tarrying with the Negative.* Durham: Duke University Press.

Žižek, S., 1997. "Multiculturalism, or, The Cultural Logic of Multinational Capitalism." *New Left Review*, 225(September–October).

Žižek, S., 1999. *The Ticklish Subject.* London: Verso.

Žižek, S., 2000a. "Class Struggle or Postmodernism?" In: J. Butler, E. Laclau and S. Žižek, eds. *Contingency, Hegemony and Universality.* London: Verso, pp. 90–135.

Žižek, S., 2000b. "Holding the Place." In: J. Butler, E. Laclau and S. Žižek, eds. *Contingency, Hegemony and Universality*. London: Verso, pp. 308–329.
Žižek, S., 2001. *On Belief*. London: Verso.
Žižek, S., 2002a. "Afterword: Lenin's Choice." In: S. Žižek, ed. *Revolution at the Gates*. London: Verso, pp. 165–336.
Žižek, S., 2002b. *For they Know Not What they Do*. 2nd ed. London: Verso.
Žižek, S., 2005. "Against Human Rights." *New Left Review*, 34(July–August).
Žižek, S., 2006. "The Prospects for Radical Politics Today." *Critical Inquiry*, 32, pp. 237–257.
Žižek, S., 2008. *In Defense of Lost Causes*. London: Verso.
Žižek, S., 2009. *First as Tragedy, Then as Farce*. London: Verso.
Žižek, S., 2012. *The Year of Dreaming Dangerously*. London: Verso.

Chapter 5

The ambiguous remainder

Contemporary capitalism and the becoming law of the symptom

Fabio Vighi

The two strictly interrelated questions concerning the law that Žižek repeatedly confronts in his writings are the following: How does the law work? How do we subvert law? The necessary precondition to any exploration of Žižek's understanding of law is, however, the awareness that Žižek is not, strictly speaking, a legal theorist (see Dean 2004). Rather, he has developed a psychoanalytic/philosophical approach that aims to expose the law's disavowed ontological core, which intersects and conditions the fundamental categories of being. Žižek's starting point is that there is no world outside the socio-symbolic law in which we dwell; all we can do is momentarily suspend its powerful grasp in order to reset its content. Second, what allows for content-related transformation is the law's hidden contradiction, which, however, is also the crucial hinge that sustains its functioning. The law, for Žižek, is internally antagonized by an inerasable excess *which is also its condition of possibility*. It is therefore apparent that Žižek's "general theory of law" is founded upon an antagonistic substance whose dialectical role is absolutely ambiguous – which, in turn, leads to an intrinsically problematic theory of political transformation. My evaluation of Žižek's concept of law is twofold: first, I outline its theoretical orientation, tracking the roots of the psychoanalytic insight that the law is grounded in its own libidinally-invested excess; in a second move, I look at cinematic representations of such excess with a view to assessing the validity of Žižek's theory of law vis-à-vis the current configuration of global capitalism.

The scandal of the law

The basic tenet of Žižek's theory of law resides in the Lacanian axiom that the law by definition redoubles into a strictly speaking unruly (excessive, violent, obscene) remainder; as well as representing the core of the law, this remainder embodies its intrinsic weakness, its inconsistency, in other words its vulnerability and potential changeability. To put it concisely: the law's *jouissance* (its "unlawful" excess) occupies the split within law, its self-fissuring, and as such captures the essence of law. Perhaps the most succinct

Žižekian definition of the law's excess is provided by way of the tautology "law is law." There is of course an implicitly authoritarian resonance in the above tautology, and that is, in a nutshell, the *violence* consubstantial with law: "the domain of symbolic rules, if it is actually to count as such, has to be grounded in some tautological authority *beyond rules*, which says 'It is so because I say it is so!'" (Žižek 1999: 320). More generally, in every tautology (e.g., "God is God") the second term "generates the specter of an ineffable X beyond words" (Žižek 2011: 68), thus abruptly halting the potentially infinite series of determinations and providing the semblance of closure, stability, and therefore unquestionable signification. In Lacanian terms, the signifier redoubles into its own determination (it "falls into the signified") in order to prevent its infinite "sliding" into other signifiers. What this operation veils is precisely the fundamental *lack* or inconsistency that inheres in language – the fact that a signifier is always, by definition, missing. And, from a Lacanian perspective, the letter is also the "letter of the law," that is to say law is rooted in the inconsistency of language.

As we shall see, the role of the Lacanian master-signifier is, formally speaking, a tautological one, insofar as it fills in (conceals, veils) the ontological lack that pertains to the signifier. According to Žižek – as confirmed also by his essay in this collection – the violence that pertains to law cannot be shirked if the aim is to change the socio-political content of a given legal framework. In fact, it needs to be assumed in the awareness that violence can also be emancipatory. For Žižek, violence *qua* "anchoring point" of law is by definition caught in a parallax: while it serves the purpose of enforcing the law, it simultaneously embodies what Hegel called "the right to distress" *qua* legal right par excellence, "*a conflict inherent to the sphere of rights*, a conflict which is unavoidable and *necessary* insofar as it serves as an indication of the finitude, inconsistency, and 'abstract' character of the system of legal rights as such."[1] While I fully share Žižek's attempt to demystify the theme of violence as embodiment of the ontological antagonism that cuts across any socio-symbolic or legalistic framework, in this essay I want to focus less on the debate on the legitimacy of violence than on the critique of the conditions that would lead to a radical transformation which, by necessity, would appear violent. In other words, my fear is that, today, any discussion on emancipatory violence will turn out to be abstract if we neglect what I regard as the crucial step towards any potential societal transformation, namely the critical awareness of how the current developments within global capitalism are already altering the nature of the relationship between law and its excess.

Superego enjoyment

In order to tackle this question, which is centered in the assumption that the ongoing economic crisis is shifting the goalposts with regard to how law is perceived and indeed enforced, it is vital to identify the theoretical mould of Žižek's concept of law. Žižek's outlook originates in the psychoanalytic view that the law is fundamentally split between its public letter (explicit text) and its superego supplement (*jouissance*), which is central to many of Žižek's texts (especially the earlier ones): "Superego is the obscene 'nightly' law that necessarily redoubles and accompanies, as its shadow, the 'public' Law" (Žižek 1994: 54). Lacan (1991: 102) had made this point already in *Seminar I (1954–55)*: "The super-ego is at one and the same time the law and its destruction." The connection between superego (the internalized compulsion to obey) and *jouissance* (excessive, destabilizing enjoyment) as constitutive of the law may seem contradictory, and yet, precisely as a contradiction, it captures the gist of the Freudian argument that the necessary implementation of the law (civilization) requires a sacrifice of enjoyment that is compensated by libidinally-charged superego pressure. To obey the law means, effectively, to renounce our desire to transgress it – a desire which the superego predates on, thus making us feel guilty. As Kafka's books testify all too painfully, our feeling of guilt is paradoxically caused by our compliance with the law, by the simple fact that we dwell in the law, rather than from our transgressing it. The more we obey, in other words, the more the law's "nightly supplement" (the superego) makes us feel guilty. But how, exactly? It all begins with the superego's "irrational" command, whose intervention aims precisely to conceal the law's constitutive inadequacy: since the law's rational, "public" or explicit text cannot fully explain to us why we should obey instead of following our desire, it needs the help of this "brute" named superego – an internalized and therefore inescapable injunction which manipulates the libido that constituted our desire to transgress. In other (Lacan's) words, the superego captures the repressed truth of Kant's moral law.

Žižek had already made this point in *The Sublime Object of Ideology* (1989: 81):

> It is a commonplace of Lacanian theory to emphasise how this Kantian moral imperative conceals an obscene superego injunction: "Enjoy!" – the voice of the Other impelling us to follow our duty for the sake of duty is a traumatic irruption of an appeal to impossible *jouissance*, disrupting the homeostasis of the pleasure principle.... But in what precisely does this obscenity of the moral Law consist? ... we obey moral Law because it is law and not because of a set of positive reasons.

The superego command is therefore highly ambiguous and controversial: its "You must obey without asking why!" is *formally* identical to "Why have you betrayed your desire? Can't you see that you could have enjoyed (more)?" The superego command resonates with an "appeal to impossible *jouissance*," and that is why we feel guilty. The feeling of guilt arises from our failure to engage with the "impossible" (always-already missing) object of desire that constitutes the substance of what we are. Subjectivity, insofar as it is grounded in law, is therefore a priori (su)stained by guilt. Or, differently stated: since the Lacanian subject coincides with its *jouissance*, which fills in an ontological lack, any "narrative construction" such as law or subjectivity is nothing but a way of masking the Real of our desire.

Lacan developed this Freudian theme especially in his text "Kant avec Sade" and in *Seminar VII*. In this respect, a key progression needs to be highlighted concerning Lacan's thought on the subject: while in the earlier phase of his work the superego featured as the Freudian category representing the return of the part of primordial, pre-subjective *jouissance* necessarily "cut off" with the subject's submission to the law, the later Lacan tends to think *jouissance* not as a somewhat "mythical" substance *preceding* the law but as coterminous with the substantial lack inevitably *consequential* to the "grafting" of language on the subject's body. Žižek fully endorses the later Lacan's notion of the Real of *jouissance* as a lack that can only be experienced and conceptualized *after* the alienating intervention of the signifier (the symbolic order), which of course grounds any reference to law. Before the signifier there is, literally, nothing.

Law as paradox

The key political implications for the above move are, essentially, two, and constitute the basis of my argument about the ambiguity of law's excess. First, Žižek categorically rejects the idea, no matter how hypothetical or utopian, of a sustainable socio-political horizon freed from the alienating presence of the law (inclusive of its addendum): enduring freedom from the law can only mean dwelling in a psychotic hell, lacking the crucial screen/mediation provided by the big Other. Following Lacan, then, Žižek endorses subjectivity as a dimension that is inextricably tied to the presence of the big Other, the space where social rules and fantasies are always-already articulated for us. This reflects Lacan's central notion of "symbolic castration," which is fully endorsed by Žižek and plays a key role in his politics. In Hegelian terms, we would say that true freedom resides not in the infinite overcoming of a limit but in accepting the limit set by law, the fact that only within certain limitations are we capable of developing and relating to an idea and practice of freedom. Second, and crucially, Žižek's "law" includes its own potentially destabilizing excess, also understandable as the typically Hegelian contradiction which, dialectically, functions as law's unacknowledged anchoring point. In brief: the excess of the law is both the hinge that supports the explicit text of the law and the "weak point" that may allow us to reconfigure its content. The law, then, at once secures the circulation of desire and is stained by *jouissance*. The paradox is that within the law's conservative function lies its destabilizing core. The *form* of the law, therefore, does not change, since it is constituted by the overlap of explicit text and disavowed-yet-fully-operative remainder; this overlap is by definition ambiguous since it captures both the coercive capacity of the law and its intrinsic, fundamental impotence.

The analogy that comes to mind here is with Lacan's concept of the phallus as the negativized image of the penis (or the "impossible" number corresponding to the square root of –1). In his 1958 paper "The Signification of the Phallus," Lacan (2006: 581) contends that the structuring role played by the phallus in the socio-symbolic order has to do, oddly enough, with its absence from it. The phallus can "play its role only when veiled, that is, as itself a sign of the latency with which any signifiable is stuck, once it is raised (*aufgehoben*) to the function of signifier. The phallus is the signifier of this very *Aufhebung*, which it inaugurates (initiates) by its disappearance." The phallus thus derives its symbolic power from its absence from the public social field and from the visual field of representation *tout court*. Another way of putting this is that the law, in a similar manner to the penis's erection, "works" only against the background of its own impotence. If law and power are inherently inconsistent, "lacking to themselves," then, Žižek often argues, the strategy of subversion most likely to succeed involves not actively opposing the law but, as it were, endorsing its total grasp, fully identifying with it, so that its inconsistency might emerge as a destabilizing factor. Žižek's defence of the "emancipatory function of violence" is embedded in the above insight into subversion.

Staging violence

Perhaps Žižek's most memorable discussion of the above theme is the one relating to David Fincher's film *Fight Club* (1999). The basic question posed by the film's hero (Norton) is simple and, at once, absolutely pressing: how is the contemporary subject to break out of "the futility of a life filled with failure and empty consumer culture"? (Žižek 2002: 250). The answer is equally simple, though apparently absurd: through self-beating. This stratagem is rendered in what is perhaps the most significant scene of the film, when the hero, while arguing with his boss, decides to act out the latter's repressed anger by beating himself up. According to Žižek, this shockingly masochistic act represents the only way "to suspend the fundamental abstraction and coldness of capitalist subjectivity." The subversion of the law is here linked to a self-damaging act "which is equivalent to adopting the position of the proletarian who has nothing to lose." The emergence of pure subjectivity coincides with an "experience of radical self-degradation" whereby I, the subject, am emptied "of all substantial content, of all symbolic support which could confer a modicum of dignity on me" (252). The reason why such a humiliating and potentially perverse position is to be assumed, Žižek argues, is that within a disciplinary relationship self-beating amounts to the staging of the other's secret fantasy; as such, it allows for the momentary suspension of the disciplinary efficacy of the relationship by bringing to light, and assuming, the obscene supplement which secretly cements it.

Žižek's key point, however, is that this obscene supplement ultimately cements the position of the "servant": what self-beating uncovers is "the servant's masochistic libidinal attachment to his master," so that "the true goal of this beating is to beat out that in me which attaches me to the master" (252). Being aware of our state of is therefore not enough, for that very subjection is embedded in a power mechanism and, as such, inevitably eroticized, sustained by our disavowed pleasure in being caught in it:

> When we are subjected to a power mechanism, this subjection is always and by definition sustained by some libidinal investment: the subjection itself generates a surplus-enjoyment of its own. This subjection is embodied in a network of "material" bodily practices, and for this reason we cannot get rid of our subjection through a merely intellectual reflection – our liberation has to be *staged* in some kind of bodily performance; furthermore, this performance *has* to be of an apparently "masochistic" nature, it *has* to stage the painful process of hitting back at oneself.
>
> (253)

Ultimately, the passage from "oppressed victim" to "active agent of the revolution" requires a *subtractive* move whereby the subject endorses that explosive excess/symptom which anchors his identity in the texture of the law: "*the only true awareness of our subjection is the awareness of the obscene excessive pleasure (surplus-enjoyment) we derive from it*; this is why the first gesture of liberation is not to get rid of this excessive pleasure, but actively to assume it" (254).

The point is worth summarizing: through the explicit (seemingly masochistic) assumption of the law's *jouissance*, one attempts to expose what Lacan calls "the non-existence of the big Other," the foundational inconsistency or absurdity of the law itself, to which we are always-already libidinally attached. In his essay "Coldness and Cruelty," Deleuze (1989: 40) argues that what supremely frustrates the sadistic executioner (representative of the excessive core of the law) is the masochistic fervour of his victim: "a genuine sadist could never tolerate a masochist victim." As Žižek notes (2002: 253), the reason for this frustration is that masochism forces the sadist to acknowledge that the object of his desire – the body of the other insofar as it suffers pain – is *already the object of the other's desire*, and as such it cannot be truly enjoyed. The masochist, then, steals the secret *jouissance* of the law, thus making visible the extent to which the law is dependent on, even enslaved to, the lack that pertains to the economy of desire. The *jouissance* staged by the masochist affirms its speculative identity with the *jouissance* of the law-enforcing executioner, hence revealing the strict correlation between the neutral yet coercive character of the law and the groundlessness of desire. As Lacan (1998: 2–3) put it at the beginning of *Seminar XX*, the law basically enjoys. And if the law, in its deepest connotation, mobilizes *jouissance*, this means that it is driven by an irrational and strictly speaking unlawful "will to enjoy."

The crucial element that emerges from this picture is the law's fundamental imbalance, which leads to its vulnerability. Žižek, then, following Lacan, turns around Kant's claim that the moral law is the measure of the subject's freedom: it is not that the unbearable pressure of the moral law coincides with disinterestedness and freedom, but that freedom can only be given as an unbearable pressure to face the empty kernel of the law. Bringing together freedom and the staging of self-beating thus targets precisely the tautological foundations of the law: the real scandal is, as Deleuze (1989: 82–85) put it by way of a comment on Kant's *Critique of Practical Reason*, that "the law ... is self-grounded and valid solely by virtue of its own form ... the object of the law is by definition unknowable and elusive." Such a perspective implies that "the object of the law and the object of desire are one and the same, and remain equally concealed"; or, as Lacan (1981: 275–76) commented at the end of *Seminar XI*, that

> the moral law ... is simply desire in its pure state, the very desire that culminates in the sacrifice, strictly speaking, of everything that is the object of love in one's human tenderness – I would say, not only in the rejection of the pathological object, but also in its sacrifice and murder. That is why I wrote *Kant avec Sade*.

This position can also be elaborated in terms of guilt. If the gap that separates the law from its positive content makes the subject a priori guilty (for, as in the supreme example of Kafka's novels, the subject never knows where he stands with respect to the "irrational" law), it is only the subject's full assumption of this indelible guilt that can break the vicious circle of law and sin, i.e., law and its transgressive supplement. Žižek, in the wake of Alain Badiou (1997), often contends that the question of how to suspend the vicious circle of law and its transgression was confronted by Saint Paul. Paul's wager is that the only way to break out of the superego's injunction to sin is via love; however, what should be emphasized is that Pauline Love coincides with the intrinsically violent dimension of the Fall (Christ on the cross), the traumatic – once again, *subtractive* – moment when we "lose everything," endorsing the fundamental contingency of any symbolic construct and renouncing our attachment to the world.

Subtractive strategy

Although in his most recent books Žižek has de-emphasized the theme of emancipatory self-directed violence in order to privilege a more formalistic definition of *jouissance* as the intrinsically neutral binding core of any symbolic/ideological framework, the basic argument has remained fundamentally identical. Let us take, by way of exemplification, the point he makes apropos the staging of *jouissance* performed by contemporary hard rock band Rammstein, who often make use of Nazi iconography; for Žižek (2011: 372), over-identifying with the "inextricable mixture of the sacred and the obscene," with the "unleashed brutality" staged by Rammstein, effectively liberates *jouissance* from its articulation in an oppressive ideology (in this case, Nazi ideology), thus making it available for its radical reconfiguration in a different symbolic/ideological edifice (though Žižek does not elaborate on this): "Rammstein undermine totalitarian ideology not with an ironic distance towards the rituals they imitate, but by directly confronting it with its obscene materiality and thereby suspending its efficacy" (387). One can easily recognize in this brief example, which is one among many, Žižek's typical theorization of subversion as predicated upon over-identification with the violent, disavowed yet also liberating libidinal core of the ideological/legal system. The aim is, first, to unbind a given symbolic context from its anchoring in *jouissance*, thus rendering it inefficient; and, second, to free *jouissance* itself, "making it available" for a different symbolic order. The first aim is subtractive or internally disabling, while the second is constructive.

I have already argued (see Vighi 2010) that if there is a weak point in this brilliant conceptualization of subversion – which, it must be said, allows one to unmask the intrinsic hypocrisy of much radical, "critical-utopian" (to use Žižek's own words) leftist thought[2] – it lies in the excessive weight it grants the first subtractive move, which implies that the more urgent second (constructive) one is left largely unattended. To put it bluntly: while the current crisis of global capitalism is already doing the "subtracting job" for us, what is glaringly missing from today's horizon is a theory that conjoins law and *jouissance* in a radically novel way, one which would allow us to overcome the deadlock or contradiction within capitalism whose harsh consequences we are now being subjected to.

Furthermore, the issue of subtraction is much trickier than we might believe when theorizing it. While it is true that capitalism is continually displacing ever-larger masses of people who are increasingly excluded from its dynamics, at the same time the "work of subtraction" is hindered by the very capitalist fantasy, which continues to sustain the system even at a time when it has clearly encountered its internal limit, producing "human waste" rather than economic growth. I believe this specific point was recently made by Woody Allen's film *Blue Jasmine* (2013), which speaks to the following paradox: even if the ongoing capitalist crisis is emphatically telling us that our productive system has no future whatsoever,[3] what counts is that our libidinal attachment to the fantasy it engenders (the ubiquitous commodification of our lives) is keeping it artificially alive. Jasmine (Cate Blanchett), the delusional protagonist of the film, should be seen as an incarnation of our obstinate refusal to mourn the actual death of capitalism as a growth-producing economic system. In the second part of this essay I will draw on film to attempt to assess how Žižek's concept of law fares with regard to the current turn within global capitalism.

Cinematic visions of law's symptom

A brief reference to Pier Paolo Pasolini's infamous film *Salò, or the 120 Days of Sodom* (1975) allows us to clarify the connection between law and its nightly superegoic supplement. The film's protagonists are four fascists, representative of Law as such, who abduct 18 young men and women, take them to a palace and abuse them in a number of sadistic ways. The law, then, is here explicitly associated with a form of obscene enjoyment that internally derails it. More to the point, to grasp the film's most significant theme it is crucial to realize that the fascists/libertines' perverted desire is characterized as *a form of pleasure beyond the pleasure principle*, a form of enjoyment unable to satisfy itself as it encounters its limit in the empty kernel of the desired object (the other's body). What is generally missed by critics is that *Salò* does not merely revolve around perverted pleasure, but rather around its endless pursuit. Proof of this is that despite their vaunted expertise in all fields of sexuality, the libertines dismiss their own orgasm (and the comfort that derives from it). The truth about their perversion is thus to be found in the limitless repetition of the act they stage, which is based on the rejection of pleasure in favor of *jouissance*. What we have is therefore the passage from desire to drive: from the awareness that the encounter with the object of desire is impossible (desire), to the awareness that the disturbing Real of enjoyment (*jouissance*) will stick to us whatever we do, like a curse (drive). And what these "Sadean executioners" discover at the end of their journey into the dark realm of *jouissance* is that the impossibility of (attaining) the object coincides with the impossible/disavowed/excessive kernel of the law they personify. Such a realization cannot but have devastating consequences: as the final part of the film suggests, it leads to the collapse of their psychic balance.

The image from the film that demonstrates this point most effectively is the shot of the madly enraged Monsignor cracking his whip in the courtyard. Here we witness the purposeless fury of the law's own obscene double, which betrays the groundlessness of law as such. The terrifyingly frustrated expression of the Monsignor suggests that torture has turned into a kind of self-torture, for the more he inflicts pain on his victims, the more he effectively "whips himself," feeding into his drive not to reach the object.[4] This uncovering of the inner volatility (and thus fragility and changeability) of the law acquires an even more stringent significance if observed from the standpoint of Pasolini's notorious anti-capitalist stance. His wager here seems to be that at a time when resisting or escaping the rule of capital is a desperate, near-impossible task, the most effective line of attack lies in assuming capitalism's own explosive imbalance, which simultaneously implies that we are only able to gain a distance from the law by identifying with its shadowy kernel. And precisely because it endorses over-identification with the law, Pasolini's strategy, like Žižek's, is at the opposite end of today's hegemonic postmodern attitude of taking an ironic distance towards anything concerning power and ideology. Ultimately, *Salò* confronts head-on *the scandal of the law*, the fact that the letter of the law is moored in the pure, implicitly self-destructive drive expressed by its nightly supplement. And Žižek's Lacanian point about the connection between superego and Kant's moral law is precisely that they are a manifestation of drive, they embody *jouissance*, and as such they are, inevitably, self-destabilizing.

"The fucking rules!"

Cinema is, in this sense, a perfect vehicle for scrutinizing the paradox of the unruly core of the law. One of the crucial lessons of contemporary Hollywood cinema lies in its representation of the connection between paternal authority and violence. Perhaps the prototype of this kind of Hollywood character is Mr Eddy from David Lynch's *Lost Highway* (1997), a mobster whose paternal role reaches its obscene "truth" in the scene where he tracks down a tailgater and, in a bout of shocking rage, beats him black and blue while shouting the following, seemingly contrapuntal, injunctions:

> Don't tailgate! Don't you ever tailgate! Do you know how many car lengths it takes to stop a car at 35 miles per hour? Six fucking car lengths! That's a hundred and six fucking feet, mister! If I had to stop suddenly, you would have hit me! I want you to get a fucking driver's manual, and I want you to study that motherfucker! And I want you to obey the goddamn rules! Fifty-fucking-thousand people were killed on the highways last year because of fucking assholes like you! Tell me you're going to get a manual!

As Žižek (2000: 18) puts it in his comment on this scene, "one should risk taking the figure of Eddy thoroughly *seriously*, as someone who is desperately trying to maintain a minimum of order, to enforce some elementary "fucking rules" in this otherwise crazy universe." The fact that it is an underworld figure who desperately seeks to enforce the law is both a symptom of the erosion of legitimate symbolic authority in our contemporary society (see McGowan 2007: 249) and a metaphorical rendition of the intrinsic unruliness of the disavowed core of the law. In fact, I would argue that in presenting these pivotal characters as criminals, Hollywood cinema only attempts to ideologically displace the truth about law. One should therefore apply Žižek's dialectical (Hegelian) wisdom: the distance between crime and law is internal to law – it captures law's "headless" character, its fundamental pointlessness which is at once represented and concealed by its violence (crime).

What is absolutely central in the scene from *Lost Highway* is the way the physical and verbal violence supplement the letter of the law as spelt out by Mr Eddy, who is therefore not simply a thug but a perfect incarnation of the functioning of the law through its unlawful redoubling (Kant's categorical imperative). Imagine the same scene with a police officer stopping the car for tailgating: if we read the above quotation without the obscene language we get the perfectly logical, rational argument that a police officer would have used to caution the offender. And Žižek's point about the split within law is that this logical application of the letter of the law would resonate precisely with the obscene superego excess the film so accurately depicts. In this respect, Žižek (1994: 60) reads (critically) Althusser's example about interpellation (a policeman suddenly shouting at you "Hey, you there!") precisely as a manifestation of the overlapping of law and its underside: although I am innocent in the eyes of the law, I cannot help developing "an indeterminate Kafkaesque feeling of 'abstract' guilt, a feeling that, in the eyes of Power, I am a priori terribly guilty of something." The gist of Žižek's point about the ambiguity of the law's remainder is succinctly rendered in the following passage:

> The paradox here is that the obscene superego underside is, in one and the same gesture, the necessary *support* of the public symbolic law and the traumatic vicious circle, the impasse that the subject endeavours to *avoid* by way of taking refuge in the public Law – in order to assert itself, public Law has to resist its own foundation, to render it invisible.
>
> (61)

Let us recall David Cronenberg's *A History of Violence* (2005); what thrills us in this film are the "two faces" (metaphorically and literally) of the father: Tom Stall (Viggo Mortensen), a peaceful, modest, law-abiding diner owner, leading a seemingly ordinary life in a small provincial American town, suddenly turns into a furious "killing machine" in order to protect his family and, more generally, his unassuming way of life. Although we soon find out that, before seeking redemption and a new "small-town" life, Tom used to work for the mob as an assassin (with his real name of Joey Cusack), the film's central theme, which impresses us beyond the narrative twists, remains that of the "shocking" overlap between the "calm face" of public paternal authority and the deranged, strangely sadistic enjoyment of its superegoic supplement. In this respect, one of the most powerful scenes occurs towards the end, when Tom/Joey is confronted outside his house by the gangsters he used to work for, who are seeking revenge for his betrayal. The moment his teenage son is apprehended by the gangsters, who demand to exchange him for Joey himself, we witness a sudden, disturbing turn in the hero's facial expression: his hitherto calm, reassuring features take on a wild, near-psychotic look, inundated with a sort of reckless *jouissance* which explodes in the following violent confrontation.

Law, violence, and the collapse of symbolic efficiency

An interesting representation of redoubled paternal authority, comparable to that of Cronenberg's film, runs through Nicolas Winding Refn's *Drive* (2011) as well as the subsequent *Only God Forgives* (2013). In this respect, the originality and intrinsic merit of *Drive* is that it places "paternal authority" in a world whose symbolic efficiency has clearly collapsed. In *Drive*'s wasteland, a universe where the "old values" are no longer operative, the hero's determination in protecting his neighbours Irene and her young son Benicio acquires a "miraculous" significance independently of the intrinsic romanticism of the story. What matters to our approach, however, is once again the split character of authority, which here is brought to new heights by the unnamed Ryan Gosling character (a getaway driver employed by criminals). The scene where the driver encounters the hitman in the elevator and violently kills him while Irene watches in horror is reminiscent of the scene from *History of Violence* described above, since it plays out the same elementary self-splitting of law: the tenderness with which the driver kisses Irene before reducing the gangster to a pulp should not be seen as a sign of his twisted psychic economy but as a powerful rendition of the inherent dark truth concerning law.

Only God Forgives, Refn's follow-up to *Drive*, is, in its overtly Oedipal narrative, even more explicitly concerned with exactly the same theme of the overlap between authority and its violent underside. The image that, at different points in the film, iconically captures the necessity of what Lacan would call the "paternal metaphor" consubstantial with law is the cutting off of a hand: unambiguously, this violent, emasculating gesture asserts the necessity of "symbolic castration" – where "castration," despite being "symbolic," should nevertheless be read as a traumatic (and liberating) experience. In this respect, Refn's film is unashamedly centered on a representation of brutal authority which proclaims at once its necessity and its contingency, insofar as the functioning of law is shown as depending on its strictly-speaking criminal core, which also captures its precariousness.

The basic structure of the plot easily lends itself to a symbolic interpretation: Julian (Ryan Gosling) and Billy (Tom Burke) are two American expatriate brothers running a drug smuggling business in Bangkok, and should be seen as contemporary incarnations of lawless *jouissance* – which is why they are, in different ways, highly disturbed characters. In fact, the beginning of the film reminds us that, in psychoanalytic terms, it is impossible to live a life completely absorbed in *jouissance*, since it can only turn into a nightmarish and deeply traumatic drive. When the only command addressed to the subject is the superego command to enjoy, one can rest assured that such enjoyment will at some point morph into some sort of pathology. The problem presented by Refn's film is therefore a very pressing one: what options are we left with, today, in a world where the symbolic law has subsided and its symptom ("Enjoy!") has effectively taken its place, becoming the *explicit* injunction that runs our existence? Fully aware that our "society of enjoyment" does not merely imply a general attitude of bored, vacuous hedonism, but more crucially the frightening prospect of a life trapped in perversion, the film offers us two potential outcomes in the fates suffered by the two brothers. While Billy's sexual perversion is so pathologically excessive (psychotic) that it can only meet its satisfaction in death, Julian's is more complex, articulated as it is around his impotence. We soon understand that such impotence is rooted in the character's twisted relation to his despotic mother Crystal (Kristin Scott Thomas) – a wonderful incarnation of the cynical, ruthless and vulgar heart of globalized capitalism – who had apparently ordered him to kill his real father.

The film makes it abundantly clear that the missing figure in this context of unbound yet profoundly self-crippling *jouissance* is precisely that of the "traditional" Father – or, more precisely, of the Lacanian "Name-of-the-Father," the signifier which, by curtailing *jouissance*, opens up for the subject the path of law, of the "liberating alienation" in the big Other. In the absence of the "paternal metaphor," then, there emerges its obscene unacknowledged double, which captures the essence of law. This is the gist of Žižek's argument apropos such films as Rob Reiner's *A Few Good Men* (1992) and Francis Ford Coppola's *Apocalypse Now* (1979):

> While the explicit law is sustained by the dead father qua symbolic authority (Lacan's "Name of the Father"), the unwritten code is sustained by the spectral supplement of the Name of the Father, the

> obscene spectre of the Freudian "primordial father" ... the total Master who dares to confront face-to-face the Real of terrifying enjoyment.

The crucial point here is that such a figure, for Žižek, emerges "not as a remainder of some barbaric past, but as the necessary outcome of modern Western power itself" (Žižek 2008: 148–149).

In Refn's film the character of the "total Master" is played by Chang (Vithaya Pansringarm), an almost mythical police lieutenant who, like the protagonist of *Drive*, conflates ruthlessness and compassion, brutality and tenderness.[5] Julian's relation to Chang is, inevitably, characterized by a mixture of fascination and aggressiveness. In this respect, the telling passages, early on in the film, are those where Julian has visions of meeting Chang in a dark room, with Chang cutting his hands off. The metaphor is all too obvious: Julian desperately craves the sort of "symbolic castration" that Chang can provide, since presumably only at that stage will he be able to do away with the incestuous attachment to his mother and relate in a (neurotically) "normal" way to his desire. Eventually, he will achieve precisely such "castration," as the last time we see him, in the film's penultimate scene, he is in a field with Chang, who appears to cut off both of his hands with his sword.

The interesting thing here is that Oedipus is, as it were, transposed into a post-Oedipal context, where symbolic efficiency has vanished and has been replaced by "the obscene spectre of the Freudian 'primordial father'" as the sole guarantee of the law. The comparison with *Apocalypse Now* is particularly tempting: while at the end of Coppola's film the "son" (Captain Willard, played by Martin Sheen) successfully brings to completion his "top secret" mission and kills the spectre of *père-jouissance* (Kurtz, played by Marlon Brando), thus re-establishing the symbolic authority of the explicit text of the law (here represented by the American army), in *Only God Forgives* this option is no longer available: the Name of the Father, the very idea of a symbolic agency exercising any kind of pacifying and enabling function, is irredeemably lost, and we are plunged instead into a universe of perverted *jouissance* that, at best, can be tamed by a law that does not hide but openly endorses its obscene core. The difference is substantial: if in Coppola's film the law is still split between explicit public text and obscene addendum, being represented by two distinct "bodies" (the American army and Kurtz), with Refn the split is internal to the same "body" (Chang).

The critical implication contained in Refn's film is that in our contemporary universe it has become impossible to "unmask the law" – to denounce its obscene underside – *since there is nothing left but this underside*, which, it would seem, one can only hope (as Refn, romantically, does) to supplement with a Master (the God of the Old Testament) who, although brutal, is also fundamentally benevolent. It would be interesting, in this respect, to compare *Only God Forgives* with the Coen brothers' *No Country for Old Men* (2007), for the two films respond in a radically different manner to the same devastating awareness relating to the collapse of the symbolic law: the God-like vengeance of Chang in *Only God Forgives* is replaced by the self-conscious, deeply disillusioned loss of efficiency of the official law – represented by sheriff Ed Tom Bell (Tommy Lee Jones) – in *No Country for Old Men.* The Coen brothers' film a priori rejects Refn's transcendental romanticism and, instead, delivers a further dose of negativity: the desolate scenario of the corrupt Western world dominated by unscrupulous thirst for money (the film's classic theme) is not only, here, so pervasive as to have completely disabled the traditional letter of the law; it also redoubles itself immanently into an absolutely enigmatic figure of Mastery (Anton Chigurh, played by Javier Bardem) who is completely devoid of positive features, indeed epitomizing ontological negativity per se (chance, contingency, or even death qua Absolute Master).

The above films' portrayal of the "collapsing" of the rational/symbolic "scaffolding" of law into its libidinal underside is indeed characteristic of our times and should be regarded as one of the most insightful, even "prophetic" features of contemporary Hollywood cinema. In such portrayals we get a glimpse of truth about our post-Oedipal "society of enjoyment," finally freed from the law's annoying prohibitions and their "ridiculous" figures of authority; such truth is, when brought down to its basic formula, the truth of a generalized condition of perversion with strong psychotic tendencies. This outcome is inevitable for a society that has seamlessly disposed of the symbolic law (the efficiency of the performative dimension of the signifier, redoubled into its "dark underside"), since such a society disavows what Lacan calls the "lack in the Other," which represents the only possibility of effecting change.

As Žižek (1999: 247–257) has remarked, perversion is definitely *not* subversive, since it denies the desire of (emanating from) the Other – in other words it forecloses the very split character of the socio-symbolic order, thus precluding any intervention into its negativity. The pervert's enjoyment depends upon a "mortified" other, reduced to a lifeless object, drained of all desire. Ultimately, this is why Lacan refers to the discourse of the University as the modern perversion of the discourse of the Master: it is characterized by a totalizing, systematic knowledge about the Other, which functions as an injunction ("You must know (what the Other wants)!").

Law and capitalist jouissance

So what about the intrinsically perverted "law of capitalism"? The assumption – widely shared among Lacanians – is that the decline of symbolic efficiency (the contraction of the "paternal metaphor") has been accelerated, historically, by the collapse of the Communist bloc and subsequent globalization of capitalism. We are increasingly drawn into a constellation whose symbolic space is organized and regulated not only by capital but especially by its "regime of enjoyment," which has effectively replaced the "traditional" efficiency of the explicit text of the law. Events which in the past might have damaged (or have been regarded as dangerous for) a given socio-symbolic entity are today quickly reabsorbed within a ubiquitous economy of enjoyment which tends to strengthen rather than undermine the system. However "scandalous" the exposure of certain "hidden truths" may be, it is more likely to be consumed and digested as a spectacle than pose a threat to the status quo. It is within this globalized and emasculating regime of enjoyment, which effectively stifles the possibility of encountering *jouissance*, that a systemic crisis has recently struck, testing the resilience of the capitalist matrix.

In respect of my analysis of Žižek's concept of law, what we are witnessing today begs the following question: when a systemic crisis hits a "society of enjoyment," where the symbolic law has lost its traditional efficiency, what is the most likely scenario to emerge? In my view, the answer is the one provided by *Only God Forgives*, though most likely *without* the film's romantic allure or hopeful naivety: the intervention of an authoritarian master who, unlike the traditional one, will not make a secret of his "obscenity," of his shameless enjoyment. Žižek hinted at this type of new mastery in a number of recent works, such as his essay "Berlusconi in Tehran":

> It is democracy's authentic potential that is losing ground with the rise of authoritarian capitalism, whose tentacles are coming closer and closer to the West. … Both Putin and Berlusconi rule in democracies which are gradually being reduced to an empty shell … Berlusconi is a significant figure, and Italy an experimental laboratory where our future is being worked out. If our political choice is between permissive-liberal technocratism and fundamentalist populism, Berlusconi's great achievement has been to reconcile the two, to embody both at the same time.… Yet we shouldn't be fooled: behind the clownish mask there is a state power that functions with ruthless efficiency. Perhaps by laughing at Berlusconi we are already playing his game. A technocratic economic administration combined with a clownish façade does not suffice, however: something more is needed. That something is fear, and here Berlusconi's two-headed dragon enters: immigrants and "communists" (Berlusconi's generic name for anyone who attacks him, including *The Economist*).
>
> (Žižek 2009: 4–5)

This analysis should be endorsed and supplemented with the full acknowledgement, and critique, of the impact carried by the current crisis, which exacerbates the turn toward authoritarianism already inherent to the post-1989 paradigm. China, as Žižek has re-emphasized in his essay for this collection, is perhaps the most unequivocal contemporary example of the alliance between capital and non-democratic politics. The danger we are facing today is that, in order to survive its crisis and retain global supremacy as a socio-economic system, capitalism will continue to unashamedly promote, and identify with, the "direct rule of law," with all its unpleasant consequences. In the present conditions, with ever-increasing masses of people "falling off" the social order sustained by the capitalist economy, it is to be expected that the conservation of such order will determine a shift in the functioning of the law: the hidden, symptomatic excess of the law will progressively morph into the explicit and ruthless application of the law. This turn will no doubt increase the visibility of the pathological imbalance of a socio-political framework governed by the interests of capital. However, it would be foolish to believe that this alone will suffice to engender any radical transformation. Ultimately, only a relentless critical effort aimed at unmasking the objective causes of the capitalist demise, combined with the drive to think new post-capitalist scenarios, will prevent the full-fledged unfolding of barbarism.

Notes

1 See Žižek's piece in this collection.

2 In the Afterword to the paperback edition of *Living in the End Times*, Žižek (2011: 403–404) denounces "the comfortable subjective position of radical intellectuals, best rendered by one of their favored mental exercises throughout the twentieth century: the urge to 'catastrophize' the situation." He adds that "perhaps what the unfortunate intellectuals cannot bear is the fact that they live a life that is basically happy, safe and comfortable, so that, in order to justify their higher calling, they are obliged to construct a scenario of radical catastrophe." Žižek here quotes a very well-chosen line from George Orwell's *The Road to Wigan Pier*: "every revolutionary opinion draws part of its strength from a secret conviction that nothing can be changed."

3 I have tackled the specific issue of the capitalist crisis in the forthcoming *States of Crisis and Post-Capitalist Scenarios* (edited with Heiko Feldner and Slavoj Žižek) and *Critical Theory and the Crisis of Contemporary Capitalism* (co-authored with Heiko Feldner).

4 Gary Indiana (2000: 59) rightly notes that

> the libertines experience arousal almost exclusively as a species of rage.... There is, of course, nothing tender or romantic in Sade; but there is, in everything, selfish pleasure. Pasolini's heroes appear to experience their own depravity as an unassuageable irritant, no less than their victims' experience of submission.

5 Refn himself defined his character as a kind of Angel of Vengeance, a man that believes himself to be God "[i]n the sense that God in the Old Testament is

saying I can be cruel, you have to fear me as I can be kind, you have to love me" (in Umstead 2013).

References

Badiou, Alain (1997) *Saint Paul: La fondation de l'universalisme.* Paris: Presses Universitaires de France.

Dean, Jodi (2004) "Žižek on Law," *Law and Critique* 15: 1–24.

Deleuze, Gilles (1989) *Masochism.* New York: Zone Books.

Indiana, Gary (2000) *Salò, or the 120 Days of Sodom.* London: BFI.

Lacan, Jacques (1981) *The Seminars of Jacques Lacan, Book XI: The Four Fundamental Concepts of Psychoanalysis.* London and New York: W. W. Norton.

Lacan, Jacques (1991) *The Seminars of Jacques Lacan, Book I: Freud's Papers on Technique, 1953–54.* London and New York: W. W. Norton.

Lacan, Jacques (1998) *The Seminars of Jacques Lacan, Book XX: On Feminine Sexuality. The Limits of Love and Knowledge.* New York, London: W. W. Norton.

Lacan, Jacques (2006) *Ecrits: The First Complete English Edition.* London and New York: W. W. Norton.

McGowan, Todd (2007) *The Impossible David Lynch.* New York: Columbia University Press.

Umstead, Ben (2013) "'Ask Not What Art Is, but What it Is Not': Nicolas Winding Refn and Cliff Martinez on *Only God Forgives,*" *Twitch* (17 July 2013). Available at http://twitchfilm.com/2013/07/interview-nicolas-winding-refn-and-cliff-martinez.html [accessed 20 January 2014].

Vighi, Fabio (2010) *On Žižek's Dialectics: Surplus, Subtraction, Sublimation.* London and New York: Continuum.

Žižek, Slavoj (1989) *The Sublime Object of Ideology.* London and New York: Verso.

Žižek, Slavoj (1994) *The Metastases of Enjoyment.* London and New York: Verso.

Žižek, Slavoj (1999) *The Ticklish Subject.* London and New York: Verso.

Žižek, Slavoj (2000) *The Art of the Ridiculous Sublime.* Seattle: University of Washington Press.

Žižek, Slavoj (2002) *Revolution at the Gates.* London and New York: Verso.

Žižek, Slavoj (2008) *Violence: Six Sideways Reflections.* London: Profile Books

Žižek, Slavoj (2009) "Berlusconi in Tehran," in *London Review of Books,* 31(14), 23 July: pp. 3–7.

Žižek, Slavoj (2011) *Living in the End Times* (revised edition). London and New York: Verso.

Intermission

Chapter 6

Superheroes and the law

Batman, Superman, and the "big Other"

Dan Hassler-Forest

Since the beginning of the twenty-first century, Western popular culture has been immersed in fantasy, arguably more than ever before. This fantasy takes many forms, from the hobbits and elves of Tolkien's Middle-earth to the vampires of *Twilight* or the zombies of *The Walking Dead*. These fantasies play a crucial role in the construction of identity within the multiple contradictions of late capitalist culture: "fantasy is a means for an ideology to take its own failure into account in advance" (Žižek 1989: 142). But among the large variety of cross-media fantasy figures and franchises, most of which are spearheaded by big Hollywood blockbusters, the superhero has maintained the most consistent degree of visibility and popularity in the early twenty-first century. Having found in digital cinema an appropriate vessel for this elaborate and reliably spectacular form of popular mythology, superheroes have reached a level of popularity that for the first time exceeds that of comic books' "Golden Age" of the late 1930s and 1940s.

Drawing upon a massive stable of existing characters, many of which are instantly familiar to global audiences after countless years of low-brow pop-cultural iterations, the producers can draw upon a seemingly inexhaustible variety of ready-made situations featuring iconic characters and well-known themes. This overwhelming volume of archival continuity makes the superhero trope far more flexible than most other figures in popular fantasy: the *Harry Potter* franchise for instance relies not only on a limited series of source novels, but also on a specific group of actors who have appeared over the years in the lead roles. The flexibility of *The Lord of the Rings* and its associated franchise is similarly limited, depending again on a collection of narratives and on director Peter Jackson's recognizable aesthetic.

But besides the superhero's unique wealth of character, incident, and mythology, there are other elements at play in the genre that help explain its massive impact on our contemporary media landscape. The figure's long and complex history associates the superhero specifically with discourses of American national and cultural identity, to an immeasurably greater extent than any of the other aforementioned popular fantasies. Giving physical form to abstract notions of nationalism, justice, and the law, superhero characters embody ideological values even more explicitly than similar characters like James Bond or Jason Bourne. Whether they do so ostentatiously, like Captain America or Superman, or with some degree of ambivalence, like Spider-Man or the Incredible Hulk, superheroes can certainly be described as – to borrow a famous Žižekianism – ideology at its purest.

The question then becomes: what kind of ideology does the superhero in fact represent? And more specifically in the context of this collection: what do these movies tell us about our understanding of Law? In my book *Capitalist Superheroes* (2011) I argued that the contemporary superhero – with very few exceptions – embodies and even mythologizes the contradictory values of neoliberalism. The most popular figures, such as Iron Man, Batman, and Spider-Man, effectively humanize institutional discourses that glorify real-world practices of surveillance and torture, while the characters' various personal traumas legitimize their violent and unilateral response to external threats. These superheroes thus sustain a popular and banal mythology of superhuman powers that all too frequently provides a thinly veiled allegory of geopolitical power and agency (see also Dittmer 2013). In this sense, contemporary superhero movies valorize not only specific historical and political practices, such as the post-9/11 War on Terror, but also Hardt and Negri's notion of American "Empire" as a form of power that operates out of a supposedly universal and benevolent interest.

The superhero therefore comes to stand for a Law that functions differently from the actual laws that govern juridical processes at the local, national, and international levels. Operating by very definition outside the realm of any actually-existing legal framework, the superhero acts instead in the arena of Stuart Hall's "common sense," negotiating tensions and contradictions that provide a relatable and historically specific context for the viewer. The superhero provides a fantasy of a shared Law that operates along the lines of Lacan's "big Other": the symbolic fiction that structures our perception of daily reality. Unencumbered by the oblique workings of bureaucracy, democratic processes, or institutional inefficiency, superheroes mobilize a popular fantasy of the "big Other" as a moral and ethical code that continues to organize structure and meaning even in our famously post-ideological world.

But do superheroes in fact share this condition? Are they all the embodiments of a neoliberal fantasy that would see the world's problems repeatedly solved through the intervention of benevolent capitalists? And assuming that there is in fact some degree of variety within the genre in its current form, does this variety result in a wider selection of ideological alternatives, or do all roads once again lead back to the mythologization of patriarchal capitalism?

In this chapter I will first develop a basic typology that offers theoretical differentiation between the two most basic superhero archetypes, most specifically in how they relate to different notions that govern our understanding of the Law. I will draw primarily on Žižek's frequent but scattered and often fragmentary writing on superhero movies (including his elaborate discussion of *The Dark Knight Rises* (2012) included in this volume), as well as his theoretical discussion of Law, religion, and ideology in his classic books *The Fragile Absolute* (2001), *The Ticklish Subject* (1999), *The Sublime Object of Ideology* (1989), and some of his more recent books on Hegelian philosophy and neoliberal capitalism. By elaborating the relationship between Žižekian theory and the contemporary superhero movie, the chapter will shed new light on the historically specific fantasies that constitute the big Other under neoliberal capitalism.

Superman and Batman: transcendence vs. immanence

Any basic division between different types of superhero must begin with the difference between what have become the two classic archetypes: Superman and Batman. As the two very first incarnations of the superhero figure, they established templates that have not only survived as the two most popular and recognizable icons of superhero fiction, but have been copied, plagiarized, and parodied countless times across many different media. This is not only because they were the first two popular icons clearly identified as "superheroes": costumed crime-fighters operating outside of the law in a never-ending fight for justice, aided by either supernatural physical powers (Superman) or enough wealth to make the massive effort and expense feasible (Batman). It is also because they embody two quite specific and complementary modes of philosophical thought.

This difference in the source of their superpowers also establishes an important distinction between the political views they represent: Superman is an alien being from another planet whose powers are naturally his. Existing on Earth as a powerful god among men, he quite obviously represents an ideal of transcendence: a provocative incarnation of a goal to which humanity can aspire, but which can never be fully attained. In his stories, Superman quite literally exists as a beacon for normal humans to point at in excitement and admiration: "It's a bird.... It's a plane.... It's Superman!" As pointed out so gleefully in Quentin Tarantino's *Kill Bill, Vol. II* (2003), it is not a question of Clark Kent ever *becoming* Superman. Rather, he exists in a pure state of Being, his masquerade as the "bookish reporter" functioning not only as a disguise but as "Superman's critique on the whole human race."

The relationship between billionaire Bruce Wayne and his alter ego Batman, on the other hand, is quite different. After the traumatic loss of his parents, Wayne decides to perform the role of Batman, which is often presented as his "more authentic" self: only by putting on the Batman suit and mask can he truly be who he is, facing his past tragedies and inner fears by cathartically punishing criminals. His identity therefore comes to exist in a state of continuous fluctuation between these two states, locked into a perpetual process of Becoming. In this state of permanent flux, he is never entirely the masked vigilante, nor completely the playboy billionaire who is presented as even more of a performance than his secret and more violent self. While Superman thus represents a relatively pure state of Transcendence, Batman/Bruce Wayne maintain a model of Immanence.

What makes both these archetypes so interesting is their relationship to a more general understanding of the contradictory functioning of the Law. In *The Ticklish Subject*, Žižek cites the following passage from Kant's *Über Pedagogik* (*Kant on Law*):

> It is discipline which prevents man from being turned aside by his animal impulses from humanity, his appointed end. Discipline, for instance, must restrain him from venturing wildly and rashly into danger. Discipline, thus, is merely negative, its action being to counteract man's natural unruliness.... Unruliness consists in independence of law. By discipline men are placed in subjection to the laws of mankind, and brought to feel their constraint.
>
> (1899: 3–5)

Batman and Superman embody two phantasmic remedies for this Kantian notion of "man's natural unruliness," as the embodiments of a Law that is able to extend beyond the limitations of institutionalized modern bureaucracy. Their primary task in these fictional worlds is the apprehension of society's unruly elements, using their powers to catch criminals who are able to circumvent the inefficient and corrupt legal institutions.

But they are at the same time also representations of a quite radical form of self-discipline: Bruce Wayne is able to transform himself into Batman, the superhero who must break the letter of the Law in order to serve its spirit more effectively. By imposing upon himself the strongest kind of discipline, including a moral and ethical code that guides and limits his actions, he becomes the symbolically acceptable avenger, ceaselessly battling the unruly elements of society as the Law's perverse but necessary supplement. For Superman too, discipline is redoubled, but works in reverse: rather than disciplining his body and mind to become a greater force to fight crime, he must curtail his natural abilities so they do not alter the coordinates of our social totality. His actions are therefore limited to interventions in more mundane emergencies such as traffic accidents, bank robberies, and the occasional attack by hostile alien forces.

Batman: plugging the gaps in the law

With the current trend of "realistic" and ambiguous superhero movies, many critics have been tempted to read them as direct allegories for state and/or corporate power as it exists in the world today. Žižek himself has done this on a few occasions, for instance in his reading of Bane in *The Dark Knight Rises* as a revolutionary leader whose "spirit of sacrifice" mobilizes a movement of "people power" in Gotham City (2012b). But as Mark Fisher has pointed out, reading the film in this overly literal way requires one to "squint quite hard" in order to make this interpretation work by deliberately ignoring several of the film's many striking contradictions (2012).

The trick in making theoretical sense of these ostentatiously ridiculous superhero figures is to take them seriously, but to do so in a way that takes into account the texts' basic incoherence. This involves first the acknowledgment of the deep contradictions embedded within the fantasies these films represent, which pose obvious challenges to traditional interpretive processes that tend to pre-suppose a largely coherent narrative text. For instance, Tim Burton's magnificent film *Batman Returns* (1992) includes a moment close to the end where Batman/Wayne finally faces the narrative's true villain Max Shreck (played by Christopher Walken). The morally ambiguous Catwoman (played by Michelle Pfeiffer) plans to execute Shreck in this final confrontation, while Batman tries to persuade her to hand Shreck over to the legal authorities. Catwoman dismisses his apparent devotion to the Law's formal structure mockingly: "Don't be naive! The law doesn't apply to people like him – or us."

Batman's response is both surprising and entirely predictable: "Wrong on both counts!" How to make sense of this insistence that he is not above the Law after we have previously seen him deliberately and quite sadistically burning a criminal alive, running over countless henchmen with his Batmobile, and generally operating as an urban vigilante whose actions, no matter how violent or illegal, function both entirely outside the Law while simultaneously acknowledged as its own ("extra-legal") extension?

The answer must lie in understanding these films' dialectical navigation of fantasies that relate back to our postmodern predicament of radical insecurity. As Žižek has argued many times, our age of hedonistic individualism, multiculturalism, and moral relativism is best understood via its relation to the Lacanian concept of the "big Other," which he describes as "the order of symbolic fictions which operate on a level different from that of direct material causality" (1999: 389). The big Other operates as a structuring virtual framework, regulating the way in which we see ourselves as subjects, especially in relation to power:

> In one of the Marx Brothers' films, Groucho Marx, caught in a lie, answers angrily: "Whom do you believe, your eyes or my words?" This

> apparently absurd logic expresses perfectly the functioning of the symbolic order, in which the symbolic mask-mandate matters more than the direct reality of the individual who wears this mask and/or assumes this mandate. This functioning involves the structure of fetishistic disavowal: "I know very well that things are the way I see them [that this person is a corrupt weakling], but none the less I treat him with respect, since he wears the insignia of a judge, so that when he speaks, it is the Law itself which speaks through him." So, in a way, I actually believe his words, not my eyes – that is to say, I believe in Another Space (the domain of pure symbolic authority) which matters more than the reality of its spokesmen.
>
> (1999: 389)

This strange double logic helps us understand the apparent contradiction in this example from *Batman Returns*: experiencing two irreconcilably different takes on the superhero's legal status, which are we to believe? Our eyes, which tell us that this bizarre costumed vigilante does indeed exist outside of the Law, as he intervenes violently and unilaterally in moments of crisis? Or our ears, which tell us reassuringly that even these colorful comic book figures do not live outside the reach of the Law?

The only answer that can help us understand these fictions' appeal is, of course, both. While everybody knows that Catwoman's claim is accurate, Batman could never explicitly acknowledge this, as the big Other requires him to maintain a certain appearance: even for himself, the basic truth that the Law does not apply to him must always be disavowed, or else his own symbolic fiction would break down. We acknowledge that these films do not operate as coherent theses that should be taken seriously and interpreted as literal allegories, but as popular fables that allow viewers to navigate the tension between irresolvable contradictions that inform our daily life under "capitalist realism" (Fisher 2009). More specifically, the contradictions these superheroes tend to embody relate to Žižek's description of the postmodern "nonexistence of the big Other" (1999: 389), which adds an additional layer of negation to this already contradictory concept.

First, the big Other as a form of symbolic fiction is already factually nonexistent: it exists only as a regulatory device that imparts a sense of structure and order to the radically (and terrifyingly) inconsistent Real. The individual subject requires the sense that behind all the chaos and indeterminacy of daily life there exists somewhere a governing instance that ultimately keeps track of everything: an "Other Scene in which the accounts are properly kept" (412). The problem with postmodern (or more specifically neoliberal) capitalism is that precisely this shared belief in any such big Other has dissolved: "Not only do we not know what our acts will amount to, there is even no global mechanism regulating our interactions

– this is what the properly 'postmodern' nonexistence of the big Other means" (ibid.).

In this sense, the big Other's nonexistence has been redoubled: in the age of individualist relativism, a widely shared faith in a single set of values obviously can no longer be publicly maintained. This is precisely how many critics have theorized the cultural dominant of postmodernism, as "the name for the complex of crises that the decline of the belief in the big Other has triggered" (Fisher 2009: 45). But even without an actual system of religion, ideology, mythology, or any other culturally determined set of values, we still require a sense of the big Other, even if it is only as an order of appearances:

> So that's the tragedy of our predicament: in order to fully exist as individuals we need the fiction of a "big Other." There must be an agency which as it were registers our predicament, an agency where the truth of ourselves will be inscribed, accepted. An agency to which we confess.
>
> (Žižek, *The Pervert's Guide to Ideology*, film, 2012)

This is precisely where an inherently contradictory form of popular mythology such as that of the superhero begins to make sense. The fantasy of the superhero revolves around the existence of a regulatory power which exists separately from the juridical framework that defines the Kantian definition of Law. In Deleuze's reading of Kant's ethical philosophy, "the law is no longer regarded as dependent on the Good, but on the contrary, the Good itself is made to depend on the law" (*Coldness and Cruelty* 1991: 82). This perception of the formal (empty) structure of the Law preceding any actual ethical content leads us directly to the forms of modern bureaucracy as described by Kafka, where one is always in some way guilty:

> Since, in the case of the Law, its *Das-Sein* (the fact of the Law) precedes its *Was-Sein* (what this Law is), the subject finds himself in a situation in which, although he knows there is a Law, he never knows (and a priori cannot know) what this Law is – a gap forever separates the Law from its positive incarnations. The subject is thus a priori, in his very existence, guilty: guilty without knowing what he is guilty of (and guilty for that very reason), infringing the law without knowing its actual regulations.
>
> (Žižek 1999: 447)

This traumatic gap between the formal structure of the law and its unclearly defined moral and ethical content is conveniently filled in by the operations of the superhero. While on the one hand, a character like Batman exists in order to enforce discipline on mankind's aforementioned "unruly nature," he does so on the other hand without being a part of the Law's institutional structure. In many versions of the Batman narrative, including *Batman Returns* and the popular 1960s TV series, he operates as the police force's enforcer, receiving a phone call whenever there's a mystery they cannot solve, or when limitations imposed on them prevent them from taking action.

The superhero's ambiguous relationship to the Law frequently leads to the character's status as an outlaw figure: someone who does Good, unhindered by the bureaucracy, inefficiency, and corruption of official law enforcement, and whose actions are defined entirely by a vaguely defined but universally recognized code. But since this "positive incarnation" of the Law directly contradicts what Žižek describes as the nature of postmodern society, superheroes "are often seen as terrorists to the societies that they are a part of, but to the reader, existing outside of the fictional world, the truth of their heroic actions is better understood for the struggle that it is" (Wolf-Meyer 501). The characters' therapeutic dimension therefore resides in the way they represent a form of big Other that allows the reader/viewer to fruitfully navigate one of our social order's most basic contradictions.

Christopher Nolan's acclaimed film trilogy prominently explores this superhero's basic relationship with the Law, introducing the character in the first film *Batman Begins* (2005) as the Law's illegal but necessary supplement, using his corporate capital and personal ingenuity to fight urban crime where the corrupt and inefficient police cannot. While his existence is secretly tolerated by Gordon, the righteous law enforcement officer who is continuously frustrated in his desire to do Good, the institution of the police force perceives him as a threat and treats him like a criminal. Nevertheless, in this first installment Batman can still defend the system "with morally acceptable methods" (Žižek 2012).

The second film *The Dark Knight* (2008) culminates in Batman assuming the responsibility for crimes that are not his, having spent most of the narrative trying to find a way to legalize his functions by transferring them to District Attorney Harvey Dent. Batman is forced to conspire with Gordon in a deliberate deception deemed necessary to maintain social order: the people's need for a regulating fiction that allows them to keep their faith in the system – in other words, the continued existence of the big Other – depends upon the official reproduction of a lie for the greater good. In Žižek's words, "one has to break the rules in order to defend the system" (ibid.). Even in the final film in the trilogy, *The Dark Knight Rises* (2012), Batman's ambiguous death/retirement does not end the necessity to maintain his supplemental function that counterbalances the Law, as the young officer Blake has already grown disillusioned with the corruption and inefficiency of the police force and is clearly destined to continue Wayne's mission after his disappearance.

Therefore, whether Batman functions as an unofficially condoned extension of the Law or as its illegal but necessary supplement, he exists in either case to fill the gap between the Law and its positive incarnations. Within the narratives, his existence is necessary for the protection of society, but even more to maintain belief in the symbolic structure that gives our social totality the appearance of cohesion. In other words, he safeguards the continued existence of the big Other, for which the empty container of modern law is never sufficient.[1] The dark knight continues to rise over and over again in order to become the kind of positive incarnation of the Law that plugs a gap left by our lack of faith in the big Other. But while Batman comes into being in order to fill this gap in our symbolic order, how then does the transcendent figure of Superman relate to our experience of the Law and the big Other?

Superman: truth, justice, and the way of *agape*

If Batman comes into existence because of fundamental shortcomings in our experience of the contingent nature of the Law, Superman arrives on earth as the pure embodiment of the Good assumed to underlie the Law's functioning. While Bruce Wayne decides to *become* Batman in response to the insufficient functioning of law enforcement, Clark Kent only needs to discover the fact that he *is* Superman in order to take on his identity. To put this in more philosophical terms: Batman is by definition a fully immanent character, as his existence is predicated on a context where his existence is called for, while his dual identity keeps him locked into a perpetual state of (Hegelian) Becoming. Superman, on the other hand, seems to be a transcendental figure who embodies an ideal that persists outside of any given socio-historical context.

It should come as little surprise that Batman's perpetual state of Becoming has proved to be far easier to present in the age of neoliberal capitalism than that of Superman. Indeed, his famous motto of "truth, justice, and the American way" is generally perceived as old-fashioned and outdated by audiences most keenly attuned to irony and political pragmatism. In the context of capitalist realism, our reality is experienced as "infinitely plastic" (Fisher 2009: 54), or what Jameson has described as a "purely fungible present in which space and psyches alike can be processed and remade at will" (1998: 57). And unlike Batman, Superman is for all intents and purposes indestructible, a two-dimensional embodiment of committed idealism that is difficult to align with our supposedly post-ideological times.

Historically, Superman's greatest popularity occurred from the late 1930s until the mid-1950s, when the discursive construction of American geopolitical exceptionalism was also at its peak. A second wave of public interest accompanied the first major superhero films that appeared in the late 1970s and early 1980s, each of which were blatant examples of Jameson's "nostalgia mode" in their neo-conservative glorification of Eisenhower-age values (1991: 296). But before long, he fell out of fashion again, with Frank Miller's influential comic book *The Dark Knight Returns* (1986) portraying his once-meaningful idealism as a simplistic, outdated, and easily misled handmaiden to America's cynical political leaders. With capitalism quickly reaching the point where the problem was no longer "how to contain and absorb energies from outside," its neoliberal form arises at the point where it must function "without an outside it can colonize and appropriate" (Fisher 2009: 8).

As part of the twenty-first-century superhero movie cycle, the blockbuster film *Superman Returns* (2006) made an attempt to re-establish Superman as a mythological character with relevance for a contemporary global audience, striving for a sense of historical currency by multiple references to the terrorist attacks of 9/11, and by playing up the nostalgia mode that previously pervaded neo-conservative culture. In the film's narrative, Superman abandoned the people of earth five years before the film begins, following the publication of Lois Lane's Pulitzer Prize-winning editorial "Why the World Doesn't Need Superman." The allegorical reference to recent history could hardly be clearer: in the carefree arrogance that followed the end of the Cold War, the post-ideological United States no longer seemed to require any form of true idealism. Superman, as the physical embodiment of those ideals, therefore abandons America in the very year in which the terrorist attacks of 9/11 created the kind of epochal singularity that rewrites history.

The narrative world of *Superman Returns* demonstrates clearly the need for renewed faith and idealism, which the character's heroic reappearance does indeed bring about within the film. Repeated shots show large audiences gazing in awe at the Man of Steel, a figure whose incredible powers are matched by his graceful and completely unselfish humility. A recurring motif is his willingness to sacrifice himself in shots that replicate messianic poses from the Judeo-Christian religious tradition, while the dialogues with the spirit of his deceased father Jor-El illustrate the divine lineage and tradition of continuity that his presence aims to restore.

Even more than the earlier cycle of Superman films, *Superman Returns* is preoccupied with establishing a Biblical visual and thematic vocabulary that portrays the protagonist as mankind's true savior, while the plot hinges on the redemption of America through its shared faith in this alien Messiah. It makes sense therefore to consider the figure of the superhero, and that of Superman in this film in particular, in relation to Žižek's discussions of Christianity and its political and even revolutionary potential. He discusses this in most detail in his book *The Fragile Absolute* (2001), where he develops St. Paul's concept of Christian love, or *agape*, as a way to disentangle the Law from its inherent transgression.

To Žižek, *agape* as a form of radical solidarity with the Other is one of the kernels that fuels social movements and the desire for political change – just as he employs Che Guevara's famous definition of love as the revolutionary's guiding force, which he subsequently applies to his reading of the character Bane in *The Dark Knight Rises*. This Paulinian *agape* is clearly central to the desire for Good that drives most superhero narratives, but most particularly in the case of Superman:

> What many people may find problematic in the Pauline *agape* is that it seems to *superegotize* love, conceiving it in an almost Kantian way – not as a spontaneous overflow of generosity, not as a self-assertive stance, but as self-suppressing *duty* to love neighbors and care for them, as hard *work*, as something to be accomplished through the strenuous effort of fighting and inhibiting one's spontaneous "pathological" inclinations.
>
> (Žižek 2001: 92)

This self-suppressing duty to care for others clearly connects to the discipline discussed earlier in relation to Kantian law. But it finds its most extreme form in the case of Superman, because he has no actual human identity to fall back on: even when pretending to be reporter Clark Kent, this is only part of his never-ending work to benefit mankind. While most other superheroes are motivated in their heroism by more individualistic reasons, such as the customary traumatic experience of personal loss, Superman operates entirely out of *agape* and its self-suppressing sense of duty.

As a singular text in the character's long and very diverse history, *Superman Returns* embraces this aspect thoroughly, which might help explain the film's disappointing performance and unpopular reputation among fans of the genre. The crucial component to the twenty-first-century genre superhero's success, after all, has been the humanization of these iconic comic book characters. Moving away from the figure's more two-dimensional origins, the most successful superhero films, from *Spider-Man* (2002) to *The Dark Knight* (2008) to *Iron Man 3* (2013), have focused above all on the superhero's relatable human qualities. Both form and content of these massively popular films give credence to Žižek's more recent remark on the neoliberal emphasis on emotion and "humanization":

> There is a very thin line separating this "humanization" from a resigned coming to terms with lying as a social principle: what matters in such a humanized universe is authentic intimate experience, not the truth.
>
> (2011: 59)

The "humanization" at stake here in fact revolves around a stubborn commitment to a form of "authentic intimate experience" that is quite cynical: as a form of constitutive ideology, this emphasis privileges emotion as authentic expression within a larger social context where lying has indeed become a grounding principle.

In these superhero narratives, we sympathize with the main characters not because of their ideals but, on the contrary, precisely because they have abundant flaws that make them relatable. In his book *Why We Love Sociopaths* (2012), Adam Kotsko even argues that the neoliberal social order makes it impossible for us to establish positive models for behavior because it can offer "no convincing account of what it would look like to do things right" (6). Twenty-first-century culture therefore offers a wide variety of iconic characters and public figures whose transgressions are an essential part of their appeal. The enormous popularity of superheroes played by Christian Bale, Robert Downey Jr., and Tobey Maguire is therefore remarkably similar to the cult of personality that has surrounded neoliberal politicians such as George W. Bush, Tony Blair, Geert Wilders, Silvio Berlusconi, and Barack Obama, just as it has celebrity CEOs like Steve Jobs, Rupert Murdoch, and Donald Trump.

Because this process of humanization is constructed around flaws and idiosyncrasies that make these figures emotionally relatable, a virtually flawless and indestructible character such as Superman is difficult to reconstruct in this way. An illuminating comparison can be drawn with the recent Superman film *Man of Steel* (dir. Zack Snyder, 2013), which was much more successful than Bryan Singer's 2006 film, at least in establishing a renewed franchise. In this new reinvention of the character, the focus is moved from religious motifs to "emotional realism." Every effort is made to present Superman as conflicted, traumatized, and fallible, in ways that strongly resemble the formula employed in the Batman films directed by Christopher Nolan (who co-produced *Man of Steel*).

The earlier film versions of Superman emphasized his exceptional nature as self-evident and unquestioned, operating in close connection with geopolitical discourses of American exceptionalism and implicitly expressing the "American conception of the world as an assumed self-evident ideal of human universalism" (Kooijman 2008: 39). In the historical context of World War II and the Cold War, one can see how a character who embodies such ideals could be popular, appealing directly to a shared symbolic order that constituted a set of values and beliefs that made up the big Other. But with the rapid dissolution of the Soviet Union and (the appearance of) really-existing global alternatives to capitalism, we witness the accelerated growth of neoliberalism and its post-ideological assault on all forms of idealism:

> Capitalism is the first socio-economic order which de-totalizes meaning: there is no global "capitalist worldview," no "capitalist civilization"

> proper: the fundamental lesson of globalization is precisely that capitalism can accommodate itself to all civilizations, from Christian to Hindu or Buddhist, from West to East. Capitalism's global dimension can only be formulated at the level of truth-without-meaning, as the "real" of the global market mechanism.
>
> (Žižek 2010a: 365)

The version of Superman we encounter in *Man of Steel* answers most directly to capitalism's radical de-totalization of meaning, in which we witness an endless assault on "any aura of authentic nobility, sacredness, honor, and so on" (Žižek 2001: 11). Now, we see for the first time a drawn-out process of the character *becoming* Superman, as he moves grimly from one job to another, intervening in the occasional catastrophe but generally avoiding occasions where he might show his true powers. He is emphatically presented as conflicted and deeply troubled, his trauma resulting from an irresolvable tension between the various rules and prohibitions articulated by his two father figures.

In the previous film franchise, as in most other versions of the character's origin story, the instructions of his biological father command him expressly to embody the ideals of a universal Good:

> Live as one of them, Kal-El, to discover where your strength and your power are needed. Always hold in your heart the pride of your special heritage. They can be a great people, Kal-El, they wish to be. They only lack the light to show the way. For this reason above all, their capacity for good, I have sent them you ... my only son.[2]

This semi-messianic directive is later supplemented by the instructions of his adopted father Jonathan Kent, who teaches the character humility and compassion. Not long before dying of a heart attack, this secondary patriarchal voice adds the human element to Superman's alien origins:

> When you first came to us, we thought that people would come and take you away because if they found out about the things you could do, well, that worried us a lot. But then a man gets older and he thinks very differently, starts to see things very clear. And there's one thing I do know, son. And that is, you are here for a reason. I don't know whose reason it is, or whatever the reason ... maybe it's ... I don't know ... but I do know one thing: it's not to score touchdowns.

His instructions are obviously no less religious in tone than the words of Kal-El's biological father, but they complete the aforementioned concept of American exceptionalism as a benevolent and paradoxically humble ideal. Together, the sets of instructions and prohibitions placed upon

Superman by his two father figures (who may as well be Jehovah and Joseph) perfectly complement each other, resulting in a thinly veiled and only slightly secularized Christ figure.

Man of Steel revisits this familiar origin story, but in such a way that the revised versions of these father figures are set up to create a massive conflict within the character. Jor-El's largely similar words to his son now foreground the notion that he has has free choice in deciding upon his destiny:

> Your mother and I believed Krypton lost something precious: the element of choice, of chance. What if a child dreamed of becoming something other than what society had intended for him or her? What if a child aspired to something greater? You were the embodiment of that belief, Kal.

Rather than the usual pre-ordained savior, this screenplay deliberately complicates the character's psychological profile by having him choose between good and evil. Even if the end result of this "free choice" is quite obviously a foregone conclusion, one can easily see the potential for drama in this addition to the mythology, like the obvious temptation to use his powers not out of *agape* but selfishly, to serve his own personal interests. Complicating things further, the prohibitions placed upon the young Clark Kent by his adopted father put enormous pressure on him not only to choose his own path, but all the flashbacks in the film reveal that he was in fact forbidden to use his powers at all. Becoming Superman therefore by definition involved breaking the father's prohibition (or Lacan's famous "*non du père*").

Man of Steel thus attempts to change Superman's archetypal popular myth of Being into one of Becoming, thereby signaling a transition from transcendence to immanence. This transformation can be seen as the genre's response to what Žižek has termed "the antinomy of post-modern individuality: the injunction to 'be yourself,' to disregard the pressure of your surroundings and achieve self-realization by fully asserting your unique creative potential" (2001: 458). In order to appeal to a twenty-first-century audience, Superman is changed into a mythical figure whose idealism becomes entirely secondary to this endless process of self-actualization.

The last and perhaps most crucial element in this transformation is Superman's new relationship with the Law, as represented in the film by the American military. While most versions show him catching evildoers on his own initiative before handing them over to the authorities, this incarnation hardly acts at all until the army gives him permission. The movie poster, showing Superman in handcuffs and surrounded by military guards, perfectly encapsulates the changed relationship between this superhero and the Law: no longer truly functioning as a transcendent ideal for others to strive towards, but as a purely pragmatic extension of American military power. And while the final scene in the film jokingly establishes that this new WMD will maintain some degree of separation from the military, he simultaneously reassures them that Superman can be counted upon to protect American interests:

ARMY GENERAL: How do we know that one day you won't act against America's interests?

SUPERMAN: I grew up in Kansas, general. I'm about as American as it gets. Look, I'm here to help. But it has to be on my own terms. And you have to convince Washington of that.

Like many other recent superhero films, such as the Batman trilogy, the Iron Man series, and the Avengers cycle, Superman thus comes to represent the fruitful collaboration between the American military and its many private partners: another among many powerful subcontractors who serve American geopolitical interests, while simultaneously giving physical shape to the discursive elements that make up American exceptionalism.

Conclusion

By becoming part of this neoliberal ethics of emotional realism and continuous self-actualization, this new incarnation of Superman, like Batman and most other recent superhero franchises, expresses our changed perspective of the Law and Lacan's big Other. Of course the big Other still exists, because it remains "a symbolic fiction [that] is constitutive of reality: if we take away the fiction, we lose reality itself" (Žižek 2011: 92). But in the age of capitalist realism, the coordinates of the big Other have changed. It has become harder for us to relate to any kind of transcendent ideal, as our reality has been increasingly defined in the relative terms of a logic of immanence. Or, as Žižek has put it: "We no longer 'really believe,' we just follow (some of) the religious rituals and mores out of respect for the 'lifestyle' of the community to which we belong" (2004).

It has long been commonplace to state that superheroes have become a new form of popular mythology.[3] Those who have argued against this notion, such as Umberto Eco, have done so from a limited and by now certainly quite dated understanding of the superhero's complex cultural, social, and ideological functions. But while it would be a mistake to interpret the superhero genre's still-growing popularity as an expression of enduring human nature, a closer analysis of superhero narratives can teach us a great deal about our era of capitalist realism. While the superhero figure has a strong utopian potential, especially in a character like Superman, I have argued in this chapter that the recent development of the genre reflects the dominant values of neoliberal capitalism by privileging emotional realism and an ethical model of immanence and pure contingency over the transcendent ideals previously embodied by many of these characters.

Following Žižek's point that our age is marked by a dissolution of a shared faith in the big Other, the twenty-first-century superhero movie offers further evidence of our predicament: occasional attempts to re-establish a sense of idealism, such as *Superman Returns*, are no longer perceived as meaningful, while Christopher Nolan's entirely cynical Batman films are heralded as profound political commentary. While part of the superhero's role is obviously still to provide the positive incarnation absent from the Law in its modern form, these films demonstrate that even this function must now be defined in negative terms. If, as David Harvey once noted, it is still the case that "the difficulty under capitalism … is to find a stable mythology expressive of its inherent values and meaning" (1990: 217), then the superhero clearly still offers at least the closest approximation of just such a mythological structure.

Notes

1 Significantly, many Batman stories contain scenes where individual characters (most often young children) briefly encounter the superhero and thereby become believers in him, completely independent from what the superhero's official legal status as criminal, outlaw, vigilante, or fairy tale might be. This demonstrates that the existence of the big Other is fundamentally a matter of faith.

2 The prohibition that accompanies this directive is the instruction in *Superman: The Movie* (1978) not to interfere directly in human history, which we can interpret as a narrative trick designed to avoid the many political, religious, and other complications that would surely accompany the existence of a superhuman being in actual history, an idea that author Alan Moore explored most directly in his comic book *Watchmen* (1986).

3 See for instance Richard Reynolds' book *Superheroes: A Modern Mythology* (1992).

References

Dittmer, Jason. *Captain America and the Nationalist Superhero: Metaphors, Narratives, and Geopolitics.* Philadelphia: Temple University Press, 2012.

Eco, Umberto. "The Myth of Superman." *Dialectics*, 2(1), Spring 1972: 14–22.

Fisher, Mark. *Capitalist Realism: Is There No Alternative?* Hants: Zero Books, 2009.

Fisher, Mark. "Batman's Political Right Turn," *Guardian*, 22 July 2012. www.theguardian.com/commentisfree/2012/jul/22/batman-political-right-turn (Accessed: 10 December 2013).

Hall, Stuart. *Culture, Media, Language: Working Papers in Cultural Studies, 1972–1979.* London: Hutchinson, 1980.

Hardt, Michael and Antonio Negri. *Empire.* Cambridge, MA: Harvard University Press, 2001.

Harvey, David. *The Condition of Postmodernity: An Enquiry into the Origins of Cultural Change.* Oxford: Blackwell, 1990.
Jameson, Fredric. *Postmodernism, or, The Cultural Logic of Late Capitalism.* Durham, NC: Duke University Press, 1991.
Jameson, Fredric. *The Cultural Turn: Selected Writings on the Postmodern 1983–1998.* London and New York: Verso, 1998.
Kooijman, Jaap. *Fabricating the Absolute Fake: America in Contemporary Pop Culture.* Amsterdam: Amsterdam University Press, 2008.
Lacan, Jacques. *Écrits: The First Complete Edition in English.* Trans. Bruce Fink. New York: W.W. Norton and Co., 2000.
Morris, Tom and Matt Morris, eds. *Superheroes and Philosophy; Truth, Justice and the Socratic Way.* Chicago: Open Court, 2005.
Reynolds, Richard. *Superheroes: A Modern Mythology.* Jackson: University Press of Mississippi, 1992.
Wolf-Meyer, Matthew. "The World Ozymandias Made: Utopias in the Superhero Comic, Subculture, and the Conservation of Difference." *Journal of Popular Culture,* 36(3), 2003: 497–517.
Williams, Evan Calder. *Combined and Uneven Apocalypse.* Hants: Zero Books, 2011.
Wright, Bradford W. *Comic Book Nation: The Transformation of Youth Culture in America.* Baltimore and London: Johns Hopkins University Press, 2001.
Žižek, Slavoj. *The Sublime Object of Ideology.* London and New York: Verso, 1989.
Žižek, Slavoj. *The Ticklish Subject: The Absent Centre of Political Ontology.* London and New York: Verso, 1999.
Žižek, Slavoj. *The Fragile Absolute: Or Why is the Christian Legacy Worth Fighting For?* London and New York: Verso, 2001.
Žižek, Slavoj. *Welcome to the Desert of the Real.* London and New York: Verso, 2002.
Žižek, Slavoj. "Passion: Regular or Decaf?" *In These Times,* 27 February 2004. www.inthesetimes.com/article/146/ (Accessed: 4 May 2010).
Žižek, Slavoj. *In Defense of Lost Causes.* London and New York: Verso, 2008.
Žižek, Slavoj. *Living in the End Times.* London and New York: Verso, 2010a.
Žižek, Slavoj. *The Parallax View.* London and Cambridge, MA: MIT Press, 2010b.
Žižek, Slavoj. *Less than Nothing: Hegel and the Shadow of Dialectical Materialism.* London and New York: Verso, 2012a.
Žižek, Slavoj. "The Politics of Batman." *The New Statesman,* 23 August 2012b. www.newstatesman.com/2012/08/people's-republic-gotham (Accessed: 12 December 2012).
Žižek, Slavoj. *The Year of Dreaming Dangerously.* London and New York: Verso, 2012c.

Part II

Hegel and consequences

Chapter 7

Bartleby by nature

German idealism, biology, and the Žižekian compatibilism of *Less Than Nothing*

Adrian Johnston

Slavoj Žižek, over the entire ongoing course of his sustained philosophical labors, wrestles again and again with versions of the perennial mind–body problem as itself one of the biggest of big questions in the history of Western philosophy. Likewise, he also repeatedly confronts the equally daunting and persistent freedom–determinism divide from various angles. As a single, massive summation of Žižek's current theoretical framework, *Less Than Nothing: Hegel and the Shadow of Dialectical Materialism* extends and develops his dialectical/transcendental materialist ways of treating these two fundamental philosophical topics. Therein, he does so primarily through staging encounters between, on one side, classical German philosophy (*à la* Immanuel Kant, J.G. Fichte, F.W.J. Schelling, and G.W.F. Hegel) and, on another side, today's empirical, experimental sciences of nature (especially quantum physics and biology).

To those unfamiliar with Žižek, this interfacing of German idealism and natural science likely would sound like a recipe for yet another death match between partisans of freedom (represented by German idealism) and advocates of determinism (represented by natural science) on an old *Kampfplatz* devoid of hope. But, as anyone familiar with Žižek's ideas already knows, such is never the case for him. Žižek is well aware of how the original forms of the idealisms of the late-eighteenth/early-nineteenth-century German-speaking world (especially the idealists' philosophies of nature and the natural sciences) have been rendered partially problematic and limited in connection with an intervening two hundred years of significant scientific advances.[1] Nonetheless, not only does he seek to salvage for the present what from German idealism has continued to remain enduringly valid and valuable for the past two centuries – he also arguably shows why and how contemporary understandings of various matters, including nature as per those sciences concerned with it, can and must be altered in response to redeployments of Kantian and post-Kantian philosophical systems.

In *Less Than Nothing*, Žižek begins approaching the issue of autonomy via the now-familiar pairing of Kant with Lacan. Specifically, as in much of his prior corpus, he has recourse to Lacan's concept of the "act."[2] Žižek states: "For Lacan, properly ethical acts are rare: they occur like 'miracles' which interrupt the ordinary run of things; they do not 'express' the entire 'personality' of the subject, but function as a break in the continuity of 'personal identity'."[3] On the next page, he adds:

> An ethical act is one that does not comprise or express the entire person, but is a moment of grace, a "miracle" which can occur also in a non-virtuous individual.
>
> This is why such acts are difficult to imagine, and why, when they do occur, one tends to invent a narrative which normalizes them.[4]

With such phrases as "the ordinary run of things," "entire 'personality' of the subject," " 'personal identity,' " "entire person," and "individual," Žižek is designating a dimension featuring centrally in both Kant's and Lacan's conceptions of ethics: in Kant, the all-too-human phenomenal "I," the empirical "me" with its self-seeking pathological inclinations aimed at private gratification, pleasure, satisfaction, etc.; in Lacan, the ego entwined through the related pleasure and reality principles with Imaginary–Symbolic realities. A basic stance held in common between Kant and Lacan is their shared insistence that the domain of this type of personal identity is not all there is to subjectivity – or, one even could say, that the subject proper is something different-in-kind from such selfhood.[5]

Amply supported by earlier investigative efforts into Lacan's heterodox Kantianism by both himself and others, Žižek therefore feels licensed to draw a straight line closely connecting the categorically imperative moral law of pure rational duty *à la* Kant with the circuits of *désir* and *jouissance* operating "beyond the pleasure principle" *à la* Lacan.[6] Of course, 1920's *Beyond the Pleasure Principle* is the text in which the later Sigmund Freud introduces his hypothesis of the *Todestrieb*. Hence, Žižek's identification of this particular "beyond" as a direct link of commonality between Kant and Lacan is of a piece with his larger endeavor to establish an equivalence between the autonomous subject as per Kantian and post-Kantian German idealism and the death drive as per Freudian–Lacanian psychoanalysis (he repeatedly insists that this synthesis of freedom as per idealism and *Todestrieb* as per analysis is the core concern of his entire *oeuvre*[7]). Žižek further reinforces the bond between Kant and Lacan through stressing that both Kantian and Lacanian ethics equally eschew reliance upon, in Lacan's terms, a hypothesized "big Other" as an ethical "subject supposed to know," namely, a transcendent, omniscient authority eternally guaranteeing the ultimate rightness (or wrongness) of one's decisions and deeds.[8] Thus, the decontextualized formal emptiness of Kant's categorical imperative, as itself the cornerstone of his metaphysics of morals, is depicted as a virtue rather than a vice insofar as its formal emptiness condemns the ethical subject to being responsible for freely determining each and every specific instantiation of this imperative – with this depiction implicitly going against Hegel's recurrent criticisms of the empty formalism of Kantian philosophy generally and his practical philosophy especially.[9]

Žižek proceeds, in *Less Than Nothing*, to lend additional precision to the notion of the act he appropriates from Lacan. Specifically, he situates it as part of a tripartite distinction between "acting out," "*passage à l'acte*," and "*Tat-Handlung*."[10] Not only, as seen above, are there threads of continuity conjoining Kant and Lacan, especially at the level of ethics – Fichte, with his (post-)Kantian re-founding of transcendental idealism on the basis of the spontaneous subject of practical philosophy, foreshadows Lacan's concept of the act with his pivotal idea of the "*Tat-Handlung*." The Fichtean *Tat-Handlung* ("fact/act") can be understood here as a structural dynamic in which subjectivity, as acting agency, and objectivity, as produced action, are moments of one and the same unity (in the case of the theory of self-consciousness central to Fichte's philosophy, the "I," in being conscious of itself, is simultaneously and irreducibly both the transcendental subject "intellectually intuiting" itself as well as the object thereby intuited).[11]

However, Žižek's Lacanian retrieval of Fichte already tacitly entails certain non-negligible modifications of the Kantian and Fichtean conceptions of transcendental subjectivity. In particular, Kant's and Fichte's presuppositions and posits apropos the relation (or lack thereof) between the transcendental and the empirical are implicitly challenged by the Žižekian Lacanianization of Kant and Fichte themselves:

> what about the retroactivity of a gesture which (re)constitutes this past itself?
>
> This, perhaps, is the most succinct definition of what an authentic *act* is: in our ordinary activity, we effectively just follow the (virtual-fantasmatic) coordinates of our identity, while an act proper involves the paradox of an actual move which (retroactively) changes the very virtual "transcendental" coordinates of its agent's being – or, in Freudian terms, which not only changes the actuality of our world but also "moves its underground."... while the pure past is the transcendental condition for our acts, our acts not only create new actual reality, they also retroactively change this very condition.[12]

Or, as Žižek rearticulates this much later, "Every authentic act creates its own conditions of possibility."[13] Now, neither Kant nor Fichte temporalizes the transcendental of their transcendental idealisms, with their idealistic subject *qua* set of possibility conditions for empirical, experiential structures and phenomena itself remaining beyond, behind, or beneath anything and everything situated in time. Arguably, transcendental subjectivity as per Kant's and Fichte's idealisms is unchanging, a constant relative to the variables of temporally volatile empirical beings and happenings. One must bear in mind that Žižek here stretches Fichte's concept of the *Tat-Handlung* to cover (Lacanian) acts other than just the (f)act of the "I"'s self-positing (something Fichte would not do) and assumes a more Hegelian (than Fichtean) dialectical-speculative, reciprocal interpenetration of self-form (i.e., acting subject) and non-self-content (i.e., objects as what are acted upon as well as performed acts themselves). Given this, Žižek's subjectivity of the act (in both senses of the genitive), if it still can be described as "transcendental," is doubly temporal, namely, both, one, chronological, genetic, and historical as well as, two, after-the-(f)act *à la* Freudian-Lacanian *Nachträglichkeit/ après-coup* (i.e., deferred action as signaled in the verb tense of the future anterior). That is to say, the Žižekian acting subject, as the non-empirical locus of ineliminable autonomy, freedom, spontaneity, etc., changes in its very transcendental contours and configurations as it moves forward in linear time precisely thanks to this subject being (auto-)affected by the effects/influences of its own acts flowing backward in retroactive time – with this whole circuit in its entirety amounting to a temporally elongated dynamic of self-reflexivity stretching out over past, present, and future.

Although Žižek already moves beyond Fichte while still explaining the latter's often misunderstood idealist philosophy, he also carefully highlights Fichte's extrapolations from and progress beyond Kant's transcendentalism. In particular, Žižek employs Fichte so as to render Kant more exact and true to himself. On Žižek's construal of the Fichtean version of Kantian transcendental idealism, transcendental subjectivity, as free *qua* autonomous and spontaneous, is neither merely a phenomenal object-as-appearance (nonetheless, the Žižekian German idealist subject indeed is enmeshed with appearances[14]) nor immediately a noumenal thing-in-itself (however, as Žižek rightly observes, Kant sometimes conflates transcendental subjectivity with *das Ding an sich* as "this I, or He, or It (the thing), which thinks"[15]). As Žižek points out, Fichte's rejection of Kant's thing-in-itself – he shares this precise rejection in common with F.H. Jacobi, Schelling, and Hegel, among others[16] – is motivated, at least in part, by a desire to foreclose a specific possibility (one entertained by Kant himself[17]): subjectivity rests on an underlying noumenal seat and, at this supersensible level, everything really is determined, namely, no autonomy/spontaneity is to be found there. In other words, by jettisoning *das Ding an sich* and, along with it, the (occasional) Kantian equation of the transcendental "I" immanent to the realm of phenomenal appearances with a noumenal "x" transcendent vis-à-vis this same realm, Fichte moves to safeguard the freedom esteemed as of unsurpassably great importance by him, Kant, and the German idealist movement in its entirety. With Žižek's reconstruction of Fichte's theory of the subject (as itself absolutely central to the latter's entire philosophical edifice as a subjectivist transcendental idealism[18]), there remains, in the post-Kantian aftermath of the dissolution of anything and everything noumenal, only the lone plane of multiple different phenomena and the kinetic negativity of (self-)positing subjectivity internal to this same plane.[19]

In relation to the immediately preceding, Žižek, as is to be expected from the author of *Less Than Nothing*, proceeds to highlight Hegel's crucial step beyond Kant and Fichte. As regards what is alleged to be "Kant's and Fichte's inability to conceive positively of the ontological status of this neither-phenomenal-nor-noumenal autonomous-spontaneous subject," he proposes that "Hegel's solution here involves the transposition of the epistemological limitation into ontological fact: the void of our knowledge corresponds to a void in being itself, to the ontological incompleteness of reality."[20] Despite Žižek's implicitly self-critical insistence, at other points in *Less Than Nothing*, on reconceptualizing the shift from Kant to Hegel as a matter of the latter "deontologizing" (rather than "ontologizing") the former, this is an instance of him sticking to his older narrative according to which Kantian epistemological ignorances can and should be transformed into Hegelian ontological insights.[21] Incidentally but interestingly, in the context of critiquing Quentin Meillassoux's "speculative materialism" much later in *Less Than Nothing*, Žižek cautions that not all minuses at the level of epistemology are to be automatically and immediately transubstantiated into pluses at the level of ontology (given that Meillassoux performs with respect to David Hume and his problem of induction an ontologization of this empiricist's epistemology akin to what Žižek's Hegel does apropos Kant[22]). He warns that, "not every epistemological limitation is an indication of ontological incompleteness."[23] The main question this raises is: What are the criteria, whether philosophical and/or empirical, for determining if and when an apparent absence of knowledge is actually the real presence of a true direct rapport between thinking and being?

That said, Žižek seems faithfully to follow Hegel's criticisms of the subjectivist essence of Kant's and Fichte's idealisms (as first formulated by Hegel in his 1801 *Differenzschrift* and repeated regularly by him thereafter).[24] Both Kant and Fichte, in Žižek's Hegelian eyes, spoil many of their best insights into transcendental subjectivity by self-(mis)interpreting their own theories of the subject in subjectivist *qua* transcendent (as distinct from transcendental) terms. The two giants of transcendental idealism (representing the first main phase of German idealism, the one preceding the rise of objective and absolute idealisms with Schelling and Hegel) succeed at disclosing an incomplete, disunited phenomenal field of dialectically unstable organizations and operations, including a more-than-phenomenal subjectivity nonetheless inextricably intertwined with this same field. But, each in his own manner, they shrink back from the ultimate ontological consequences potentially to be unfurled out of their philosophical efforts: Kant tends to treat his own critical–transcendental analyses as strictly epistemological and sometimes succumbs to the temptation to hypothesize (or, one might say, hypostatize) a noumenal self as a transcendent "I"-Thing; both Kant and Fichte, as subjectivists in Hegel's sense, are extreme and stubborn anti-realists, treating their own discourses as exclusively about (self-)conscious thinking *für sich* and not also non-conscious being *an sich*. For Žižek, if a Fichtean in particular wants to defend the reality of freedom as amounting to the authentic, radical causal efficacy of non-appearing subjectivity (i.e., the [self-]positing transcendental subject) and its corresponding appearances, then he/she should become a Hegelian by, as Hegel might phrase it, thinking subject also as substance (to invert a famous turn of phrase from the preface to the *Phenomenology of Spirit*).[25] That is to say, in order for the autonomous/spontaneous subject of Fichte's philosophy to be robustly and unambiguously non-epiphenomenal, it and the surface of phenomena to which it remains immanent must, in the absence of a Kantian-style noumenal Elsewhere (as an other world of things-in-themselves transcending this world here), be ontologized – and this if only by default insofar as the phenomenal here and now is the one and only existence that enjoys being in the wake of the dissolution of any absolute Outside of noumena. Despite his repudiation of Kant's *Ding an sich*, Fichte still fails to abandon the anti-realist subjectivism closely associated with this very Thing.

As regards a properly Hegelian sublation of the idealist accounts of freedom within the Kantian and Fichtean edifices, Žižek expresses this with the help of Lacanian language. Near the end of the third chapter of *Less Than Nothing* (the chapter entitled "Fichte's Choice"), he suggests:

> what kind of structure do we have to think so that it effectively involves the subject, not only as its epiphenomenal "effect," but as its immanent constituent? Lacan's answer, of course, is that the condition of freedom (of a free subject) is the "barred" big Other, a structure which is inconsistent, with gaps.[26]

This line of thought subsequently is reiterated: "we are free because there is a lack in the Other, because the substance out of which we grew and on which we rely is inconsistent, barred, failed, marked by an impossibility"[27] and "I am free if the substance of my being is not a full causal network, but an ontologically incomplete field."[28] To cut a long story short, Žižek has in mind, across the span of these quoted remarks, both socio-symbolic and natural-real versions of the Lacanian barred big Other. Put differently, the "structures" that must be "inconsistent," "incomplete," and the like for the effective existence of non-epiphenomenal autonomous/spontaneous subjectivity are those of the substance(s) both of non-human nature and of the "objective spirit" of cultural-linguistic symbolic orders (i.e., barred Reals as well as barred Symbolics).[29] Put in Hegelian terms, Hegel and Lacan, for Žižek, sublationally raise Kant and Fichte to the dignity of their Notions by ontologizing their epistemological/subjectivist negativities as necessary non-subjective conditions for their transcendental subjects.[30]

Less Than Nothing goes on to spend sustained energy in explaining the details of nature as, in Lacanese, the lacking Other of a barred Real of material substances at odds with each other (of course, Schelling's and Hegel's post-Fichtean, absolute idealist philosophies of nature, within the history of German idealism, already prepare the ground for much of what Žižek does here, as he well knows[31]). Žižek's aim in so doing is, as I indicated a moment ago, to establish the ultimate ontological-material bases *qua* necessary conditions of possibility for free subjects immanently transcending these same bases. In addition to working through core components of the freedom-determinism question/problem via an enchaining together of Kant, Fichte, Hegel, and Lacan, he also brings into the conversation references to biology and cognitivism. Žižek refers specifically to arguments in Daniel Dennett's 2003 book *Freedom Evolves*.[32] One straightforward way to rearticulate Žižek's compatibilism is to observe that, for both him and Dennett, incompatibilists, as anti-naturalistic dualists, rely upon a useless standard of freedom whose uselessness is due to an empty abstraction: the vacuous pseudo-idea of a wholly pure "I" completely devoid of content by virtue of this self's transcendence of anything and everything determinate. One way to make this point is to assert that the standard image of "imprisonment" in deterministic nature entails a false distinction between prisoner (i.e., the incompatibilist's self) and prison (i.e., what the incompatibilist [mis]perceives in the guise of deterministic nature as this self's Other). Arguably, Kant and Fichte (unlike Schelling and Hegel) both flirt with, if not outright embrace, such incompatibilism, at least sometimes and to certain degrees.

In *Less Than Nothing*, a position in Anglo-American Analytic philosophy of mind (i.e., a specific brand of compatibilism bearing upon the freedom–determinism issue) is defensibly situated as, unbeknownst to itself, a permutation of the "system-program" of post-Fichtean German idealism (especially as per Schelling and Hegel) to think subject also as substance.[33] In other words, if there really is such a thing as free subjectivity (*qua* autonomous, spontaneous, and self-determining), then, for a thoroughly materialist theory of such a subject, this freedom must be rendered as an outgrowth of natural substances. To again resort to a Hegelian style of phrasing, to the extent that there is a true and irreducible distinction between determination (via natural substance) and self-determination (via more-than-natural/denaturalized subjectivity), this must be a distinction internal to determination itself. Furthermore, not only, at the level of a theoretical-philosophical ontology, are there reasons to insist upon the immanence of the subjective to the substantial (*contra* any dualistic transcendence in which subjects stand entirely over and above all material actualities) – Žižek, fully in line with Hegel, also suggests that the unreal, impossible purity of the voided "I" of incompatibilisms is objectionable at the level of a practical-philosophical ethics and/or politics insofar as its purity comes at the price of not being able to be either motivated by or committed to doing anything specific. Such a content-less, indeterminate "I" is reminiscent of versions of the "beautiful soul" (and similar figures/shapes of consciousness) harshly derided throughout Hegel's writings.[34]

Although Dennett, with his thesis in *Freedom Evolves* that there is no inconsistency in claiming that human beings are naturally determined to be free, himself indicates much of what I just explained, Žižek consistently exhibits a comparatively stronger, clearer, and more unambiguous fidelity to staunch anti-reductionism and related greater wariness of a biologizing naturalism that would risk compromising or mitigating the freedom of concern to both himself and Dennett. The distinguishing feature of Žižek's own version of compatibilism is his emphasis on antagonism, inconsistency, and so on. In *Less Than Nothing*, he quickly moves to develop this feature through interrelated invocations of retroaction and incompleteness:

> We are ... simultaneously less free and more free than we think: we are thoroughly passive, determined by and dependent on the past, but we have the freedom to define the scope of this determination, to (over)determine the past which will determine us ... I am determined by causes, but I (can) retroactively determine which causes will determine me: we, subjects, are passively affected by pathological objects and motivations; but, in a reflexive way, we have the minimal power to accept (or reject) being affected in this way, that is, we retroactively determine the causes allowed to determine us, or, at least, the *mode* of this linear determination. "Freedom" is thus inherently retroactive: at its most elementary, it is not simply a free act which, out of nowhere, starts a new causal link, but a retroactive act of determining which link or sequence of necessities will determine us. Here, one should add a Hegelian twist to Spinoza: freedom is not simply "recognized/known necessity," but recognized/assumed necessity, the necessity constituted/actualized through this recognition.[35]

In the immediately following paragraph, Žižek proceeds to link this retroaction to a certain sort of incompleteness:

> The key philosophical implication of Hegelian retroactivity is that it undermines the reign of the Principle of Sufficient Reason: this principle only holds in the condition of linear causality where the sum of

> past causes determines a future event – retroactivity means that the set of (past, given) reasons is never complete and "sufficient," since the past reasons are retroactively activated by what is, within the linear order, their effect.[36]

The above points are recapitulated subsequently in *Less Than Nothing*.[37] There is an enormous amount in need of unpacking in these quotations (this requisite labor will occupy me for some while in what follows). To begin naturally enough at the start of the first of these two quoted passages, Žižek alludes to a paraphrase transposing Freud's statement "the normal man is not only far more immoral than he believes but also far more moral than he knows"[38] into "the normal man is not only far more determined than he believes but also far freer than he knows" (this exact paraphrase is deployed by both Zupančič and me[39]). Although Žižek does not do so in this instance, he elsewhere explores a more psychoanalytic angle apropos the matters at stake in this context by speculating about agency, choice, freedom, and the like (also on the basis of German idealism) specifically in relation to the Freudian–Lacanian unconscious.[40] However, in *Less Than Nothing*, he indeed rightly rebukes those, such as Robert Pippin (and Manfred Frank), who erroneously conflate the analytic unconscious with the id *qua* roiling primitive ocean of animalistic organic instincts and thereby oppose such crude mindedness to the subjective self-reflexivity so powerfully thematized within the tradition of German idealism. As Žižek quite correctly observes, Lacan's "return to Freud" brings out how the unconscious (as unthought thinking or unknown knowing) is intimately folded within the very reflexivity of self-relating/reflecting subjectivity *à la* Kant, Fichte, Schelling, and Hegel.[41] That noted, Žižek's above depiction of subjects as simultaneously more and less free than they think can be taken in both psychoanalytic and non-psychoanalytic senses, depending on whether one is considering freedom and determinism as unconscious *qua* defensively occluded from thought (i.e., as per the analytic unconscious bound up with intra-psychical defense mechanisms) or as unconscious *qua* simply non-conscious (i.e., as per non-analytic notions about what remains unthought).

Furthermore, Žižek's ensuing specifications regarding what he means by individuals being simultaneously "less free and more free than we think" hint at an intricate tapestry of references in the background of his claims and arguments. Identifying in order of historical chronology the different constituents involved in this complex contextual framing of his remarks, Kant is the first major presence casting a long shadow over these considerations. To be more precise, Žižek here appropriates Henry Allison's interpretation of Kantian practical philosophy via what Allison calls the "incorporation thesis."[42] According to this Žižekian appropriation of

Kant and Allison together, the Kantian subject's free self-determination amounts to its ability spontaneously to decide which potential determinants of its actions will have been these actions' actual determinants. One should notice that, perhaps under Allison's influence, Žižek here offers a more sympathetic depiction of Kant's ethical subjectivity by comparison with his above-highlighted, Hegel-inspired indications suggesting that Kant, given the incompatibilism of his anti-materialist/naturalist dualisms, renders the properly ethical subject empty, ineffective, and impotent through "purifying" it of all relations to any and every real or possible determinate content. Allison's Kant sidesteps the dead-end of sterile, vacuous indeterminism insofar as he insists that the actor's autonomy consists precisely in a second-order power to "incorporate" (i.e., freely identify with and opt to be determined by) omnipresent and ultimately unavoidable first-order determinants, with the latter including an ever-varying array of empirical entities and events along with the self's responses to them (also, much of this resonates both with Lacan's 1959 description of desire per se as always "in the second degree" *qua* "desire of desire"[43] as well as, in the Analytic philosophical canon, Harry Frankfurt's seminal 1971 paper "Freedom of the Will and the Concept of a Person"[44]).

In fact, the Allisonian incorporation thesis provides Žižek with a means of discerning a Hegelian dimension within the structures of the Kantian metaphysics of morals. Specifically, he mobilizes Hegel's distinction between "presupposing" (associated by Hegel with the "in itself" [*an sich*]) and "positing" (associated by Hegel with the "for itself" [*für sich*]) in characterizing freedom *à la* Kant as enacted in "the free positing of our presuppositions"[45] (this Hegelian distinction is important for Žižek throughout his corpus[46]). On Žižek's construal of Kant's practical philosophy here, the subject's capacity to be spontaneously self-determining consists in nothing more than its ability freely to determine (i.e., posit) which potential determinants (i.e., presuppositions as the palpable background of various pressing circumstances, inclinations, situations, urges, and so on) will be actually determining of its effectively realized conduct. Through the present moment of such an autonomous decision, the subject chooses which past influences bearing upon this *hic et nunc* will become, in the immediate future, what will have been the decisive, sufficient motivators of its consequent eventual deed. What is more, this Žižekian Hegelianization of Kant (via Allison) also tacitly relies on the Hegelian logic of cause and effect, according to which the effect is the cause of its cause. That is to say, a potential cause becomes an actual cause only after the (f)act of generating an ensuing actual effect; the logical status of "cause" is conferred upon something *après-coup* through the retroaction of something else subsequently being conceptualizable as an "effect" in connection with this prior something.[47] Or, one could say, the effect posits its cause as its preceding presupposition.

Before I highlight another Hegelian facet of Žižek's compatibilist reinterpretation of the freedom-determinism problem in Kantian and post-Kantian German idealism, I wish to bring to the fore another contemporary reference silently hovering in the wings of the passages currently under discussion. Although not in *Less Than Nothing*, Žižek elsewhere directly cites Benjamin Libet's neurobiological research.[48] Libet is the experimental investigator credited with discovering the late quality of conscious awareness (an approximately five-hundred-millisecond delay of onset) of an impulse to action in relation to the non-conscious initiation of the synaptic firing sequences that, left to run their course, will eventuate in the performance of this very action.[49] I will come back to Žižek's glosses on Libet's findings in due course, since both sides of the Libet–Žižek pairing address the freedom-determinism difficulty from combined philosophical, psychoanalytic, and scientific perspectives. For now, suffice it to note Libet's hypothesis according to which "free will," although not responsible for the originally neuronal triggering of intentions-to-act (hence the threatening character of Libet's discoveries for advocates of traditional versions of free will), nonetheless is an effective reality as a power to veto these synaptic sequences once consciousness becomes aware of them after an approximately five-hundred-millisecond delay (but before these sequences fully run their course and terminate in an action).[50] Implicitly endorsing Libet's hypothesis, Žižek takes it to dovetail with his interpretation of Kantian ethical subjectivity (as per Allison's incorporation thesis), with Libet's vetoing consciousness being the neurobiological epitomization of Kant's autonomous agent "positing its presuppositions." On this Žižekian reading, the presuppositions are the neuronal firing patterns initially arising non-consciously and automatically within the central nervous system. And the subsequent, lagging first-person introspective awareness of these patterns correspondingly posits, through how it denies (by vetoing) or permits (by not vetoing) them to pass on to eventual actualizations (as behaviors, performances, etc.), what will and will not have been the causally efficacious presuppositions behind the conscious subject's manifested conduct. For Žižek, this amounts to a materialist-*qua*-neuroscientific substantialization of a Kantian model of subjectivity. Again, I will return to this Libet-related content soon enough.

Once more referring back to the two block quotations above from *Less Than Nothing*, Žižek's invocations of the modality of necessity as per Hegelian philosophy cannot but prompt associations to Hegel's treatments of necessity in relation to contingency as its modal complement. Throughout his career-long engagement with Hegel, Žižek consistently insists that, contrary to certain popular (mis)representations of this giant of German idealism, Hegel does not privilege necessity over contingency (as, for example, metaphysically real logical and/or world-historical Ideas/Spirits *qua* timeless teleological dictators reigning from on high over the empirical-material realities of finite spatio-temporal creatures and creations). On the contrary – the Žižekian Hegel prioritizes contingency over necessity, making the latter a secondary outgrowth of the former.[51] And, without getting bogged down in details for the time being, there indeed is significant support in Hegel's own texts for this Žižekian interpretive line.[52] Hence, Žižek's invocations of a Hegelian dialectic between necessity and freedom in the above-quoted passages from *Less Than Nothing*, considering both Hegel's speculative-dialectical logic of necessity and contingency as well as Žižek's frequent emphasis on contingency's centrality in Hegelian philosophy, lead straight to the following question: How are the concepts of freedom and contingency compared and/or contrasted by Žižek? As with the Libet material, I will circumnavigate back to this critical query shortly.

Apropos the role of retroaction in the preceding, this temporal topic brings up Žižek's reliances on Freud, Lacan, and Alain Badiou. *Pace* the vulgar misunderstanding according to which time in psychoanalysis is no exception to the commonplace assumption that it flows in only a single linear-chronological direction (with analysis presumably just stressing the past's determination of the present), Freudian-Lacanian *Nachträglichkeit/après-coup* underscores the pivotal and pervasive workings of "deferred action" *qua* the backwards-flowing influence of the present and future on the past.[53] Of particular relevance and importance in the current context, retroactive temporality is integral to the later Lacan's conception of the "act," a concept that has come over the years to occupy a place at the very heart of Žižek's theoretical apparatus. Succinctly stated, for Lacan, whether or not a given action (as a piece of comportment, a deed or doing) will have been an act (as a true disruption of established Imaginary–Symbolic reality[54]) gets determined after the (f)act.[55] For Žižek, as he emphasizes repeatedly, whether or not a given instance of behavior is to count as free, as a manifestation of freedom, is also a matter of retroactivity's future anterior.[56]

However, there nonetheless appears to be a non-negligible difference between the act *à la* Lacanian psychoanalysis and autonomy *à la* Žižekian German idealism (with the latter as the activity of spontaneously positing one's presuppositions). Although both involve retroactivity, the distinct facets of subjectivity illuminated here by Lacan and Žižek seem to contrast markedly. The account of the subject entailed by Lacan's theory of the act stresses the subject's non-existence prior to the act that brings it into being.[57] Lacan emphasizes that his subject of the act definitely is not an already-there locus of (self-)awareness whose deliberations and reflections precede and produce the act in question. Due both to the act's relationship to the analytic unconscious as well as to the act's dependence for its deferred, belated act-level status on its ensuing resonances/dissonances with trans-subjective socio-symbolic matrices, the Lacanian act is more the prior cause than the subsequent effect of its subject. And, whatever freedom is involved with the *après-coup* subject of the act, it looks to be distinct from Kantian-style freedom as consisting in a capacity for willful, conscious self-determination[58] (if only, as per Žižek's appropriations of Allison and Libet, as a power selectively to incorporate, through blocking vetoes, which presently palpable inclinations and influences will and will not be allowed to determine realized courses of acting).

Furthermore, Žižek's quasi-Lacanian German idealist depiction of freedom similarly sometimes gives the impression of cross-resonating also with Badiou's (partially Lacan-inspired) theory of "evental" subjectivity. But such echoes, while not entirely misleading – Badiou too sketches a dynamic of retroactive positing of presuppositions in his portrayal of subjects of events[59] – arguably distort as much as they disclose. In certain respects, Badiou's account of the event–subject rapport is closer to Lacan's of the act–subject one than is Žižek's more Kantian characterization of free agency[60] (and this apart from the various discrepancies between Lacan's and Badiou's concepts of act and event respectively[61]). Other potentially relevant details aside, the Badiouian subject of the event, like the Lacanian subject of the act, in no way whatsoever pre-exists the given event to which it owes its very (coming into) being.[62] Moreover, in addition to the Kantian and post-Kantian characteristics of Žižekian autonomous agency (with its reflective/reflexive vetoing powers of self-determination), Žižek's specific synthesis here of German idealism and neurobiology (via Libet) likely would be unappealing to Badiou, considering the latter's aversions to the German idealists and the life sciences.

Finally, and once again with reference to the two related passages from *Less Than Nothing* I quoted earlier (in particular, the second of these), Žižek interestingly draws a radical conclusion about the principle of sufficient reason from his compatibilist considerations of subjective freedom. The free subject's ability in the present to determine what past forces and factors will become the causes determining this same subject's activities renders the past by itself "insufficient." In other words, the past alone, as the ensemble of presuppositions *qua* influences pressing upon the present, lacks the capacity directly to posit (*qua* cause, command, determine, dictate, etc.) realized effects at the level of subjects' cognition and comportment. Or, put differently once more, preceding chains of entities and events, with respect to free actors, transition from insufficiency to sufficiency only *après-coup* through the subsequent supplements of choices to block (or not to block) their translations into materialized decisions and deeds.

As regards his reflections on the principle of sufficient reason, Žižek's opening up of the past by decompleting it through its reciprocal relations with ever-unfurling presents and futures cannot but call to mind a theme recurrent throughout his works, including *Less Than Nothing*: an ontology of incompleteness. Often with reference to Lacan's notion of the "not-all" (*pas tout*) and related dictum according to which "the big Other does not exist" (*il n'y a pas de grand Autre*), Žižek regularly stresses that both Imaginary–Symbolic realities as well as the Real of being-in-itself are "barred," namely, detotalized and permeated with antagonisms, conflicts, gaps, ruptures, tensions, and the like.[63] In remarks from *Less Than Nothing* I already cited some time ago, he identifies a Hegelian–Lacanian ontology of non-wholeness as providing the ultimate meta-transcendental basis of transcendental subjectivity itself *qua* spontaneous and self-determining. For Žižek, genuine freedom, as non-epiphenomenal subjective autonomy, is possible only if the Real of being *an sich* is not "complete" as a causally closed One enjoying seamless self-consistency. The insufficiency of the realized past alone, as per Žižek's take on the principle of sufficient reason, looks to be of a piece with his recurrent emphasis on ontological incompleteness.

However, at this juncture, two possibly major problems for Žižekian compatibilism can and should be made explicit. First, a danger of vicious circularity seems to threaten Žižek's explanation apropos the rapport between present subjective freedom and past objective (in)sufficiency. On the one hand, the positing activity of the subject's spontaneous self-determination through its veto power (as per the combination of Kant, Allison, and Libet) retroactively renders the presuppositions of already-there potential determinants insufficient on their own apart from this positing; on the other hand, this very same insufficiency of these past presuppositions appears to be itself an ontological-temporal and meta-transcendental condition of possibility for this very same subject's autonomy *qua* free (self-)positing. Succinctly stated: no free present, no insufficient/incomplete past; no insufficient/incomplete past, no free present. How, if at all, does Žižek avoid falling into this trap?

Second, there arguably are, as I noted earlier, cross-resonances between Žižek's Hegelian recasting of Allison's Kantian incorporation thesis and his repeated insistence that Hegel ultimately prioritizes contingency over necessity. However, if such reverberations indeed are audible (even if not entirely intended), then it sounds as though Žižek is in danger of indefensibly equivocating between contingency and freedom by associating autonomous spontaneity with a modality involving arbitrariness, capriciousness, chanciness, randomness, and so on. Bluntly stated, contingency as mere indetermination is far from being freedom as full-blown self-determination. This certainly is the view of the vast majority of Western philosophers past and present, holding with special strength for Kant and his German idealist successors. As will be seen shortly, Žižek's references to quantum physics, particularly in *Less Than Nothing*, often only intensify the sense that he illegitimately conflates the indeterminate with the self-determinate. So, does Žižek actually operate with a subtle, refined distinction between contingency and freedom despite the worrying impression that he fails to recognize or respect this distinction?

At one moment during his speculations regarding theoretical physics in *Less Than Nothing*, Žižek invokes the now-familiar compatibilist (mis)use of quantum indeterminacy as a means to debunk materialist/naturalist determinisms of a Laplace's-demon type.[64] To believe that simply exorcizing this demon is tantamount to establishing the causally efficacious reality of robust human freedom obviously would be to rely on the invalid equation of the indeterminate with the self-determinate. Subsequent quantum-physical moments in *Less Than Nothing* only partly indicate Žižek's innocence of this equivocation. On the one hand, he clearly identifies and rejects this very equivalence (with reference back to Lenin's 1908 *Materialism and Empirio-Criticism*).[65] But, a few pages later in *Less Than Nothing*, Žižek arguably muddies the waters again as regards this distinction between the mere absence of determination and the full presence of freedom. Redeploying lines of reflection going back to earlier works of his such as 1996's *The Indivisible Remainder: An Essay on Schelling and Related Matters*,[66] he argues for a blurring of the nature-culture distinction such that quantum indeterminacy becomes a proto-subjective power already there within natural substance conceived along the lines of a certain Schellingian *Naturphilosophie*.[67] Having critically considered much of this content elsewhere,[68] I will be highly selective in my responses in this context. To begin with, autonomous spontaneity is an integral feature of the human subject *qua parlêtre* according to Žižek's combination of German idealism and Lacanianism. Hence the parallels he draws between symbolic-linguistic human *Geist* and quantum objects and processes risk falling afoul of his own Leninist "denouncing" of "spiritualist appropriations of quantum physics."[69]

However, the recourse to Schellingian philosophy of nature holds out the promise of an absolute idealist defusing of this danger.[70] Schelling's "potencies" (*Potenzen*) can be interpreted as integrally of a piece with a non-reductive realist naturalism involving a strong emergentism in which emergent powers exhibit a speculative–dialectical continuity-in-discontinuity (*à la* Schellingian–Hegelian identity-in-difference[71]) vis-à-vis the ontological grounds out of which they emerge[72] (with Žižek identifying three such potencies/powers, namely, his "ontological triad of quantum proto-reality (the pre-ontological quantum oscillations), ordinary physical reality, and the 'immaterial' virtual level of Sense-Events"[73]). Therefore, following this Schelling, Žižek consistently could deny that material/natural indetermination is equivalent to more-than-material/natural self-determination (i.e., that contingency does not equal freedom) while, at the very same time, treating human autonomy as internally arising out of natural heteronomy. Moreover, absolute idealism (whether Schelling's or Hegel's) permits a non-panpsychist (i.e., an anti-spiritualist) panlogicism in which the recognition of structural and dynamical isomorphisms between human and non-human dimensions (as in, for example, "to suppose that the symbolic order pre-exists in a 'wild' natural form"[74]) is hardly tantamount to a one-sided anthropomorphizing of nature.[75] Instead, as Žižek's handling of the nature-culture distinction already suggests, rendering cultural subjectivity immanent to natural substantiality (in line with the absolute idealist agendas of Schelling and Hegel[76]) does not reduce one pole of the distinction to the other. Rather, it thoroughly sublates (*als Aufhebung*) the traditional, *Verstand*-style dichotomy between non-human nature and non-natural culture by transforming both sides of this distinction simultaneously and in tandem with each other.

As I have argued on prior occasions, there are multiple empirical-scientific as well as theoretical-philosophical reasons for hesitating to endorse unreservedly Žižek's mobilizations of quantum physics.[77] Without recapitulating those arguments here, I simply will reiterate my claim that, at least for now, the life sciences, much more than the physical sciences, are the real main proving grounds for a materialist theory of subjectivity (or, more exactly, a materialist ontology that is distinctive precisely in containing within itself, as a core feature, such a theory – the dialectical and/or transcendental materialisms forwarded by both Žižek and me contain this theoretical feature). Hence, from this perspective, it is better to consider Žižek's compatibilism within the register of (to use the Schellingian language he favors) the "potency" of biology (especially the neurosciences). It is unclear in *Less Than Nothing* whether he intends to extend his compatibilist position to cover the "lower potency" of quantum physics. Žižek therein refrains from directly basing human freedom on quantum indeterminacy, although he seems still to edge towards this gesture. Indeed, some of Schelling's philosophy pushes strongly in this very direction with the idea of subjective spontaneity as the resurgence, at a higher power (that of *Existenz*), of the groundlessness of the *Ur/Un-Grund*[78] (this middle-period [1809–1815] discourse already is foreshadowed by the early appropriations of Baruch Spinoza in the philosophies of nature and identity, with the autonomous "I" being the resurfacing, among the determinate products of *natura naturata*, of the primordial productive force of freely active *natura naturans*[79]). Recourse to Schelling might exacerbate the temptation dubiously to short-circuit the level distinction between, on the one hand, natural quantum objects and processes as neither sentient nor sapient and, on the other hand, significantly larger spiritual (*als* Hegelian *Geist*) structures and dynamics as uniquely human sentience and sapience. In, for instance, *The Indivisible Remainder*, Žižek appears openly to flirt with this very temptation.[80]

Nonetheless, through his recourse to Libet's research (strongly implicit in *Less Than Nothing* and explicit elsewhere), Žižek himself offers the beginnings of an anchoring of his compatibilism in the life sciences. Two of his direct references to Libet, one in 2004's *Organs without Bodies* and the other in 2006's *The Parallax View*, are particularly revealing of Žižek's specific compatibilist position as combining German idealism, psychoanalysis, and neurobiology. Addressing "Benjamin Libet's (deservedly) famous experiments" in *Organs without Bodies*, he states:

> What makes them so interesting is that, although the results are clear, it is not clear what they are arguments *for*. It can be argued that they demonstrate how there is no free will: even before we consciously decide (say, to move a finger), the appropriate neuronal processes are already underway, which means that our conscious decision just takes note of what is already going on (adding its superfluous authorization to a fait accompli). On the other hand, consciousness does seem to have the veto power to stop this process already underway, so there seems to be at least the freedom to *block* our spontaneous decisions. And yet, what if our very ability to veto the automatic decision is again conditioned by some "blind" neuronal processes? There is, however, a third, more radical option. What if, prior to our conscious decision, there already was an *unconscious* decision that triggered the "automatic" neuronal process itself?
>
> Prior to Freud, Schelling developed the notion that the basic free decisions made by us are unconscious. So, with regard to Libet's experiment, from the Freudian standpoint, the basic underlying problem is that of the status of the Unconscious: are there only conscious thoughts (my belated conscious decision to move a finger) and "blind" neuronal processes (the neuronal activity to move the finger), or is there also an unconscious "mental" process? And, what is the ontological status of this unconscious, if there indeed is one? Is it not that of a purely virtual symbolic order, of a pure logical *presupposition* (the decision *had to be made*, although it was never effectively made in real time)?[81]

The immediately following paragraph proceeds thus:

> It is with regard to such questions that the cognitivist project seems unable to provide a materialist answer. It either denies them or takes refuge in a "dualist" idealist position. When Daniel Dennett almost compulsively varies the theme of how dangerous "Darwin's idea" is, one is tempted to raise the suspicion that his insistence conceals/reveals the opposite fear: what if Darwin's idea (the radical contingency of evolution, the emergence of intentionality and mind itself out of a blind process of genetic variations and selection) is the one whose message is pacifying (take it easy, there is no meaning or obligation in our lives ...)? What if, in a Kierkegaardian way, the true

> "danger," the truly unbearable trauma, would be to accept that we *cannot* be reduced to an outcome of evolutionary adaptation, that there is a dimension eluding cognitivism? No wonder, then, that the most succinct definition of cognitivism is internalized behaviorism: a behaviorism of the interior (in the same way that, in contrast to a Jew, a Christian has to be "inwardly circumscised").
>
> That is to say, does it not (re)apply the behaviorist reduction (a reduction to observable positive processes) to internal processes: mind is no longer a black box, but a computational machine?[82]

The invocations both of the Schellingian cutting deed of the primordial, unconscious decision (*Ent-Scheidung*) founding one's character in the always-already past pre-history of one's actual life history as well as of the Freudian "choice of neurosis" (*Neuronenwahl*) as the eclipsed origin of one's symptom-ridden selfhood are Žižekian staples.[83] Having discussed Žižek's appropriations of these two related notions at length before,[84] I here will restrict myself to playing devil's advocate on behalf of the cognitivism Žižek seeks to undermine in these passages.

Although I am convinced that the more expansive systematic framework of Žižek's ontology can and does justify his above-articulated interpretation of Libet and corresponding critique of Dennett et al., I nevertheless view the critical formulations in the preceding two quotations as inadequate on their own by virtue of being vulnerable to a quick retort from proponents of more deterministic flavors of cognitivism. Žižek momentarily entertains the hypothesis that the veto power uncovered by Libet's experiments is not an incarnation of the subject's free spontaneity, but itself merely another heteronomous effect of underlying neurological and evolutionary causal determinants ("And yet, what if our very ability to veto the automatic decision is again conditioned by some 'blind' neuronal processes?"). As seen, he immediately proceeds to counter-propose "a third, more radical option," namely, a hybrid Schellingian-Kierkegaardian-Freudian idea according to which an unconscious-but-subjective choice and/or act irreducible to anything bodily precedes and provokes the neuronal firing sequences involved in the very capacity of consciousness to block other such sequences. But, without additional supporting argumentation, what prevents the opening up of an interminable, irresolvable tit-for-tat regress? Such a regress would consist in the cognitive determinist replying to this Žižekian philosophical/psychoanalytic move by grounding Žižek's (unconscious) autonomy in a yet deeper neurobiological and/or evolutionary-genetic asubjective, unfree basis – with Žižek in turn positing behind the cognitivist's deeper basis an even more primordial "abyss of freedom."... and on and on *ad nauseum*. This essentially would be to fall back into the confines of Kant's "third antinomy," thereby lending it further plausibility (an undesirable outcome for Žižek's post-Kantian compatibilism). Moreover, this situation resonates with a bit of humor, one nicely capturing the peculiarity of the Schellingian temporality of the decision/deed, utilized by Bruno Bosteels in a Badiouian critique of Žižek:

> a joke ... puts two fools together in an insane asylum as they get caught up in a heated shouting match. The first yells: "You're a fool!" And the second: "No, *you*'re a fool!" "No, *you*!" and so on, back and forth, until the first person finally shouts out with a certain pride: "Tomorrow, I will wake up at five a.m. and I will write on your door that you're a fool!" to which the second person answers smilingly: "And I will wake up at four a.m. and wipe it off!"[85]

In order to block this regress, to avoid such a degenerative slide into a Kantian-style antinomic impasse, the Žižekian compatibilist should not rely so heavily upon a not-unambiguously-materialist conception of human freedom (i.e., Schelling's *Ent-Scheidung* and Freud's *Neuronenwahl* as appropriated by Žižek) as a foil against the reductive naturalist materialism of certain brands of cognitivism. Instead, what is needed so that this compatibilism can overcome these determinist cognitivisms while itself remaining firmly materialist and (quasi-)naturalist (and yet simultaneously staunchly anti-reductive) is nothing less than a metaphysics of nature in which anything resembling Laplace's demon and the absolutizing of the Newtonian mechanics of efficient physical causes (assumed as valid in Kant's *Critique of Pure Reason* generally and "third antinomy" therein specifically) is decisively refuted. A *Naturphilosophie* achieving this would establish at least the preliminary necessary (albeit not necessarily sufficient) meta-transcendental conditions of possibility for the autonomous subjectivity Žižek's compatibilism wishes to save and defend. This would be a twenty-first-century philosophy of nature embodying the "Spinozism of freedom" as "The Earliest System-Program of German Idealism" pursued by Friedrich Hölderlin as well as both Hegel and Schelling, the latter two each developing post-Kantian philosophies of nature.[86]

Before turning to Libet's reflections and speculations as regards his own research, Žižek's glosses on him in *The Parallax View* are worth quoting and examining. Žižek elaborates:

> there is another lesson to be learned from Libet: the function of *blocking* as the elementary function of consciousness. This negative function is discernible at two main levels: first, at the level of "theoretical reason," the very strength of consciousness resides in what may appear to be its weakness: in its limitation, in its power of abstraction, of *leaving out* the wealth of (subliminal) sensory data. In this sense, what we perceive as the most immediate sensual reality is already the result

> of complex elaboration and judgment, a hypothesis which results from the combination of sensual signals and the matrix of expectations. Secondly, at the level of "practical reason," consciousness, while in no way able to instigate a spontaneous act, can "freely" impede its actualization: it can veto it, say "No!" to a spontaneously emerging tendency. This is where Hegel comes in, with his praise of the infinite negative power of abstraction that pertains to understanding: consciousness is possible only through this loss, this delay with regard to the fullness of immediate experience – a "direct consciousness" would be a kind of claustrophobic horror, like being buried alive with no breathing space. Only through this delay/limitation does the "world" open itself to us: without it, we would be totally suffocated by billions of data with, in a way, no empty breathing space around us, directly part of the world.[87]

This recourse to the distinction between theoretical and practical philosophy brings Kant's shadow into view. In particular, the aspects of Hegel's philosophy mobilized by Žižek here – the abstracting negativity associated with Hegelian subjectivity, so crucial in both the *Phenomenology of Spirit* and elsewhere,[88] cuts across the theoretical-practical divide in this block quotation from *The Parallax View* – are partially foreshadowed, as is often the case with Hegel, by Kant. More precisely, the first *Critique*, especially with its "Transcendental Deduction" (with its transcendental unity of apperception[89]) as well as its "Axioms of Intuition," "Anticipations of Perception," and "Analogies of Experience"[90] (all of this under the heading of the "Transcendental Analytic" with its "Analytic of Principles"), powerfully presents the case that what is experienced by human beings as their reality is not some brute, raw, primitive givenness (i.e., direct disclosures of mind-independent objective things and occurrences manifest and registered as presumably simple, immediate sensory-perceptual data). Rather, on the Kantian picture inspiring subsequent assaults on "the myth of the given" from Hegel to Wilfrid Sellars,[91] John McDowell, and Pippin, "what we perceive as the most immediate sensual reality is already the result of complex elaboration and judgment, a hypothesis which results from the combination of sensual signals and the matrix of expectations" (as Žižek puts it above).

Furthermore, when Žižek says "the very strength of consciousness resides in what may appear to be its weakness: in its limitation, in its power of abstraction, of *leaving out* the wealth of (subliminal) sensory data," he alludes to psychoanalysis in addition to German idealism. Freud's metapsychological conception of what he labels the "perception-consciousness system" indicates that one of the (if not the) principle functions of awareness is not receptively to open up to influxes from the wider world, but, by contrast, to cancel, dampen, diminish, reduce, or screen out these very influxes. That is to say, on an analytic account, consciousness functions more to block out than to let in sensory-perceptual impressions (Freud explicitly speaks of a "shield against stimuli"). And, of course, such restrictive and restricted awareness operates not only against external natural and socio-cultural realities – it also functions intra-psychically so as to repel and exclude from (self-)awareness unbearably extimate aspects of psychical reality (i.e., as Žižek would label them, "things from inner space").[92]

In terms of the practical-philosophical upshots of Libet's work on Žižek's reading, a connection can be established to another neurobiological investigator: Antonio Damasio. In particular, Damasio's early "somatic marker hypothesis" (as per his 1994 book *Descartes' Error*) is relevant here.[93] In the preceding block quotation, Žižek speaks of how "a 'direct consciousness' would be a kind of claustrophobic horror … we would be totally suffocated by billions of data with, in a way, no empty breathing space around us, directly part of the world." At the level of *praxis*, the Libetian delaying and blocking functions of consciousness, especially when parsed in conjunction with a Žižekian combination of German idealism and psychoanalysis, are bio-material conditions of possibility for decision-making. Without these filters, the human mind would be paralyzed into inactivity through being thoroughly overwhelmed by an indigestible poverty of riches such that, neither in its cognitions nor comportments, would it be able to act as a free agent. Likewise, Damasio demonstrates that affectively charged somato-psychical centers of intra-neuronal/mental gravity, ones situated below the threshold of explicit self-awareness, are crucial to the reliability and effectiveness of conscious operations of reasoning and deliberating about choices. *Pace* commonsensical folk wisdom past and present, neuropathological cases in which the emotional dimensions of individuals' brains/minds are diminished or destroyed do not result in people who, by virtue of the minimization or elimination of feelings and passions, are better, more rational decision-makers; these patients, who indeed can and do reason "in cold blood," turn out to make either poor decisions or no decisions at all (i.e., they are worse than average at choosing or even too impaired to be able to choose to begin with). Damasio's observational and experimental findings appear to lend further support to Žižek's hypotheses about the practical implications of Libet's neurobiologically grounded buffers/screens.

But what about Libet himself? What does he have to say apropos the multiple issues raised by Žižek's analyses? Not only do Libet's presentations of his specific empirical discoveries (i.e., those concerning the approximately five-hundred-millisecond time lag for the onset of conscious awareness regarding neural firing sequences) reinforce much of what Žižek does with these same discoveries – Libet's broader theoretical speculations are startlingly in line with some of the philosophical and psychoanalytic angles of Žižek's musings. To start at the broadest of philosophical levels, Libet espouses what fairly could be described as an emergent dual-aspect monism. In other words, Libet's preferred ontology and corresponding theory of subjectivity are surprisingly proximate to Žižekian transcendental materialism. For Libet, more-than-material mind emerges from material brain, with the former thereafter becoming irreducible to the latter.[94] He even proposes that this asserted strongly-emergent irreducibility of the mental to the physical/organic could, at least in principle, be experimentally tested. If and when sufficiently sophisticated surgical instruments and techniques allow for isolating areas of the brain while still keeping them alive (i.e., surgically severing all of these areas' synaptic connections to the rest of the brain's neural networks while leaving the blood vessels sustaining these areas of living tissue fully intact), it will be seen whether the cognitive, emotional, and/or motivational capacities correlated with these thus-isolated areas remain integrated within the synthetic mental sphere of consciousness. If so, this would suggest that conscious mindedness possesses a functional unity independent (at least in certain respects) of its material basis in the anatomy and physiology of the central nervous system.[95] Despite Žižek's ambivalence about emergentism – in *Less Than Nothing*, he voices reservations about it despite also conceding (at least tacitly) that he nevertheless relies upon a robust version of it (one admitting "downward causation") – his transcendental materialist compatibilism, like Libet's emergent dual-aspect monism, posits the immanent genesis of thereafter-irreducible mind/subject from matter/substance.[96]

The cross-resonances between Žižek and Libet reverberate more profoundly still. Even though Freud had to fight fiercely against a long-standing, deeply-entrenched assumption according to which the mental and the conscious are co-extensive and equivalent, one of Freud's historical triumphs (despite the somewhat spurious appearance of his contemporary defeat) is that nobody in the "psy-" disciplines nowadays seriously questions the notion that much of mental life transpires below the radar of explicit cognizance. Libet echoes this post-Freudian consensus with his repeated assertions that a sizable amount of neuronal and mental processes integral to cognitive, emotional, and motivational functioning remains implicit *qua* non-conscious.[97] But, if this were all that he echoed, the connection with psychoanalysis would be tenuous indeed; the Freudian unconscious proper is not merely the absence of consciousness. However, Libet goes further here in two ways. First, he suggests that, in the roughly five-hundred-millisecond interval between an initiated neural firing sequence and a belated awareness of this sequence as an intention-to-act, unconscious defense mechanisms might be able to take advantage of this interval so as to distort, inflect, modify, nudge, etc. how late-to-arrive consciousness takes note of and responds to the underlying intention in question.[98] Hence, Libet avowedly sees his research as uncovering a fundamental feature of neurobiologically based mental life whose existence lends support to core Freudian views. Second, he maintains that the time lag his investigations reveal shows that any region of the brain capable of affecting consciousness also can work unconsciously (because every such region works in and through the temporal gaps of delays).[99] Additionally, like Freud and Žižek, Libet emphasizes that the delayed temporal quality of consciousness acts as a filter protecting minded awareness against the potential incapacitating flood of sensory-perceptual overloading.[100]

At one point, Libet comments, "Perhaps all conscious mental events actually *begin unconsciously* before any awareness appears."[101] In light of Žižek's mobilization of Schelling et al. against cognitivism in *Organs without Bodies* – as I explained a short while ago, Žižek there argues that the *Ent-Scheidungen* of unconscious decision-making are the non-neurobiological possibility conditions for the neurobiological structures and dynamics highlighted by Libet's investigations – everything hinges on the ontological standing of Libet's unconscious beginning. Whether with Libetian emergent dual-aspect monism or Žižekian transcendental materialism – both positions share in common a compatibilist orientation, among other things – there are, to put this in Hegelian parlance, a number of presuppositions in need of positing.

As seen earlier, Žižek, in *Organs without Bodies*, asks apropos his anti-cognitivist unconscious, "what is the ontological status of this unconscious, if there indeed is one? Is it not that of a purely virtual symbolic order, of a pure logical *presupposition* (the decision *had to be made*, although it was never effectively made in real time)?" Žižek's invocation of "a purely virtual symbolic order" arguably refers to his combination of the concepts of Hegelian "objective spirit" and the Lacanian big Other (i.e., the cultural-linguistic symbolic order). The "virtual reality" in question here is that of the trans-individual networks of collective beliefs, customs, habits, institutions, laws, mores, practices, rituals, traditions, and so on. These matrices of material and more-than-material shared configurations structure individuals who become and remain proper subjects through how these individuals internalize and instantiate such configurations (although, at the same time, because Hegel, Lacan, and Žižek are not classical metaphysical realists, objective spirits, symbolic orders, and the like are not transcendent realities unto themselves and, hence, exist only in and through their specific instantiations at the level of particular individuals[102]). Thus, as regards the hybrid Schellingian–Kierkegaardian–Freudian unconscious he mobilizes against certain cognitivisms, Žižek appears to be making the Hegelian–Lacanian suggestion that the virtual-yet-objective reality of a *geistige grand Autre* condemns particular persons to the abyssal freedom of groundlessly, spontaneously deciding how to subjectify themselves in response to the coordinates of this pre-existent, partially deterministic order (with the very "barring" of this big Other as inconsistent, conflicted, etc. being a crucial part of what allows and pulls for acts of underdetermined decisions as necessary moments of processes of subjectification). Put differently, a web of real abstractions composing a given socio-historical context into which specific individuals factically are hurled always-already compel these individuals to choose their subjectivities on the basis of this web's parameters and permutations.[103] And yet, what would prevent Žižek's cognitivist adversary from promptly responding with the claim that this primordial subjectifiying *Ur*-choice (i.e., Schelling's *Ent-Scheidung* and/or Freud's *Neuronenwahl*) vis-à-vis "a purely virtual symbolic order" is itself just another heteronomous effect determined by such causes as electro-chemical reactions in the brain or genetically encoded evolutionary dictates?

Assuming that the Žižekian anti-cognitivist unconscious indeed is to be understood along the lines sketched in the preceding paragraph, it plausibly could be maintained that Žižek and Libet both need a theory of subjectivity drawing on models of "extended mind" (as these models are dubbed in Analytic philosophy of mind). Especially for Žižek's compatibilism, part of what makes his philosophical-psychoanalytic subject irreducible to the bio-materiality of its corresponding central nervous system alone is its being bound up with and distributed over the "virtual" extension constituted by everything associated with Hegel's objective spirit and/or Lacan's symbolic order, an expanse vastly exceeding single, isolated organisms. Žižekian subjectivity is brought into effective existence by virtue of the mediating influences of trans-individual, socio-linguistic forces and factors[104] (however, Žižek also nonetheless justifiably insists in turn upon the irreducibility of this subjectivity to the spiritual/social mediators helping to generate and sustain it[105]).

Given the implicit extended-mind dimensions of Žižek's compatibilist picture of autonomous, full-fledged subjectivity, this picture requires explicit posits (with the support of accompanying argumentation) at two levels. To employ a combination of Freudian and quotidian terms, what is called for are interlinked, coordinated phylogenetic and ontogenetic renditions of the emergence of the cultural out of the natural. At the ontogenetic level, fundamental questions of the following kind would have to be asked and answered[106]: How is the anatomy and physiology of the human animal receptive to being permeated and modulated by external milieus, especially of a socio-linguistic sort? Why are these overriding (or, as Lacan would prefer, overwriting) impositions from without not only not rejected like failed organ transplants by the libidinally charged bodies onto which they are impressed, but instead supported and perpetuated by these very bodies? What accounts of the constituents and operations of both the individual's central nervous system as well as the mediating matrices of trans-individual symbolic orders (and the interactions between these two dimensions) explain the asserted autonomy of signifier-entangled subjectivity, itself a transcendence-in-immanence with respect to its corporeal grounds as themselves necessary conditions for any and every subject's existence? How does the reflexivity/recursivity of the subject of the signifier enable it to become non-epiphenomenally self-determining (*à la* Kantian and post-Kantian German idealist depictions of subjective spontaneity) despite it remaining ontologically dependent upon the physical basis of its underlying bodily being (particularly its brain)? How and why does "natural" substance become (also) "cultural" subject? How and why is the latter free in and through the former?

At the phylogenetic level, a related series of queries likewise proliferates for Žižekian compatibilist transcendental materialism:[107] what larger-scale philosophy of nature and the natural sciences is required to substantiate the move of barring Laplace's demon (as a figure representing reductive, totalizing determinisms in general)? What is involved in the genesis of human out of natural history? Assuming human history in fact does so, how does it achieve (at least partially) a separateness from natural history? How and why does nature permit and participate in this, namely, a break with it permitted and catalyzed from nowhere other than within itself? What exactly would a *Naturphilosophie* with an ontology of self-sundering, auto-denaturalizing nature look like that is both uncompromisingly materialist and (quasi-)naturalist *qua* responsible with respect to the empirical, experimental sciences of nature? And how are these phylogenetic topics to be systematically interfaced with the ontogenetic ones outlined above?

I would be the first admiringly to acknowledge that Žižek should be credited both with articulating many of the key insights establishing the theoretical foundations for a possible transcendental materialist compatibilism and with richly elaborating these insights in relation to German idealism and Lacanian metapsychology (not to mention Badiou's philosophy). What is more, he has done much to reactivate, within the context of European philosophical traditions and their offshoots, serious engagements with the natural sciences of a sort foreshadowed by Schellingian and Hegelian philosophies of nature as well as certain Marxian dialectical materialisms (precursors largely overshadowed and overlooked during roughly the past one hundred years of "Continental philosophy" as dominated by anti-realist idealisms, constructivisms, and relativisms). However, as the plethora of questions raised in the preceding two paragraphs already indicates, I also would contend that much still remains to be done in consolidating and solidifying a transcendental materialism non-reductively yet (quasi-)naturalistically and materialistically resolving the antinomies between the autonomous/free and the heteronomous/determined. Further expansions and elaborations of philosophically and psychoanalytically informed inquires concerning, in particular, evolutionary theory, epigenetics, neuroplasticity, emergentism, recursion, downward causation, extended mind, and Analytic philosophy of mind in general are requisite if Žižekian transcendental materialism is to continue to develop and advance further. Žižek deserves recognition not only for his trailblazing labors of paving lengthy portions of the path of this novel materialism – his work thus far also outlines with precision what still must be accomplished in the years ahead by him, his sympathetic-yet-critical others, and an interdisciplinary "general intellect" conditioning whatever future philosophical breakthroughs along these materialist lines might be possible.

Notes

1 Slavoj Žižek, *Less Than Nothing: Hegel and the Shadow of Dialectical Materialism*, London: Verso, 2012, pp. 457–458, 461–463.
2 Adrian Johnston, *Badiou, Žižek, and Political Transformations: The Cadence of Change*, Evanston, IL: Northwestern University Press, 2009, pp. 144–156.
3 Žižek, *Less Than Nothing*, p. 121.
4 Ibid., p. 122.
5 Ibid., p. 123.
6 Ibid., pp. 123, 265–266, 310.
7 Slavoj Žižek, *The Indivisible Remainder: An Essay on Schelling and Related Matters*, London: Verso, 1996, p. 73; Slavoj Žižek, "Preface: Burning the Bridges," *The Žižek Reader*, ed. Elizabeth Wright and Edmond Wright, Oxford: Blackwell, 1999, p. ix; Slavoj Žižek, "Liberation Hurts: An Interview with Slavoj Žižek with Eric Dean Rasmussen," www.electronicbookreview.com/thread/endconstruction/desublimation, 2003; Slavoj Žižek and Glyn Daly, *Conversations with Žižek*, Cambridge: Polity, 2004, pp. 61, 64–65, 135; Žižek, *Less Than Nothing*, pp. 492–493, 830; Adrian Johnston, *Žižek's Ontology: A Transcendental Materialist Theory of Subjectivity*, Evanston, IL: Northwestern University Press, 2008, pp. 105, 109, 126, 166, 181–194.
8 Žižek, *Less Than Nothing*, pp. 127–128.
9 G.W.F. Hegel, *Faith and Knowledge*, trans. Walter Cerf and H.S. Harris, Albany: State University of New York Press, 1977, pp. 67, 73, 76–78; G.W.F. Hegel, *Philosophy of Mind: Part Three of the Encyclopedia of the Philosophical Sciences with the Zusätze*, trans. William Wallace and A.V. Miller, Oxford: Oxford University Press, 1971, §467 (p. 226); G.W.F. Hegel, *Elements of the Philosophy of Right*, ed. Allen W. Wood, trans. H.B. Nisbet, Cambridge: Cambridge University Press, 1991, §6 (pp. 39–40), §135–137 (pp. 162–165); G.W.F. Hegel, *Lectures on the History of Philosophy, Volume Three*, trans. E.S. Haldane and Frances H. Simson, New York: The Humanities Press, 1955, pp. 460–461, 471–474.
10 Žižek, *Less Than Nothing*, pp. 209–210.
11 J.G. Fichte, "Review of *Aenesidemus*," *Fichte: Early Philosophical Writings*, ed. and trans. Daniel Breazeale, Ithaca: Cornell University Press, 1988, pp. 64, 75; J.G. Fichte, "Concerning the Concept of the *Wissenschaftslehre* or, of So-called 'Philosophy'," *Fichte*, p. 126; J.G. Fichte, "Outline of the Distinctive Character of the *Wissenschaftslehre* with Respect to the Theoretical Faculty," *Fichte*, p. 267; J.G. Fichte, "A Comparison between Prof. Schmid's System and the *Wissenschaftslehre*," *Fichte*, p. 328; J.G. Fichte, *The Science of Knowledge*, trans. Peter Heath and John Lachs, Cambridge: Cambridge University Press, 1982, pp. 40–42, 93, 96–98; J.G. Fichte, *The Vocation of Man*, trans. William Smith, La Salle: Open Court, 1965, p. 70; Dieter Henrich, "Fichte's Original Insight,"

trans. David R. Lachterman, *Contemporary German Philosophy*, ed. Darrel E. Christensen, Manfred Riedel, Robert Spaemann, Reiner Wiehl, and Wolfgang Wieland, University Park: Pennsylvania State University Press, 1982, pp. 25–26, 48.

12 Žižek, *Less Than Nothing*, p. 214.

13 Ibid., p. 649.

14 Adrian Johnston, "'Freedom or System? Yes, please!': How to Read Slavoj Žižek's *Less Than Nothing: Hegel and the Shadow of Dialectical Materialism*," *Repeating Žižek*, ed. Agon Hamza, Durham: Duke University Press, 2014 (forthcoming).

15 Immanuel Kant, *Critique of Pure Reason*, trans. Paul Guyer and Allen Wood, Cambridge: Cambridge University Press, 1998, B156 (p. 259), A346/B404 (p. 414), A350–351 (pp. 416–417).

16 Johnston, "'Freedom or System? Yes, please!'".

17 Immanuel Kant, *Critique of Practical Reason*, trans. Lewis White Beck, New Jersey: Prentice Hall, 1993 (third edition), p. 154; Immanuel Kant, *Grounding for the Metaphysics of Morals*, trans. James W. Ellington, Indianapolis: Hackett, 1993 (third edition), pp. 19–20; Johnston, *Žižek's Ontology*, pp. 63–64.

18 Johnston, "'Freedom or System? Yes, please!'".

19 Žižek, *Less Than Nothing*, pp. 147–148, 161–163, 169, 174–175.

20 Ibid., p. 149.

21 Johnston, "'Freedom or System? Yes, please!'".

22 Quentin Meillassoux, *After Finitude: An Essay on the Necessity of Contingency*, trans. Ray Brassier, London: Continuum, 2008, pp. 53, 91–92; Adrian Johnston, *Prolegomena to Any Future Materialism, Volume One: The Outcome of Contemporary French Philosophy*, Evanston, IL: Northwestern University Press, 2013, p. 150.

23 Žižek, *Less Than Nothing*, p. 907.

24 Johnston, "'Freedom or System? Yes, please!'".

25 Ibid.

26 Žižek, *Less Than Nothing*, p. 185.

27 Ibid., p. 263.

28 Ibid., p. 264.

29 Johnston, *Žižek's Ontology*, pp. xxv, 65, 77–79, 92, 107, 111–113, 122, 148, 170–171, 179–180, 189, 208–209, 272–273, 285–287; Adrian Johnston, *Adventures in Transcendental Materialism: Dialogues with Contemporary Thinkers*, Edinburgh: Edinburgh University Press, 2014 (forthcoming); Adrian Johnston, *Prolegomena to Any Future Materialism, Volume Two: A Weak Nature Alone*, Evanston, IL: Northwestern University Press, 2015 (under review).

30 Žižek, *Less Than Nothing*, pp. 282–284, 317.

31 Ibid., p. 461.

32 Ibid., pp. 211–212; Daniel C. Dennett, *Freedom Evolves*, New York: Viking, 2003, pp. 85, 90–91, 93; Johnston, *Žižek's Ontology*, pp. 204–208.

33 Johnston, *Adventures in Transcendental Materialism*; Johnston, *Prolegomena to Any Future Materialism, Volume Two*; Johnston, "'Freedom or System? Yes, please!'".

34 G.W.F. Hegel, "The Spirit of Christianity and Its Fate," *Early Theological Writings*, trans. T.M. Knox, Philadelphia: University of Pennsylvania Press, 1975, pp. 234–237, 285–286; Hegel, *Faith and Knowledge*, p. 147; G.W.F. Hegel, *Phenomenology of Spirit*, trans. A.V. Miller, Oxford: Oxford University Press, 1977, pp. 221–235, 392–393, 399–400, 403–404; G.W.F. Hegel, *Elements of the Philosophy of Right*, §13 (p. 47); Hegel, *Lectures on the History of Philosophy, Volume Three*, p. 510; G.W.F. Hegel, "Review of Solger's *Posthumous Writings and Correspondence*," trans. Diana I. Behler, *Miscellaneous Writings of G.W.F. Hegel*, ed. Jon

Stewart, Evanston, IL: Northwestern University Press, 2002, pp. 394–395; G.W.F. Hegel, "Review of Göschel's *Aphorisms*," trans. Clark Butler, *Miscellaneous Writings of G.W.F. Hegel*, pp. 410–411, 418.

35 Žižek, *Less Than Nothing*, pp. 212–213.

36 Ibid., p. 213.

37 Ibid., pp. 465–466.

38 SE 19: 52.

39 Alenka Zupančič, *Ethics of the Real: Kant, Lacan*, London: Verso, 2000, pp. 28, 39; Alenka Zupančič, *Das Reale einer Illusion: Kant und Lacan*, trans. Reiner Ansén, Frankfurt am Main: Suhrkamp, 2001, pp. 35, 46; Johnston, *Žižek's Ontology*, p. 102.

40 Johnston, *Žižek's Ontology*, pp. 93–122.

41 Žižek, *Less Than Nothing*, pp. 553–554.

42 Henry Allison, *Kant's Theory of Freedom*, Cambridge: Cambridge University Press, 1990, p. 40; Henry Allison, "Spontaneity and Autonomy in Kant's Conception of the Self," *The Modern Subject: Conceptions of the Self in Classical German Philosophy*, ed. Karl Ameriks and Dieter Sturma, Albany: State University of New York, 1995, p. 13; Johnston, *Žižek's Ontology*, p. 104.

43 Jacques Lacan, *The Seminars of Jacques Lacan, Book VII: The Ethics of Psychoanalysis, 1959–1960*, ed. Jacques-Alain Miller, trans. Dennis Porter, New York: W.W. Norton and Company, 1992, p. 14.

44 Harry G. Frankfurt, "Freedom of the Will and the Concept of a Person," *The Journal of Philosophy*, vol. 68, no. 1, 14 January 1971, pp. 5–20; Adrian Johnston, "Drive between Brain and Subject: An Immanent Critique of Lacanian Neuropsychoanalysis," *The Southern Journal of Philosophy*, vol. 51: "Spindel Supplement: Freudian Futures," 2013, pp. 81–82; Johnston, *Prolegomena to Any Future Materialism, Volume Two*.

45 Žižek, *Less Than Nothing*, pp. 465–466.

46 Slavoj Žižek, *Le plus sublime des hystériques: Hegel passe*, Paris: Points Hors Ligne, 1988, p. 77; Slavoj Žižek, *The Sublime Object of Ideology*, London: Verso, 1989, p. 169; Johnston, *Žižek's Ontology*, pp. 18–19, 146–148, 151–152, 160.

47 G.W.F. Hegel, "The Philosophical Encyclopedia [For the Higher Class]," *The Philosophical Propaedeutic*, ed. Michael George and Andrew Vincent, trans. A.V. Miller, Oxford: Blackwell, 1986, §51 (p. 133); G.W.F. Hegel, *Science of Logic*, trans. A.V. Miller, London: George Allen and Unwin, 1969, p. 559; G.W.F. Hegel, *The Encyclopedia Logic: Part I of the Encyclopedia of the Philosophical Sciences with the Zusätze*, trans. T.F. Geraets, W.A. Suchting, and H.S. Harris, Indianapolis: Hackett, 1991, §153–154 (pp. 227–230); G.W.F. Hegel, *Lectures on Logic: Berlin, 1831*, trans. Clark Butler, Bloomington: Indiana University Press, 2008, §153–154 (pp. 167–168).

48 Slavoj Žižek, *Organs without Bodies: On Deleuze and Consequences*, New York: Routledge, 2004, pp. 137–138; Slavoj Žižek, *The Parallax View*, Cambridge: MIT Press, 2006, pp. 240–241.

49 Benjamin Libet, *Mind Time: The Temporal Factor in Consciousness*, Cambridge: Harvard University Press, 2004, pp. 42, 56, 66–67, 80–81, 101–102, 107.

50 Libet, *Mind Time*, pp. 139, 208.

51 Žižek, *The Sublime Object of Ideology*, pp. 61–62; Slavoj Žižek, *The Metastases of Enjoyment: Six Essays on Woman and Causality*, London: Verso, 1994, pp. 35–36; Slavoj Žižek, "*Da capo senza fine*," *Contingency, Hegemony, Universality: Contemporary Dialogues on the Left*, London: Verso, 2000, p. 227; Slavoj Žižek, *The Fright of Real Tears: Krzysztof Kieślowski Between Theory and Post-Theory*, London: British Film Institute, 2001, p. 101; Slavoj Žižek, *For they Know Not what they Do: Enjoyment as a Political Factor*, London: Verso, 2002 (second edition), p. 169;

Slavoj Žižek, *À travers le réel: Entretiens avec Fabien Tarby*, Paris: Lignes, 2010, pp. 47–58; Žižek, *Less Than Nothing*, pp. 98, 217–223, 225, 227, 459–460, 467–469, 637–638; Johnston, *Žižek's Ontology*, pp. 126–128, 221.

52 Hegel, *Science of Logic*, pp. 545, 549–550, 553; Hegel, *The Encyclopedia Logic*, §145 (p. 219), §147 (p. 221–222); Hegel, *Lectures on Logic*, §147 (pp. 159–161); Johnston, *Prolegomena to Any Future Materialism, Volume Two.*

53 SE 1: 233; SE 2: 133; SE 3: 222; SE 10: 206; SE 12: 149; Jacques Lacan, "Position of the Unconscious," *Écrits: The First Complete Edition in English*, trans. Bruce Fink, New York: W.W. Norton and Company, 2006, p. 711; Žižek, *For they Know Not what they Do*, p. 202; Adrian Johnston, *Time Driven: Metapsychology and the Splitting of the Drive*, Evanston, IL: Northwestern University Press, 2005, pp. xxi, xxx, 9–10, 34–35, 47, 141, 193, 218–219, 226–227, 316.

54 Jacques Lacan, *Le Séminaire de Jacques Lacan, Livre XV: L'acte psychanalytique, 1967–1968* (unpublished typescript), sessions of 15 November 1967, 22 November 1967.

55 Jacques Lacan, *Le Séminaire de Jacques Lacan, Livre X: L'angoisse, 1962–1963*, ed. Jacques-Alain Miller, Paris: Éditions du Seuil, 2004, p. 367; Jacques Lacan, *Le Séminaire de Jacques Lacan, Livre XIV: La logique du fantasme, 1966–1967* (unpublished typescript), session of 7 June 1967; Johnston, *Badiou, Žižek, and Political Transformations*, p. 117.

56 Žižek, *For they Know Not what they Do*, p. 222; Slavoj Žižek, *In Defense of Lost Causes*, London: Verso, 2008, pp. 314–315; Johnston, *Žižek's Ontology*, pp. 120–121; Johnston, *Badiou, Žižek, and Political Transformations*, pp. 117, 148.

57 Lacan, *Le Séminaire de Jacques Lacan, Livre XIV*, sessions of 15 February 1967, 22 February 1967; Lacan, *Le Séminaire de Jacques Lacan, Livre XV*, session of 29 November 1967; Jacques Lacan, "L'acte psychanalytique: Compte rendu du Séminaire 1967–1968," *Autres écrits*, ed. Jacques-Alain Miller, Paris: Éditions du Seuil, 2001, p. 375.

58 Johnston, *Badiou, Žižek, and Political Transformations*, p. 110.

59 Alain Badiou, *Peut-on penser la politique?*, Paris: Éditions du Seuil, 1985, pp. 101, 107; Alain Badiou, "Six propriétés de la vérité II," *Ornicar?*, no. 33, April–June 1985, pp. 123, 141; Alain Badiou, "On a Finally Objectless Subject," trans. Bruce Fink, *Who Comes After the Subject?*, ed. Peter Connor and Jean-Luc Nancy, New York: Routledge, 1991, p. 31; Alain Badiou, "*La vérité: Forçage et innommable*," *Conditions*, Paris: Éditions du Seuil, 1992, pp. 206–207; Alain Badiou, *Being and Event*, trans. Oliver Feltham, London: Continuum, 2005, pp. 206, 209, 397–398; Johnston, *Badiou, Žižek, and Political Transformations*, pp. 33, 58–60.

60 Johnston, *Badiou, Žižek, and Political Transformations*, pp. 148–150.

61 Ibid., pp. 150–156.

62 Alain Badiou, *Ethics: An Essay on the Understanding of Evil*, trans. Peter Hallward, London: Verso, 2001, p. 43; Johnston, *Badiou, Žižek, and Political Transformations*, p. 114.

63 Johnston, *Žižek's Ontology*, pp. 108, 142–143, 165–167, 171–172, 178, 180, 189, 208; Johnston, *Adventures in Transcendental Materialism*; Adrian Johnston, "Slavoj Žižek," *The Blackwell Companion to Continental Philosophy*, second edition, ed. William Schroeder, Oxford: Blackwell, 2014 (forthcoming).

64 Žižek, *Less Than Nothing*, p. 744.

65 Ibid., p. 915; V.I. Lenin, *Materialism and Empirio-Criticism*, Peking: Foreign Languages Press, 1972, pp. 338, 342.

66 Žižek, *The Indivisible Remainder*, pp. 189–236; Žižek, *The Parallax View*, pp. 165–173; Johnston, *Žižek's Ontology*, pp. 195–203.

67 Žižek, *Less Than Nothing*, pp. 918–921.
68 Adrian Johnston, "A Critique of Natural Economy: Quantum Physics with Žižek," *Žižek Now*, ed. Jamil Khader and Molly Anne Rothenberg, Cambridge: Polity, 2013, pp. 103–120; Johnston, *Adventures in Transcendental Materialism*.
69 Žižek, *Less Than Nothing*, p. 915.
70 Johnston, " 'Freedom or System? Yes, please!' "; Adrian Johnston, "Where to Begin? Robert Pippin, Slavoj Žižek, and the True Starting Point of Hegel's System," *Crisis and Critique*, vol. 1, no. 2, 2014, special issue: "Critique Today," ed. Agon Hamza and Frank Ruda (forthcoming).
71 G.W.F. Hegel, "Fragment of a System," trans. Richard Kroner, *Miscellaneous Writings of G.W.F. Hegel*, p. 154; G.W.F. Hegel, *The Difference Between Fichte's and Schelling's System of Philosophy*, trans. H.S. Harris and Walter Cerf, Albany: State University of New York Press, 1977, p. 156; F.W.J. Schelling, *Bruno, or On the Natural and the Divine Principle of Things*, trans. Michael G. Vater, Albany: State University of New York Press, 1984, pp. 136, 143.
72 F.W.J. Schelling, *Ideas for a Philosophy of Nature*, trans. Errol E. Harris and Peter Heath, Cambridge: Cambridge University Press, 1988, pp. 30–31, 33–35, 53–54; F.W.J. Schelling, *First Outline of a System of the Philosophy of Nature*, trans. Keith R. Peterson, Albany: State University of New York Press, 2004, pp. 48, 215–217, 229–231; F.W.J. Schelling, "Presentation of My System of Philosophy 1801," *The Philosophical Rupture between Fichte and Schelling*, ed. and trans. Michael G. Vater and David W. Wood, Albany: State University of New York Press, 2012, pp. 153, 167, 194, 199; F.W.J. Schelling, "System of Philosophy in General and of the Philosophy of Nature in Particular 1804," *Idealism and the Endgame of Theory: Three Essays by F.W.J. Schelling* (1801), trans. Thomas Pfau, Albany: State University of New York Press, 1994, p. 192.
73 Žižek, *Less Than Nothing*, p. 921.
74 Ibid., p. 921.
75 Johnston, *Adventures in Transcendental Materialism* (1804).
76 Johnston, " 'Freedom or System? Yes, please!' ".
77 Johnston, "A Critique of Natural Economy," pp. 103–120; Johnston, *Adventures in Transcendental Materialism*.
78 F.W.J. Schelling, *Philosophical Inquiries Into the Nature of Human Freedom and Matters Connected Therewith*, trans. James Gutmann, Chicago: Open Court, 1936, pp. 3, 11, 13, 17–18, 24, 34, 38–40, 59–60, 86–87, 92; F.W.J. Schelling, "Stuttgart Seminars," *Idealism and the Endgame of Theory*, pp. 202, 207, 213, 225; F.W.J. Schelling, *Clara, or, On Nature's Connection to the Spirit World*, trans. Fiona Steinkamp, Albany: State University of New York Press, 2002, p. 28; F.W.J. Schelling, *The Ages of the World: Third Version c. 1815*, trans. Jason M. Wirth, Albany: State University of New York Press, 2000, pp. 56–59, 61–62, 64, 77–78.
79 F.W.J. Schelling, "Of the I as the Principle of Philosophy, or On the Unconditional in Human Knowledge," *The Unconditional in Human Knowledge: Four Early Essays 1794–1796* (1797), trans. Fritz Marti, Lewisburg: Bucknell University Press, 1980, p. 69; F.W.J. Schelling, "Treatise Explicatory of the Idealism in the *Science of Knowledge* 1797," *Idealism and the Endgame of Theory*, pp. 92–93; Schelling, *Ideas for a Philosophy of Nature*, pp. 50–51; F.W.J. Schelling, "On the World-Soul," trans. Iain Hamilton Grant, *Collapse: Philosophical Research and Development*, vol. 6, January 2010, pp. 70–71, 92; Schelling, *First Outline of a System of the Philosophy of Nature*, pp. 17, 34–35, 48, 116–117, 122–123, 196, 202–203, 205, 211, 218; F.W.J. Schelling, *System of Transcendental Idealism*, trans. Peter Heath, Charlottesville: University Press of Virginia, 1978, p. 17; F.W.J. Schelling, "Schelling in Jena to Fichte in Berlin, November 19, 1800," "J.G. Fichte/F.W.J. Schelling: Correspondence 1800–1802," *The Philosophical*

Rupture between Fichte and Schelling, pp. 44–45; Schelling, "Presentation of My System of Philosophy," (1801) pp. 142–143, 145, 149, 203–204; F.W.J. Schelling, "Further Presentations from the System of Philosophy," (1802) [Extract] *The Philosophical Rupture between Fichte and Schelling*, pp. 218–219; F.W.J. Schelling, *On University Studies*, trans. E.S. Morgan, Athens, OH: Ohio University Press, 1966, p. 65; Schelling, *Bruno*, pp. 125, 202–203; Schelling, "System of Philosophy in General and of the Philosophy of Nature in Particular 1804," p. 186; F.W.J. Schelling, *Philosophy and Religion* (1804), trans. Klaus Ottmann, Putnam: Spring Publications, 2010, pp. 8, 14.

80 Žižek, *The Indivisible Remainder*, pp. 220–228, 231.

81 Žižek, *Organs without Bodies*, pp. 137–138.

82 Ibid., p. 138.

83 Schelling, "Stuttgart Seminars," pp. 200, 205–207; Schelling, *Clara*, pp. 28, 78; Schelling, *The Ages of the World*, pp. 22–23, 38–39, 85, 100; SE 1: 231, 270–271, 279; SE 3: 220, 255; Žižek, *Le plus sublime des hystériques*, pp. 221–224, 229; Žižek, *The Sublime Object of Ideology*, p. 168; Slavoj Žižek, *Enjoy Your Symptom! Jacques Lacan in Hollywood and Out*, New York: Routledge, 1992, pp. 35–36; Žižek, *The Indivisible Remainder*, pp. 13, 33–34, 47, 53–54, 72; Slavoj Žižek, "The Abyss of Freedom," *The Abyss of Freedom/Ages of the World*, Ann Arbor: University of Michigan Press, 1997, pp. 14–15, 29–31, 33, 37, 41; Slavoj Žižek, *The Ticklish Subject: The Absent Centre of Political Ontology*, London: Verso, 1999, p. 318; Slavoj Žižek, *The Fragile Absolute, or Why Is the Christian Legacy Worth Fighting For?*, London: Verso, 2000, pp. 73, 78, 93–94; Slavoj Žižek, *On Belief*, New York: Routledge, 2001, p. 147; Žižek, *The Fright of Real Tears*, p. 151; Žižek, *Organs without Bodies*, pp. 25–26; Žižek, *Less Than Nothing*, pp. 273–275; Žižek and Daly, *Conversations with Žižek*, p. 166.

84 Johnston, *Žižek's Ontology*, pp. 90–122.

85 Bruno Bosteels, "Badiou without Žižek," *Polygraph: An International Journal of Culture and Politics*, no. 17, 2005, special issue: "The Philosophy of Alain Badiou," ed. Matthew Wilkens, pp. 241–242.

86 Johnston, "'Freedom or System? Yes, please!'".

87 Žižek, *The Parallax View*, pp. 240–241.

88 G.W.F. Hegel, *Jenaer Systementwürfe III: Naturphilosophie und Philosophie des Geistes*, ed. Rolf-Peter Horstmann, Hamburg: Felix Meiner, 1987, pp. 171–185; Hegel, *Phenomenology of Spirit*, pp. 18–19, 21; G.W.F. Hegel, "The Science of Laws, Morals and Religion [For the Lower Class]," *The Philosophical Propaedeutic*, §1 (p. 4); Hegel, "Logic [For the Middle Class]," §3 (p. 75); Hegel, *The Encyclopedia Logic*, §1–3 (pp. 24–27), §8–9 (pp. 32–33), §20 (pp. 49–51), §24 (p. 58); Hegel, *Philosophy of Mind*, §381 (pp. 11–15), §408 (p. 128), §410 (pp. 140–141), §413–414 (pp. 154–155), §422 (pp. 162–163).

89 Johnston, "Where to Begin?".

90 Kant, *Critique of Pure Reason*, A162/B202-A218/B265 (pp. 286–321).

91 Wilfrid Sellars, *Empiricism and the Philosophy of Mind*, Cambridge: Harvard University Press, 1997, pp. 14, 45.

92 SE 1: 296–297, 306–307, 312, 317–319; SE 14: 194; SE 18: 26–32, 55–56, 58, 63; SE 19: 19–26, 230, 238; Slavoj Žižek, "The Thing from Inner Space," *Sexuation*, ed. Renata Salecl, Durham, NC: Duke University Press, 2000, pp. 216–259; Johnston, *Žižek's Ontology*, pp. 160–161.

93 Antonio Damasio, *Descartes' Error: Emotion, Reason, and the Human Brain*, New York: Avon, 1994, pp. 173–175, 185, 187–189, 197–198, 212–219; Antonio Damasio, *Looking for Spinoza: Joy, Sorrow, and the Feeling Brain*, New York: Harcourt, 2003, pp. 148–150; Antonio Damasio, *Self Comes to Mind: Constructing the Conscious Brain*, New York: Pantheon, 2010, p. 9.

94 Libet, *Mind Time*, pp. 6, 17, 86–87, 163, 184.
95 Libet, *Mind Time*, pp. 172–177.
96 Žižek, *Less Than Nothing*, pp. 239, 374, 379–380, 399–401, 416, 459, 561–562, 595–597, 707–708, 726–727, 729–736, 905–906; Johnston, *Adventures in Transcendental Materialism.*
97 Libet, *Mind Time*, pp. 28, 56, 66–67, 107.
98 Ibid., pp. 71–72, 120–122, 208.
99 Ibid., pp. 118–119.
100 Ibid., pp. 115–116.
101 Ibid., p. 107.
102 Žižek, *Less Than Nothing*, pp. 285–286.
103 Ibid., pp. 185–186, 188–189.
104 Ibid., pp. 333–334.
105 Ibid., pp. 65, 414, 730, 764; Johnston, *Adventures in Transcendental Materialism.*
106 Johnston, *Time Driven*, pp. xxxvi–xxxviii, 340–341; Johnston, *Žižek's Ontology*, pp. xxv, 65, 77, 107–108, 113, 170–171, 179–180, 189, 208–209, 212–213, 269–287; Adrian Johnston, "The Weakness of Nature: Hegel, Freud, Lacan, and Negativity Materialized," *Hegel and the Infinite: Religion, Politics, and Dialectic*, ed. Slavoj Žižek, Clayton Crockett, and Creston Davis, New York: Columbia University Press, 2011, pp. 159–179; Adrian Johnston, "Reflections of a Rotten Nature: Hegel, Lacan, and Material Negativity," *Filozofski Vestnik*, special issue: "Science and Thought," ed. Frank Ruda and Jan Voelker, vol. 33, no. 2, 2012, pp. 23–52; Adrian Johnston, "Points of Forced Freedom: Eleven More Theses on Materialism," *Speculations: A Journal of Speculative Realism*, no. 4, June 2013, pp. 93–97; Johnston, "Drive between Brain and Subject," pp. 48–84; Adrian Johnston, "An Interview with Adrian Johnston on Transcendental Materialism [with Peter Gratton]," *Society and Space*, 2013, http://societyandspace.com/2013/10/07/interview-with-adrian-johnston-on-transcendental-materialism/; Johnston, *Adventures in Transcendental Materialism*; Johnston, *Prolegomena to Any Future Materialism, Volume Two.*
107 Johnston, *Prolegomena to Any Future Materialism, Volume One*, pp. 59–77; Johnston, "An Interview with Adrian Johnston on Transcendental Materialism [with Peter Gratton]".

Chapter 8

What is to be judged?

On infinitely infinite judgments and their consequences

Frank Ruda

> Though the name of the infinite judgment usually appears in the ordinary logics, it is not altogether clear what its nature really is.
>
> (G.W.F. Hegel)

Introduction

Slavoj Žižek has been said to be many things: for example a peculiar embodiment of Elvis for contemporary cultural theory, the most dangerous philosopher in the west or the world's most unlikely movie star. Yet until now he has very rarely, if at all, been considered to be a thinker of judgment.[1] But one may argue that it is precisely his theory of judgment which provides one of the most crucial building blocks of his entire enterprise. Subsequently I will demonstrate in what sense and to which extent Žižek's – highly systematic[2] – position can be read as a very fundamental contribution to a proper theory of judgment. As Žižek is also known as a perspicacious and controversial reader of Kant and Hegel, it may come as no surprise that it is as in his readings of these thinkers where he develops his own logic of judgment. In the following, I will turn first to Kant to and subsequently to Hegel. Each of these readings concludes with an account of Žižek's take on the matter. If the reader is now tempted to ask why the subsequent contribution may be legitimately included in a volume on Žižek and law, my answer is the following: the most crucial law that Žižek investigates – and thereby he not only follows Kant and Hegel but also shows his fundamentally philosophical orientation – is the law of reason.

What you are about to read is therefore not a presentation of why and how Žižek is a theorist that provides crucial insights for legal theory or something like it. What you are about to read is an attempt to demonstrate that Žižek's thought is so challenging and breathtaking because he first and foremost needs to be read as a theorist of the law(s) of reason and thought, that is: as a true philosopher. This cannot be done without returning to Žižek's sources. Hence, what you are about to read is a depiction not only of Žižek, but of the persistent relevance of Kant and Hegel for any account of judgment whatsoever.

Kant's eternal law of novelty

In his "Critique of Pure Reason" Kant claimed that to attain any true self-knowledge [*Selbsterkenntnis*] one needs to "institute a court of justice, by which reason may secure its rightful claims while dismissing all groundless pretensions ... according to its own eternal and unchangeable laws...."[3] The "Critique of Pure Reason" purposed not to install but to *be* this very court of justice, demarcating between rightful and unlawful claims of reason and preparing the foundation for a rigid rational self-critique that exorcises all illegal, i.e., irrational, actions and thoughts from its kingdom. Irrationality in this kingdom amounts to unfreedom, since the realm of reason is the realm of freedom. This means that Kant's project depicts not only the eternal laws of reason but also those of freedom, and violating a law in one of them means that reason becomes a self-incarcerating criminal in both of them; it may even lose its constitutive double citizenship.[4] But reason can only avoid this if it knows the laws it has to obey to be and remain a reasonable citizen. Kant's first critique therefore seeks to enlighten reason about these laws and seeks to awaken or actualize a certain capacity to discriminate (between wrong and right). For this sake Kant inaugurates a gigantic tribunal in which reason's own laws are made public and presented to and by reason. Adorno once remarked about Kant's critical endeavor that it "grounds objectivity in the subject as an objective reality"[5] and this objectivity is what manifests in the eternal laws of reason. Yet the judge and what is judged is reason itself and this is at the same time done according to the laws of reason – one is dealing with a true self-critique.[6]

This is also why in performing this self-critical tribunal Kant has to develop a (self-) critical theory of judgment, although of course he will unfold the proper and elaborate critique of judgment only years later. It is this very theory of judgment that is of crucial importance to Slavoj Žižek.[7] To understand why that is, one need to retrace the steps that lead Kant to his account of what he calls "the logical function of the understanding in judgments."[8]

From the very beginning of his critical enterprise Kant relies on the distinction between two types of judgments: analytic and synthetic.[9] The former are clarifications, i.e., they articulate something that is already contained in a concept;[10] the latter extend and expand a concept by adding [*hinzufügen*] a connection between one concept and another. The "entire final aim"[11] of Kant's speculative endeavor is investigating the latter. The question is thus how to add and bring about a relation between concepts in an a priori manner, namely under the condition that one cannot refer to experience to derive it. In Kant's words, the crucial question to answer is how to conceive of a "really new acquisition"[12] [*Erwerb* (B)/*Anbau* (A)]. This is the question: How does one account for something new in the domain of pure thought? What are the laws by means of which one can elaborate that something can be added to a pure concept? How does one derive such a supplement if it is impossible to derive it analytically? This is the "real problem of pure reason ..."[13] – pure reason liberated not only from experience but also from any kind of unreasonable wrongdoing. So, what is reason's eternal law of novelty?

Kant's logic of truth ...

This is (one of) *the* question(s) reason is "driven by its own need to as answer, as well as it can."[14] On his way to an answer Kant first unfolds what is famously called the transcendental aesthetic. In it, he "isolate[s] sensibility"[15] as one of the two forms of any possible cognition. Isolated sensibility, subtracted from any supplement of conceptual understanding – that is to say the pure form of sensibility, "the mere form of appearance"[16] – is what he famously accounts for in terms of space and time. After this depiction of these a priori "condition[s] of possibility of appearances"[17] as such, he turns to what he calls transcendental logic. The transcendental aesthetic deals with "the rules of sensibility in general," the transcendental logic with "the rules of the understanding in general."[18] The latter can be derived from a series of conceptual distinctions: within the realm of logic, there can be a general (lawful) depiction of these rules – and one may say that generality is what makes a rule into a law[19] – and a depiction of particular rules for particular usages. Any logic addressing particular rules for particular cases cannot be properly transcendental; it is only the general logic that is able to offer a clear-cut account of how understanding and reason function generally. Now, on the general layer of logic, one again needs to distinguish between pure transcendental logic and general yet applied logic. Although the latter entails the general rules of use and enables the purifying of common sense from problematic prejudices, it nonetheless starts from empirical conditions, namely from the psychological condition of the thinking subject. It is only the former, properly transcendental type of general logic that represents what Kant calls the "canon of the understanding and reason."[20] Only here does one deal with the pure form of thought a priori.

One can read these distinctions as increasing the degree of formal abstraction: initially there is a logic conditioned by particular usages (determined by the particular things used and/or the particular cases in which they are used), then there is a logic of the general rules of thought conditioned only by the particularity of its subject, and finally one ends with the most formal of all logical enterprises, with thought being alone with itself. This is the realm of transcendental logic. In other words: one deals first with a logic that is still conditioned by contingent empirical things, then with a logic conditioned only by the contingent empirical situation of the thinking subject,[21] and finally with unconditioned thought, liberated and purified from all (empirical) contingency.[22] Only the latter properly deals "with the laws of understanding and reason, but only insofar as they are related to objects a priori."[23] One hence enters a kingdom of pure laws, pure objectivity without (empirical) objects, an objectivity without (material) objects.

The transcendental logic is thus a purely formal enterprise. This implies that the forms (of thought) it deals with do not consider *what* is thought but only *how* it is thought, which is also why these forms of thought "are entirely indifferent with regard to the objects."[24] In this precise sense the transcendental logic contains the formal depiction of "a logic of truth"[25] – a logic which depicts the eternal laws of pure understanding and reason and can therefore present the formal structure of truth as such. If what needed to be accounted for was the eternal law of novelty, here one gets a further insight: the law of the new is that which has to be linked to truth.[26] What one hence is dealing with is the presentation of how to conceive of "acts of pure thinking."[27]

One is dealing with pure (and not empirical) concepts that solely belong to thought (and not to intuition). These concepts are not derived but "elementary"[28] and need to be presented in a systematic manner (otherwise there would be a return of empirical contingency to the very realm from which it should be excluded). Transcendental analytic again entails two sides: one dealing with elementary concepts, the other with principles. It is in the first part where Kant introduces quite some far-reaching claims: 1. If understanding is not intuition, it is a form of cognition through concepts and hence discursive.[29] This implies that Kant's logic of truth is the truth of discursivity as such (of its, as Kant says in a Walter-Benjamin-like manner, "pure use"[30]). 2. If on one hand intuition always implies some receptive affectation by an object of intuition, concepts on the other rely on functions. What is a function? A function is "the unity of the action of ordering different representations under a common one."[31] This implies for Kant that pure conceptual thought, pure thought employing concepts as its means, is constitutively linked to an activity of thought that is able to synthesize newly generated concepts.

... is in the logic of infinite judgments

After the long march through Kant one here reaches the point where he claims that thought's pure use of concepts necessarily implies "judging by means of them."[32] Something new can be generated, something can be added to an already existing concept in one way and one way only, namely by means of judgment (i.e., by means of concepts). This means that "[a]ll judgments are accordingly functions of unity among our representations" and "[w]e can ... trace all actions of understanding back to judgments."[33] In short: thought is nothing but the faculty to judge. Thought in its purest form cannot but judge, even if it only deals with itself. Yet if thinking is discursive (i.e., conceptual), concepts are fundamentally predicates of possible judgments that constitutively function by synthesizing. Concepts thereby allow for the very functioning of discursivity as such, namely for an a priori synthesis of different concepts under a common one.[34] But what if that the truth of discursivity is not as such discursive, although it nonetheless enables discursivity?[35]

Here the question of "the logical function of understanding in judgments"[36] arises. It is here that Kant introduces the famous table of different categories of judgment, which allows for a distinction between quantitative, qualitative, relational, and modal judgments. Quantitative judgments concern either all objects, a few objects, or just one unique object; relational judgments cover the relation between two concepts (categorical judgment), between two positively related propositions (hypothetical), or between two or more negatively related propositions (disjunctive). The modalities of judgments "concern ... only the value of the copula in relation to thinking in general,"[37] that is to say they may concern the relation between two concepts or propositions as being possible (what Kant calls problematic judgments, entailing hypothetical or disjunctive), being actual and true (what he calls assertoric judgments, which can include universal, particular, or singular judgments), or being necessary (apodictic judgments, which can be either affirmative or negative ones). Yet qualitatively all judgments can be distinguished as either affirmative (say: the soul *is* mortal), negative (say: the soul is *not* mortal), and infinite judgments (say: the soul is *im*mortal, non-mortal). It is this qualitative distinction that Žižek has elevated into the true Kantian revolution; he even goes so far as to claim that "this logic of infinite judgment contains *in nuce* Kant's entire philosophical revolution."[38] Why? This is easy to answer: because there is only "one" (place of the) truth of discursivity and it needs to be indicated by a qualitative difference. The truth of discursivity cannot be quantitative, or modal, or relational. It needs to be qualitative, and as the positive and negative judgment are still locatable within modal or relational categories (hence they are within discursivity), qualitative difference is the only infinite judgment.

What does Kant say about infinite judgments?

> [I]n transcendental logic infinite judgments must ... be distinguished from affirmative ones, even though in general logic they are rightly included with the latter and do not constitute a special member of classification. General logic abstracts from all content of the predicate

> … and considers only whether it is attributed to the subject or opposed to it. Transcendental logic … considers the value or content of the logical affirmation made in a judgment by means of a merely negative predicate, and what sort of gain this yields for the whole cognition.[39]

What is this to say? Kant reformulates the distinction of general and transcendental logic. General logic distinguishes between attributing a predicate to a subject and negating such a predication. Empirical subjects seem to judge either affirmatively or negatively, either "yes" or "no," whereas transcendental logic depicts how the very form of a "yes" (of something positive, discursive) can include something of a "no" (non-discursive). This is for Kant *the* formal structure of truth. This is why the distinction between general logic and transcendental logic has to do at the same time with the difference between infinite and affirmative and infinite and negative judgment. What is an infinite judgment? An infinite judgment has the form of an affirmative judgment because it attributes a predicate to a subject. Yet the qualification of its form is not enough. The predicate it assigns to the subject in question is not a positive predicate but an immanently negated predicate, a non-predicate. Therefore it takes something of the negative judgment, namely the negativity implied in the relation between the predicate and the subject. The infinite judgment inscribes this negativity to the predicate while positively affirming its assignability to a subject. The infinite judgment is that which basically manifests the insight that there is no relation, that there is only a non-relation between positive and negative judgment. The infinite judgment is a judgment that concerns a relation but which is at the same time not simply a judgment about a relation. It takes an affirmative form, yet is essentially negative; it suspends all the categories which are specific to relational judgments and is in this sense what makes pure relation or relationality as such appear. The infinite judgment is what lies at the ground of all other possible judgmental types.

Infinite judgment is a truth-judgment: not simply a true judgment, but a judgment that itself has the logical structure of the truth of discursivity. Kant's example is:

> [B]y means of the proposition "The soul is not mortal" I have certainly made an actual affirmation as far as logical form is concerned, for I have placed the soul within the unlimited domain of undying beings.… But the infinite sphere of the possible is thereby limited only to the extent that that which is mortal is separated from it, and the soul is placed in the remaining space of its domain. But even with this exception this remains infinite, and more parts could be taken away from it without the concept of the soul growing in the least and

> being affirmatively determined. In regard to logical domain, therefore, this infinite judgment is merely limiting with regard to the content of cognition in general.[40]

The infinite judgment produces a surplus of cognition – this surplus is what is depicted in the logic of truth. Truth is a surplus, this is the eternal law of the new: there can only be truth if there is a supplement to what is. Yet, via this surplus the infinite judgment also delineates a limit. What is limited is what can be regulated by a general logic. Through its peculiar kind of affirmation (of a non-predicate), the infinite judgment opens up a space which limits the jurisdiction of any general logic. Yet if transcendental logic depicts the truth of discursivity as such, what is this truth? In other terms: What is to be judged by these judgments?

Žižek, infinite judgment, or: being more Cartesian than Descartes

An immediate response to this question may be that one is still within the waters of Cartesianism. Could one not assume that the very realm of the infinite judgment refers to what Descartes developed with his famous cogito-argument, which addresses the absolutely empty point of subjectivity to which any discourse is sutured? Yes and no. Yes, because "Descartes was the first to introduce a crack into the ontologically consistent universe"[41] – into the universe governed by general logic. And Kant follows on the path opened up by Descartes' crack. General logic is not enough. But what is this crack? It is a product of Descartes' endeavor to find an absolute certainty. On this path he famously subtracts all imaginable and symbolic determinations by means of doubt and reaches the infamous *cogito ergo sum*: there exists something in reality that does not appear in it; there is something which splits reality into two. In this Kant follows Descartes: infinite judgments also delineate a realm of that which does not appear, not even in the domain of pure thought, since otherwise it could be accounted for in terms of positive or negative judgments.

But for Žižek, Descartes is not radical enough as he withdraws from his own insight: "Descartes, as it were, patches up the wound he cut into the texture of reality. Only Kant fully articulates the inherent paradoxes of self-consciousness."[42] It is only with Kant that we get "the impossibility of locating the subject in the 'great chain of being,' into the Whole of the universe."[43] Descartes accounted for the subject in terms of a "positive phenomenal entity, *res cogitans*"[44] and thereby presumed that there is a great chain in which the subject will somehow find its place (even if as the zero-point of the discourse). What Descartes was unable to conceive, according to Žižek, is the fact that his own argument prevents him from drawing the conclusions he draws. He saw that one can only attain a proper conception of the subject if one voids it of all experiential content, yet when he reached the pure form of the "I think" he immediately ascribed – via a positive judgment – an existence to this empty form. Thereby Descartes confused the "I think" with something that is part of experiential reality. Here Kant is more radical when, according to Žižek, he basically states: if one thinks that one thinks, that what is thought is minimally different from the thought itself. If one thinks "I think," it is impossible for the two to coincide. Why?

If I think anything (say I think that Hegel is cooler than Kant), the act of thinking and that which I think differ. Descartes' error emerges when I assume that if I think that "I think," I have a representation of the "I think," that is that the act of thinking and its substance can coincide. I cannot represent the act of thinking in the act of thinking, since this turns it into a substance and hence I lose the very act with which I started. This error is precisely what Kant's logic of infinite judgment prevents. This means that the very act of synthesis that Kant asserts as *necessary* element of any judgment and hence for his formal account of truth (of any discursive setting) is at the same time *impossible* and this *is* the true formal way of accounting for the truth of any discourse. Avoiding Descartes' error, Kant manifests the formal and logical "structure" of something that is absolutely necessary, yet at the same time impossible to formalize – this is what the infinite judgment does. The act of thinking and the substance of thinking can never coincide – this is the paradox of self-consciousness in Žižek's terms, as this would generate an experiential representation of something that cannot simply be experientially represented, since otherwise there is only experiential reality and one precisely loses the minimal difference that one just had attained. This is why for Kant the subject can never be integrated into any great chain of being, because it is already *immanently out of joint*.

The infinite judgment is the Cartesian truth of discursivity as such (without its Cartesian mis-conceptualization), namely that the truth of any discourse is the subject. This is to say: with Kant the subject is split between act (of thinking) and substance (of thought). This is immediately related to Kant's category of the "thing in itself" – I am in my conception of myself always separated from how I am in myself (from the thing in itself that I am), otherwise I would not be a thing in itself; and the same holds for my relation to the substance of any object whatsoever of which I can have only a phenomenal representation, which misses the thing in its substance.[45] One may yet state that the difference between the thing in itself and the Kantian subject, immanently out of joint, is that the former is "something" empty which does not appear, whereas, like in Descartes but more consistently elaborated, the subject is empty and appears as this emptiness. Kant is in very this respect more Cartesian than Descartes. The very failure to make act and substance (of the thinking subject but also of any-thing) correlate *is* the subject and this is what the infinite judgment accounts for. This is also how to grasp their limiting nature: Kant's depiction of thought by means of infinite judgments is a depiction of the limits of thought (as any thought is discursive). This limit is formally articulated by the infinite judgment. And this means through a conception of the limits of thought, one can gain a formalization of that which cannot be thought. The infinite judgment is this formalization as it precisely refers to the limit of any general(ized) logic, i.e., to the limit of that which can be positively or negatively thought. What is to be judged is that which can only be judged as being in-finite, or: un-judgeable.

Substantial un-substantiality

This does sound nice. Why does Žižek not end here? As is well known, he always argues with regard to the infinite judgment something along the following lines:

> Kant introduced the key distinction between negative and indefinite judgment: the positive judgment "the soul is mortal" can be negated in two ways, when a predicate is denied to the subject ("the soul is not mortal"), and when a non-predicate is affirmed ("the soul is non-mortal") – the difference is exactly the same as the one, known to every reader of Stephen King, between "he is not dead" and "he is undead." The infinite judgment opens up a third domain which undermines the underlying distinction: the "undead" is neither alive nor dead, but precisely the monstrous "living dead." And the same goes for "inhuman" ... "he is not human" means simply that he is external to humanity, animal or divine, while "he is inhuman" means ... that he is neither human nor not-human, but marked by a terrifying excess which, although negating what we understand as "humanity," is inherent to being human. And ... this is what changes with the Kantian revolution: in the pre-Kantian universe, humans are simply humans, beings of reason, fighting the excess of animal lust and divine madness; only with Kant and German Idealism does the excess to be fought become absolutely immanent, located at the very core of subjectivity itself.[46]

Kant's transcendental logic thus deals with an excess, a fundamental kind of negativity, un-deadness, inhumanity at the very kernel of subjectivity. What is depicted by the "un"-prefix is the core of subjectivity as such: of a subject that is constitutively out of joint. But for Žižek, Kant is again not enough – it is not enough to be more Cartesian than Descartes. Why? In a compulsion to repeat manner, one may answer, because one can and hence must also be more Kantian than Kant. Hegel has to enter the picture – maybe the only philosopher in whose regard it is difficult to be more than he was, since his whole system is about this very self-surpassing movement. Kant was in some sense unaware of his own revolutionary discovery. For him, the form of the infinite judgment still positively relates to the subject of the judgment. The infinite judgment as conceived by Kant clearly empties out the subject of all positive attributes and simply delineates its peculiar status through assigning a non-predicate. With this form one may assert that the subject of the infinite judgments is substantially incomplete, flawed, but Kant was unable to avoid that the infinite judgment amounts to stating that by assigning a non-predicate to a subject, it nonetheless depicts the *substance* of the subject in terms of a *non-predicate*, namely as a (negative) substance, which consists in the substancelessness of the subject. He still allows for the idea that un-substantiality is substance and this is a consequence of the form of his infinite judgment, namely the positive form in which a non-predicate is asserted. To put this in different terms: Kant was unable to avoid that the infinite judgment was read as a positive statement about a positive assignation of a non-predicate. For Žižek it is only with Hegel – only with the idea that first as substance then as subject – that one can overcome substantializing (the) non-substantiality (of the subject).[47]

Hegel judging

Hegel elaborates his theory of judgment in what he calls the subjective logic or the doctrine of the notion.[48] Therein one finds a tripartite structure, which divides into subjectivity, objectivity, and idea. Why does the logic of judgment locate within the depiction of the notion? Because the logic of judgment determinately accounts for the very movement of the concept in which the form of conceptual movement generates out of itself another. It has to do so, because otherwise there could not be a concept (if everything is conceptual nothing is conceptual) and hence it needs to posit that which is other than itself. And as the concept thus far has simply, as in a Kantian setting, only been a form, that which is then posited by it is content.[49] This is why "the judgment is this positing of the determinate Notions by the Notion itself."[50] This is why judging functions differently from comprehension [*Begreifen*], but only because it is another function of the notion itself. The distinction of judgments that Hegel develops in the following are therefore further determinations of the notion.[51] To put it in different terms: concepts generate content and the *initial content they generate is the form of the judgment* itself.

This content, i.e., the form of the judgment, is the relation between a subject and a predicate, yet they are indeterminate. The judgment "contains first two self-subsistents which are called subject and predicate. What each is cannot yet really be said; they are still indeterminate, for it is only through judgment that they are to be determined."[52] Judgment makes subject and predicate determinate by determining their relation. Hegel thereby can distinguish between three instances appearing in judgment: name, subject, predicate (i.e., notion before the judgment, notion in the judgment, and of course the relation between the two of them). In simple terms, the subject is that which becomes of a name after a predicate has been assigned to it. Names embody singularities such that no predicate of any general value can be assigned to them. A name in itself is nothing; what it names is hence even less than nothing. And the Hegelian twist is, of course, that any subject is in itself nothing but a name and in-itself-in-itself less than nothing. The subject is a name that received a predicate. Only a name that received a predicate is turned into a subject and therefore there is no subject without predicate (otherwise it would be a name). Hegel's argument is thus: even if one enters the realm of judgment, on one side there is just a name and this name is "subject;" on the other, there is another name: "predicate." This is why they are indeterminate. "Subject" (name) only becomes a true subject when it stands in a relation to "predicate," through which it becomes a proper predicate. This is why it is the relation that makes a predicate into a predicate and a subject into a subject.[53] So, for Hegel, judgments deal with relations that make subjects into subjects by making predicates into predicates.

This very movement is why "the Notion [that] constitutes the essential *ground* of the judgment, these determinations are at least indifferent to the extent that when one belongs to the subject and the other to the predicate, the converse relationship equally holds good."[54] The relation within judgment is twofold, but when beginning with the logic of judgment, this twofoldness does not yet exist, as there are not even two sides except in an abstract, name-like manner. The determinations of the subject and the predicate are hence indifferent. This is why Hegel asserts that there is a relation in judgment which is unable to really take into account the two particular sides of the relation: this is the positive judgment. The positive judgment deals with two names making one judgment, hence becoming subject and predicate (this is why it is logically the first derivable judgment). But can we also predicate something upon the relation between a subject and a predicate in a way that this very relation is made into being the subject? Hence can we say anything about relation proper (which is what determines the two sides)? This is what somehow happens with the negative judgment. But Hegel's idea is that these two sides (subject-predicate-relation and the subject-predicate-relation-as-subject with regard to which one can predicate on it) need to coincide. This is his infinite judgment.

Hegel's positive judgment

Hegel: "In subjective judgment we want to *see one and the same* object *double*, first in its individual actuality, and then it its essential identity or in its Notion."[55] The subject needs to be the subject and its predicate, the predicate needs to be a predicate and the subject's predicate: the subject has to be the predicate as much as the predicate has to be the subject. Yet, to achieve this infinite repetitive redoubling, the form of judgment has to reach its infinite form; only then it can adequately "restore this *identity* of the Notion, or rather ... posit it" and this "is the goal of the *movement* of the judgment."[56] Infinity is judgments' goal for it is only with the infinite judgment that judgment attains its own notion. The logic of judgment thus necessarily entails a conception of repetition – and this is why it should be also come as no surprise that something of the positive and the negative judgment will return in each step of the way of its unfolding.

In a positive judgment there is an abstract predicate (a "predicate") in an indifferent relation (a "relation") to an indeterminate subject (a "subject").[57] Its most fundamental form can hence be written down by as: "*the individual is universal*."[58] The subject is individual, the relation to the predicate is individual and the predicate is individual. So everything is individual, and thus the individual is universal. Yet if the individual is universal, it is abstract (being everything that there is and hence having no criteria to discriminate it from something else) and thus not treated as individual. The abstract predicate, which deprives the individual of its individuality, makes it hence (abstractly) universal. Yet "[t]he individual is universal" is still different from stating: "A is B." The latter is true for any sentence, yet the judgment, although being abstract with regard to all its elements, has this abstract determination as its determination and thereby turns into more than a mere sentence. One may also say that the judgment "the individual is universal" is itself an individual judgment which articulates a universal claim. It is thus more than *just one* particular sentence like "A is B." This is why Hegel claims that in it "the universal *resolves* itself into the individual [*entschließt* sich das Allgemeine zum Einzelnen]; and the judgment is this explication of the universal [das Urteil ist dieser *Aufschluß*]."[59] Even if the positive judgment is just an abstract universal way of relating individual and universal, nonetheless it presents that there is more to it than to a sentence. There are the individual, the universal, and their relation. Three is thus the number of judgment.

The individual in judgment is posited as the universal and is thereby turned into "*a thing of manifold properties*, an *actuality of manifold possibilities*, a *substance* of such and such *accidents*."[60] "The individual is universal" implies that the individual which is (the) universal can possess infinitely many properties. The predicate ("universal") is so abstract – isn't it like a name? – that its assertion enables the subject to have potentially infinitely more predicates (as this kind of universality simply asserts predictability) and thus turns out to be just one of the properties of the subject. From this side, one may also read the content of positive judgment saying the following: "*the universal is individual*"[61] – the universality is but one of many predicates of the individual whose substance is universal. Ultimately one is left with two abstract propositions, which do not even make one judgment – the positive judgment dissolves not simply into one sentence but into two, into two "identical propositions:

> The individual is individual,
> The universal is universal."[62]

Now the two determinations of the judgment have fallen completely asunder and there is nothing but two tautological self-relations. The positive judgment dissects not even into one sentence but into two: into two mere sentences of no content but a tautological assertion of identity. Before, as we has seen, "the universal is individual" expresses the content of the positive judgment (as it is expressed in an individual proposition) and "the individual is universal" its form (as the form of relating predicate to subject articulates a universal claim). The logical consequence one is facing here is that the positive judgment disseminates into two sentences; it is hence unable to generate any unification from its movement, although it presumed it. It hence falls into pure external separation. This means that one need to unify what was split into two. For this sake one also needs to negate the outcome of the positive judgment – its separation into two empty sentences – and this negation is what makes the negative judgment.

Hegel's negative judgment

The negative judgment derives from this insight into the dissemination of positive judgment, from the insight that it is not true that content is the only thing that counts in judgment and that the form is as important. It gives a too-abstract account of their relation. What Hegel calls "the true logical *content*"[63] implies that the form of the judgment is reflected as and in the content. This insight succeeds positive judgment. The negative judgment is primarily negative because it negates the positive judgment and therefore takes the following form: "the *individual is not* abstractly *universal* … the *individual* is, therefore, *in the first instance* a *particular*."[64] Yet because it needs to negate both sides, it redoubles into: "the *universal* is not abstractly *individual* … the universal is, therefore, *in the first instance* a *particular*."[65]

The move Hegel performs here is that the negative judgment negates the copula. Hence it can be rendered as stating the individual is-not the universal, or: the universal is-not the individual. The negation hence relates to the subject-predicate relation of the positive judgment and negates it by ascribing a "not" to the copula.[66] Both renderings can now according to Hegel be unified and, now, for the first time one is dealing with judgment proper: the individual is a particular. The particularity of the predicate is not an empirical but generated through a logical investigation of positive judgment. "The individual is a particular" is obviously a positive articulation of the negative judgment. One may also say that this can be rendered as: "the individual is not-universal," which is the positive expression of the negative judgment, and hence, it seems, we have reached again Kant's formula for the infinite judgment. One is now dealing with a particular relation between subject and predicate.[67] But one has established this relation at the same time in one (positive expression of the negative) judgment, but also not only through one judgment, for one needed the negation of the positive judgment.[68]

The move "from the form of the *relation* to the form of the *determination*"[69] is that one takes the form of relation (between subject and predicate) in the positive judgment itself as subject to which one negatively non-ascribed a predicate and thereby negatively determined the subject as much as the predicate. This is moving from (the form of) relation to (the form of) determination. As the negative judgment does not start with universality (simply because it is already mediated by negating the positive judgment), one starts with something not-universal and hence particular. This implies that "the negative judgment is not [the] total negation; the universal sphere which contains the predicate still subsists and therefore the relation of the subject to the predicate is essentially still positive."[70] Why is that? Because if I say "Slavoj Žižek is not-American" I only negate a determinate predicate and separate it from the universal sphere of possible predicate of Žižek. The universal sphere of determinability remains intact – if he is not American, one still may presume that he has a nationality but a different one. With regard to this universal sphere, the negative judgment retains something of the positive judgment, which is what the positive expression of the negative judgment (the individual is a particular) expresses.

The negative judgment (S.Z. is not American = the individual is a particular) negates only an individual determination of the subject and via this negation determines subject and predicate; neither the universal sphere of predicates nor the subject nor determination as such are (determinately) determined. Rather, the particularity that negative judgment refers to mediates between individual and universal, and as this is the kernel of negative judgment, it is in its general function a judgment of mediation or of relation. But this mediation does not properly work, because although it emphasizes the particularity of the individual, it does not, as it seems, emphasize the individuality of the individual, or in Hegel's words: "The individual is not an undetermined determinate, but the determined determinate"[71] and therefore it is just negating an individual predicate and leaving the universal sphere intact. This point is crucial: first the negative judgment negates an individual property (being American) but does not negate predicatability as such. It thus ends up with an idea of indeterminate determinateness (S.Z. may be many other things than not-being American), yet this indeterminate determinateness is not indeterminate in an abstract manner (as with the positive judgment), which would still imply a positive givenness of a realm of determinations to be potentially ascribed to the subject. One here rather deals with a negation of determinateness after the negation of an individual predicate happened. Therefore "the negation of the determinateness is already the second negation, and therefore the infinite return of individuality into itself."[72]

This is why the negative judgment (the individual is a particular) ultimately reads: the individual is the individual, as positing of "absolute determinateness"[73] of the subject. The subject is absolutely determined, yet only in a negative way, i.e., as being not determined by predicates. On the other side (the universal is a particular[74]) this judgment reads: the universal is the universal. Thereby the negation – of positive judgment – "must itself appear in the form of a negative judgment."[75] Only in this manner can one get rid of the last residue of positivity (an abstract realm of predicatability). This is to say if the subject (the individual is individual) is determined, yet only as being undetermined, then that which determines the subject, i.e., the predicate (the particular), is taken to be in-determining any determination. So in negative judgment one has an indeterminate determinate subject and determinate indeterminate predicate. Thereby the subject, although in an inverted form, re-appears in the predicate and vice versa. Another way of putting this is to say that there is no longer simple subject-predicate relation; there is nothing one could cling to; the subject shifts into the predicate which shifts into the subject, etc. Thus "the *whole extent* of the predicate is negated and there is no longer any positive relation between it and the subject."[76] Finally, the infinite judgment.

Hegel's infinite judgments

Žižek pointed out that

> With reference to the infamous thesis on "determinate negation," one would expect negative judgment to *succeed* infinite judgment as a "higher," more concrete form of dialectical unity-within-difference.... For Hegel, however, it is infinite judgment with its abstract, indeterminate negation which brings forth the "truth" of negative judgment – why?[77]

This is the crucial question. Why does Hegel, against the common cliché, not proceed in direction of more and more determination?[78] The first answer may be an easy one: the positive judgment was not a true judgment, yet the negative judgment was not either.[79] The infinite judgment is the truth of the two accounts of how to relate subject to predicate, i.e., it is the relation between the relation between positive and negative relation of subject and predicate. First a positive relation between subject and predicate, than a negative relation with regard to this positive relation (hence: a relation to relation), then a third version which relates to the way one relates the first two and thus to the way they relate subject and predicate. In infinite judgments one is dealing with a relation to relationality as such or to discursiveness as such. This is why it cannot simply be more determined; one here deals with the truth of discursiveness.

Yet stating that there is no truth in positive and negative judgments[80] means to also state that in them there is no relation between the relations established by them and therefore no relation to relationality. With what Hegel calls the "*negatively infinite* ... judgment"[81] one attains the negation of the negative judgment (which already negated the positive judgment). But this negation produces something "*nonsensical*,"[82] namely such judgments as "Žižek is not Africa," "Althusser is not yellow," etc. These judgments are indeed true, or better: correct, and their abstract form is "the individual is not an individual." Yet they are not really judgments: although they definitely relate subject and predicate, they at the same time do not relate them – this is what makes them nonsensical. The positive articulation of the infinite judgment seems to generate a mere tautology: "the individual is an individual," or "Žižek is Žižek." But nonetheless the individual "is posited for the first time as a *determinate determinateness* ... posited as an individual. The individual is hereby *posited* as continuing itself into *its predicate*."[83] This is why one is here dealing with a judgment that states not only "the individual is an individual" but also "the universal is a universal," since that which seems separated into the individual (1) that is an individual (2), because it re-doubles itself in its predicate, is therefore universal. And thus this judgment states that the universal is universal; it remains what it is through its separation from itself.

Yet what one ends with is that the negative-infinite judgment articulates a separation between subject and predicate that is "*too great*"[84] and hence can hardly be called a judgment any longer. But the positive-infinite judgment articulates an identity that is simply a tautology and hence it is due "to the complete lack of difference ... no longer a judgment." This is why one is oscillating within the realm of infinite judgments between too much difference (the individual is not an individual) and too much identity (the individual is the individual). Thus one is driven to think a different kind of too-muchness as the outcome of this, a too-muchness of a difference within identity, of identity in-difference. The very contradiction produced by the problematic articulations of negatively-infinite positively-infinite judgments, the wrong choice[85] between them, forces one to think that what is needed is a repetition of the movement that led to the infinite judgment in its negative and positive form. Or in different terms: their very failure forces one to think that this failure *is* another kind of judgment in which the too-much of difference and the too-much of identity correlate – a judgment in which they correlate such that there is a *minimal difference* between identity and difference,[86] one is forced to think what I want to call infinitely-infinite judgment.[87] How to do this?

Of spirits and bones

Žižek takes up Hegel's notion of infinite judgment frequently throughout his oeuvre and he also from time to time emphasizes the difference from Kant. Žižek:

> Hegel's version of "infinite judgment" is thus different from Kant's – there is a negation of negation … at work in its most famous example, "the Spirit is a bone": (1) the Spirit is a bone; (2) this is nonsense, there is an absolute contradiction between these two terms; (3) well, the Spirit *is* this contradiction. One can see the opposition between this procedure and the paradox of identity as identified by Hegel, where the very occurrence of an identical term causes surprise: A rose is … (we expect a predicate, but get) a rose. The Hegelian move is to treat this surprise/paradox as constitutive of identity: there is surprise (and a temporal logic) in both cases, but of a different kind.[88]

Žižek here takes Hegel's famous case from the *Phenomenology*, in which Hegel argues against the problematic reading of the claim that the spirit is a bone – problematic because it amounts to endorsing the reductivist claim that your bodily nature determines what and how you think. Against this Hegel asserts a more dialectical reading in Žižek's account, namely one that can also avoid the idea that one first needs to start with the bone and then one ultimately afterwards achieves spirit. Rather, one fully needs to endorse the idea that spirit is a bone[89] (one needs the failures of positive, negative, negatively-infinite, and positively-infinite judgments); only by stating this too-much of identity can one attain the idea that they are absolutely different, a too-muchness of difference. Yet if there is a contradiction between the too-muchness of identity and of difference, what one is forced to think is that these two versions of too-muchness, this *two-muchness*, is what needs to be thought. The minimal difference between two too-muchnesses is spirit. It is neither, as with Descartes, a representation of too-muchness in an empty form, nor is it, as with Kant, the substantialization of non-substantiality. What Žižek's account of judgment amounts to is to think a difference, as minimal as it may be, between a too-much of identity and a too-much of difference, between an empty form (too much of difference and of identity) and something which is radically out of place (too much of identity and of difference). To repeat Žižek's move: their minimal difference *is* the subject. Its "structure" is delineated by what I call infinitely-infinite judgment. What are its consequences? I think this is what one may call dialectics, or more precisely it is what one may call (Žižek's) dialectical materialism.

Notes

1 Even though Žižek's treatment of judgment is mentioned sometimes in secondary literature, by far the most extensive treatment of this topic in his work can be found in Adrian Johnston, *Žižek's Ontology: A Transcendental Materialist Theory of Subjectivity* (Evanston, IL: Northwestern University Press, 2008), pp. 36–37, 229–236.

2 I have depicted one possible manner of reading his work in Chapter 4 of Frank Ruda, *For Badiou: Idealism Without Idealism* (Evanston, IL: Northwestern University Press, 2015).

3 Immanuel Kant, *Critique of Pure Reason* (Cambridge: Cambridge University Press, 1998), p. 101.

4 One Kantian name for a crime in the country of reason is dogmatism (ibid., pp. 118–119); another is skepticism (ibid., p. 148).

5 Theodor W. Adorno, *Kant's Critique of Pure Reason* (Stanford: Stanford University Press, 2001), p. 2.

6 This is why Kant calls his critique "a treatise on method" (Kant, *Critique*, p. 112). Later he states that the critical enterprise is first and foremost negative, i.e., limiting its scope to a purely theoretical (and not practical) investigation, it nonetheless has positive effects akin to "the police" that "put a stop to the violence that citizens have to fear from other citizens, so that each can carry on his own affairs in peace and safety" (ibid., 115).

7 Cf. for example Slavoj Žižek, *Less Than Nothing: Hegel and the Shadow of Dialectical Materialism* (London and New York: Verso, 2012), pp. 160–171; Slavoj Žižek, *Tarrying with the Negative: Kant, Hegel and the Critique of Ideology* (Durham, NC: Duke University Press, 1998), pp. 9–44, 83–124; Slavoj Žižek, "Kant as a Theorist of Vampirism," *Lacanian Ink* 8 (Spring), 1994, pp. 19–33.

8 Kant, *Critique*, p. 206.

9 For a comment on this distinction with regard to that which accompanies all my representations, namely the "I think," cf. Žižek, *Tarrying with the Negative*, pp. 13f. For a reworking of this also, cf. Willfrid Sellars, "Is There a Synthetic Apriori?" in: *American Philosophers: The Philosophical Science in the United States*, ed. Sidney Hook (New York: Criterion Books, 1956), pp. 135–159.

10 One may say that this is Kant's account of Brandom's endeavor. Cf. Robert B. Brandom, *Making it Explicit: Reasoning, Representing, and Discursive Commitment* (Cambridge and London: Harvard University Press, 1994).

11 Kant, *Critique*, p. 143.

12 Ibid.

13 Ibid., p. 146.

14 Ibid., p. 147. In this sense reason is like an average three-year-old kid. It never stops asking: "Why?" and thereby it is ultimately driven to raise questions about

the status of the unconditional – something which cannot simply be analytically derived, but needs to be synthetically – and obviously in an a priori manner – accounted for.

15 Ibid., p. 157.
16 Ibid.
17 Ibid., p. 158.
18 Ibid., p. 194.
19 This is why Kant speaks of "absolutely necessary rules of thinking" (ibid.).
20 Ibid.
21 Kant calls this "the contingent conditions of the subject" (ibid., p. 195).
22 This is why applied general logic deals with "attention, its hindrance and consequences, the cause of error" (ibid.), whereas the pure transcendental is only concerned with "the logical form in the relation of cognitions to one another," i.e., with "the form of thinking in general" (ibid., p. 196).
23 Ibid., p. 197.
24 Ibid., p. 199.
25 Ibid.
26 Kant refers to the logic of truth as an analytic part of the transcendental logic. The critique of the idea that one thereby generates any content of truth he calls transcendental dialectic (which famously deals with the paralogisms and antinomies of reason). For the sake of the present chapter, the transcendental analytic is more relevant.
27 Ibid., p. 196.
28 Ibid., p. 201.
29 On this cf. Béatrice Longuenesse, *Kant and the Capacity to Judge: Sensibility and Discursivity in the Transcendental Analytic of the* Critique of Pure Reason (Princeton and Oxford: Princeton University Press, 1998).
30 Kant, *Critique*, 202. Kant situates truth as truth of the symbolic, which obviously is the real.
31 Ibid., p. 205.
32 Ibid.
33 Ibid.
34 I here leave aside the crucial distinction of subsuming and reflective judgments that Kant develops in his third critique, as my focus solely lies on the passages Žižek frequently refers to. On the former issue cf. Jan Völker, *Ästhetik der Lebendigkeit: Kants dritte Kritik* (Munich: Fink, 2011), and Rado Riha, *Kant in drugi kopernikanski obrat v filozofiji* (Ljubljana: Založba ZRC, 2013).
35 Of course, what stands behind this synthesizing move is what Kant calls transcendental apperception, the "I think" that accompanies all my representations. I will return to this point.
36 Ibid., p. 206.
37 Ibid., p. 209.
38 Žižek, *Tarrying with the Negative*, p. 112.
39 Kant, *Critique*, p. 207.
40 Ibid., pp. 207–208.
41 Žižek, *Tarrying with the Negative*, p. 11.
42 Ibid.
43 Ibid.
44 Ibid., p. 12.
45 Žižek argues that

> the same goes for the Kantian Thing-in-itself: how does the subject arrive at it? In abstracting from every sensible determination that pertains to the

objects of experience, what remains is the object of pure abstraction, the pure 'thing-of-thought" (*Gedankending*). In short, our search for a pure presupposition, unaffected by the subject's spontaneous activity, produces an entity which is pure positedness.

[Ibid., p. 19]

This means in the pure thing-of-thought what is encountered is again just the act of thought generating it and hence not the substance of thinking. The thing in itself is an *Un-Ding*.

46 Žižek, *Less Than Nothing*.

47 This is why, in one way or another, Quentin Meillassoux remains a Kantian, since he totalizes un-totalizability (for him: *everything is un-totalizable*). For a longer elaboration of this argument, cf. Frank Ruda, "The Speculative Family, or: Critique of the Critical Critique of Critique," *Filozofski Vestnik* 33 (2), 2012, pp. 53–76.

48 G.W.F. Hegel, *Science of Logic* (New York: Humanity, 1969), 575–825.

49 One should here be precise: Hegel indeed asserts that there is no content that is not generated by form. Yet this is far from being formalism. But it is just as far from simply being a gradual acquiring of content-determinations, as most Hegel scholars still read Hegel.

50 Ibid., p. 623. One may say that Hegel here refers to the literal reading of the German "Urteilen" as "Ur" (originary) and "teilen" (division). A simple example is: "I am I" is a judgment in the sense that I am divided from something to which I stand in an identity relation. In Hegel's words: "It is thus the original division [Teilung] of what is originally one" (ibid., p. 625).

51 Not only in the sense of deriving further formal determinations of the concept, but in the sense of literally further determining the concept.

52 Ibid., p. 623.

53 "Subject" only becomes subject after entering into relation. Yet this implies that "subject" is subject. To my mind: ""subject" is "subject/subject" is "subject"/subject" is the ultimate infinite judgment for Žižek. We will get there ....

54 Hegel, *Science of Logic*, p. 627.

55 Ibid.

56 Ibid.

57 A simple example: "The sky is blue."

58 Hegel, *Science of Logic*, p. 632.

59 Ibid., p. 633.

60 Ibid.

61 Ibid.

62 Ibid., p. 634.

63 Ibid., p. 636. The investigation of Günter Wohlfart shows one of their many limitations here, since he assumes that the distinction between form and content with regard to the positive judgment cannot properly be upheld by Hegel. Yet this is precisely Hegel's point and the true dialectical twist concerning positive judgment. Cf. Günter Wohlfart, "Das unendliche Urteil," *Zeitschrift für philosophische Forschung*, 39(1), p. 88.

64 Hegel, *Science of Logic*, 637.

65 Ibid.

66 Stupid example: "The sky is not-blue."

67 The particularity is gained by taking the subject–predicate relation as subject and negating its relation – which, as shall have become clear, is the truth of the positive judgment.

68 Hegel: "The judgment's determination as determination of the Notion, is in its

own a universal as continuing itself into its other determinations. Conversely, the relation of the judgments is the same determination as that possessed by the extremes ... the relation also has negativity in it" (ibid., p. 638).

69 Ibid.
70 Ibid., pp. 639–640.
71 Ibid., p. 640.
72 Ibid., p. 641.
73 Ibid.
74 The subject of the first version is "individual," of the second "universal."
75 Ibid.
76 Ibid.
77 Žižek, *Tarrying with the Negative,* p. 21.
78 For a reading that assumes the cliché about Hegel, cf. J.N. Findlay, *Hegel: A Re-Examination* (London: Collier Books, 1962), pp. 229f.
79 Hegel, *Science of Logic,* p. 641.
80 "The negative judgment is as little a true judgment as the positive" (ibid.).
81 Ibid., p. 642.
82 Ibid.
83 Ibid.
84 Ibid., p. 643.
85 One may repeat the old joke: "Negatively-infinite judgment or positively-infinite judgment. No, thanks. Both are worse."
86 And because they correlate, this is another version of Hegel's (in)famous identity of identity and difference.
87 One may recall, simply, that the only infinitely-infinite judgment that there is for Hegel is what he calls the idea, which is why he also calls it the "absolute judgment."
88 Žižek, *Less Than Nothing,* 534.
89 Cf. for this also the brilliant elaboration of Malden Dolar, "The Phrenology of Spirit," in *Supposing the Subject,* ed. Joan Copjec (London: Verso, 1994), pp. 64–83.

Chapter 9

The legal imaginary and the real of right

Jeanne L. Schroeder

What is law?

I start not with Slavoj Žižek, but with H.L.A. Hart, the most influential Anglophone jurisprude. Hart's positivism may seem impoverished compared to speculative theory. Nevertheless, there are surprising moments of correspondence between Hart's concept of law and Lacanian theory. As such he serves as a foil: a point of comparison to explicate a Žižekian jurisprudence.

Hart, like Jacques Lacan, recognizes that law is linguistic in nature and, therefore, necessarily incomplete. Rejecting the command theory that posits that law is founded in fear, Hart asserts that the subject comes into being through submission to the order of law. This is the "internal position" with respect to law.

Hart's concept is not so much wrong as incomplete. It captures an "imaginary" moment of legality. It however represses law's symbolic and real moments.

Moreover, Hart lacks the courage of his convictions. He eventually suggests that perhaps only "officials" have the internal position. The rest of us cringe in fear before its inexplicable violence. As such, he unwittingly anticipates Žižek's insistence that law is sustained by an obscene underside.

Unable to bear its ethical implications, Hart implies that law's incompleteness is merely empirical – not logical – in nature. We can approach a complete legal system. This enables judges implicitly to deny their guilt for their actions.

Hart's blind spots originate from his separation theory: i.e., law is independent from "morality." A Žižekian analysis shows that, far from being separated, law and "morality" are inextricably linked: morality is the real to the symbolic of law. It is not beyond the law but within it as its logically necessary limitation.

Hart

Hart addressed *The Concept of Law*[1] to undergraduates, attempting to describe law in a manner understandable to lay persons. At first reading by an attorney, his account seems familiar: it captures much of how I experienced practice. This may be why this book continues to be so influential a half century after publication. Upon further reflection, however, it is frustratingly vague and inconsistent.

Hart self-identifies as a positivist: his is not a theory, empirical study, or psychological account of law. Rather, a *concept* of law is a description of how law functions: an image of law as it is, not what it should be.

Hart rejects the "command theory" of Jeremy Bentham and John Austin that sees law as habit of obedience inculcated by threat of punishment. Hart finds this inadequate for many reasons; e.g., it doesn't describe laws that facilitate, rather than prohibit, activity. More importantly, it might explain Oliver Wendell Holmes's bad man, but it does not capture how "good people" relate to law.

Admitting that obedience to law is habitual, Hart insists that law-abiding people do not act *merely* out of fear. Rather they adopt an internal position. Hart's concept is law as rules. Playing a game is, by definition, the agreement to follow its rules because a game is constituted by its rules. Similarly, to consent to be a member of a society is to agree to be bound by its constituent laws.

One implication is that a game player may not refuse to follow a rule because she disagrees with it: I cannot decide in the middle of a chess game to move my rook diagonally. Similarly, a citizen cannot disobey a law she finds objectionable unless she is willing to pay the penalty.

Despite his use of the term "internal position," Hart's is not a psychological theory of human behavior.[2] Neither the game player nor the law follower need have any psychic investment in the rules in the sense of accepting that they are good or proper. A person with an internal position will, however, agree that violation of rules is a reason to punish the miscreant.[3]

Nevertheless, despite his disclaimers Hart's concept sometimes parallels psychoanalytical theory. Specifically, he suggests that submission to law is what makes us human.[4] Later, however, Hart posits that perhaps only "officials" have the internal position, i.e., the command theory might be correct with respect to most people. He admits that such a terrified citizenry is subhuman, "deplorably sheeplike" and headed for the "slaughterhouse."[5]

Hart asserts that the status of a law as such is independent from its moral, or indeed any, substantive content. He thinks this is necessitated by the positivist law project – to describe law as it exists, not as it should be. Normativity is moral by definition.[6]

Nevertheless, Hart insists his position is moral. Separating morality from law enables it to serve as an *external* critique of law. If we were to conceptualize morality as internal to law, people might conflate the two, presuming that existing laws are moral. In fact, some "laws may be law but too evil to be obeyed."[7]

Although Hart contrasts law to "morality" he never defines the latter (although he attempts to distinguish some aspects of moral rules from legal rules). As such, the separation thesis threatens to devolve into the truism of law is not non-law.

If law cannot be identified by content, it must be identifiable by form. Hart posits that a functioning legal system requires a set of "secondary" rules governing the "primary" rules. His secondary rule that has generated the most interest is the "rule of recognition" that tells officials how to identify what rules are laws as opposed to something else (e.g., etiquette).[8]

If officials identify the law through rules of recognition, not substance, then the law must be unambiguous, fixed, and complete. In his metaphor, law is located in a central "core" of easy cases. Hart recognizes that officials occasionally confront "hard cases" in a "penumbra" surrounding the core in which law is unclear.[9] The penumbra exists because law, like language, is incomplete or "open textured."[10]

I suggested that one reason why his account has had traction is that it captures aspects about how lawyers experience law. First, I don't want to believe I obey out of fear – I am not Holmes's bad man, but a good citizen. Second, both as attorney and law professor I often find the law certain. I have little trouble marking exams.

On further thought these comforting intuitions are incorrect, both empirically and theoretically. Despite my self-serving self-characterization, I don't know my true motives for obeying the law. I, like many if not most people, occasionally break laws when there is very little chance that I would be caught or where punishment would be minimal.

More importantly, the idea that the law is "usually" clear and unambiguous is naive at best. If most people rarely resort to the courts, this is evidence neither that they know what the law is nor that law is certain.

Finally, although Hart is no doubt correct that law and "morality" are not the same thing, every law has substantive effect and, therefore, a moral dimension. Moreover, one only says law is Law when law is monstrous. Indeed, Hart initially developed the separation thesis in a debate as to whether Nazi law was Law.

How can Hart be so right and so wrong? On the one hand, Hart's concept has strong, albeit unintended, affinities with Žižekian jurisprudence. On the other, it is inadequate because it is partial. Hart captures the legal imaginary but is incapable of recognizing its symbolic and the real aspects. As such, he violates the oath required by all witnesses in the United States. He might tell the truth, but not the whole truth.

Hart and the master's discourse

Hart's concept of law is as a master's discourse. Lacan, not a lawyer, thought that the master's discourse was primitive and unlikely to be found in the modern world, having largely been displaced by the "University discourse."[11] In contrast, Hart argues that it is the heart of any functioning legal system.[12]

$$\frac{S_1}{\$} \rightarrow \frac{S_2}{a}$$[13]

Each of Lacan's discourses is spoken by an "agent." In the master's discourse (based on Hegel's lord-bondsman dialectic) this is the master signifier (S_1). The master signifier is meaningless in the sense that it stands for nothing but itself. The master is in his position for formal, not substantive, reasons. He is obeyed because he is recognized as master, not because he deserves his position. Similarly, to Hart positive law is meaningless not in the sense that it has no content, but because its status is determined by the rule of recognition regardless of its content. The master is structurally an idiot, or in the words of Mr. Bumble, "the law is a ass."[14] This is necessitated by the very nature of mastery because justification makes mastery conditional.

The master (S_1) addresses S_2, the signifying chain of "knowledge." In the case of Hart, S_2 is the "officials" who recognize, obey, and enforce the law. Hegel asserts that, if the master is proudly ignorant, the bondsman gains knowledge from servitude – he learns how to get things done. Even if the law is formally senseless, the officials learn how to effectualize it.

So far, I am Hart's disciple: the master's discourse is a necessary moment in any legal system. Officials recognize, obey, and enforce laws just because they are laws, not because they are just. Hart's account is, nevertheless, inadequate. Lacan shows that the master's is only the first discourse. It generates three others: the university's, the analyst's, and the hysteric's. These are equally necessary aspects of law. They enable morality, expelled by law, to return to complete the critical function Hart assigned it.

Most importantly, every discourse results in a "product." In the master's discourse, this is created by expulsion. Precisely because it is missing, this product is an *object petit a*: the object cause of the discourse's desire. In the case of Hart, what is expelled is morality: that which can not be named (which is perhaps why Hart refuses to define it). However, from a Lacanian perspective, rather than separating law from morality, expulsion makes law dependent on "morality" as the desire that drives it forward. I *want* to obey law not just because, but because the law is just.

Here, I too punt on what this ghostly missing morality might be, only to presage that I identify it with what Hegel called "right": the real limit to the symbolic of positive law. In the legal imaginary, however, specific moralistic rules – Hart identifies those mandating conventional sexual practices – or policy positions stand in the place of the spectral right as the law's *object petit a*.[15]

Law is Law

Although he does not use the expression, Hart's positivism can be reduced to "law is Law." To the lay person, this assertion that positive law, no matter how immoral, is the only definition of law seems inane at best, insane at worst. But Žižek has repeatedly argued that tautology is not empty but profound in a way that Hart could nor articulate.

Sometimes tautology is the only possible definition. "[T]he very problem (obstacle) [of definition] retroactively appears as its own solution."[16] In other words,

> In this way, through the very failure of our endeavor, we circumscribe an empty place, the place of the right word – precisely the word we are trying to explain. So at some point, after our paraphrases fail, all we can do is to conclude in exasperation: "In short, it is X!" Far from functioning as a simple admission of failure, however, this can effectively generate an insight – *If*, that is, through our failed paraphrases we have successfully circumscribed the *place* of the term to be explained. At that point, as Lacan would have put it, "the signifier falls into the signified," the term becomes part of its own definition.[17]

There is a minimal difference – a parallax view – between the proposition "law is ..." and the judgement "Law." The former (which the official merely finds "on the books") has no particular status. However, this changes when the official adopts the internal position and pronounces such "law" as "Law."

Law with a capital "L" is the rule one obeys to play the game called "society." The tautology is transubstantiation in the Catholic sense of the term. When the official proclaims "this is the law" there is an imperceptible yet immeasurable difference between the words written in the statute book before and after. They are now invested with the dignity of the Law. We quake in awe before its awful, sublime violence.

In Žižek's words:

> tautology gives birth to the specter of some imponderable depth which escapes word: far from being an index of perfection, it hints at an obscene contingent underside. When do we say, "The law is the law"? Precisely when the law is encountered as unjust, arbitrary, etc., and then we add, "But, nonetheless, the law is the law."[18]

Later he continues:

> One can see ... the paradox of identity as identified by Hegel, where the very occurrence of an identical term causes surprise: A rose ... (we expect a predicate, but get) a rose. The Hegelian move is to treat this surprise/paradox as constitutive of identity: there is a surprise (and a temporal logic) in both cases, but of a different kind.[19]

Moreover, the tautology "law is Law" is a mobius strip. Positive law – the banal "black-letter" – turns out to be the august, divine institution of "Law itself" just as the man Jesus is revealed to be the Christ. But, this can equally be written as "Law is law." God could only be manifest in a lowly carpenter. The majesty of law is manifest in the practice of the sleaziest shyster and its enforcement by a bored or malicious civil servant.

The rule of recognition

Paradoxically, Hart's most and least successful idea is the "rule of recognition." If law can not be identified by substance, it must be recognizable by form. Officials do not make law, they find it through secondary rules.

At this stage, I want to raise a Žižekian point about the official as subject. The matheme of masculinity is "all subjects are submitted to the symbolic order," or perhaps better, the masculine subject is completely submitted to the symbolic order.[20] The man is the subject who, although castrated like all subjects, denies his castration, claiming to be complete and in control. In the context of law, he has the law, he knows what the law says: he merely recognizes that which is already there.

Although this is never literally true it is an imaginary moment in how we lawyers experience law. When the official speaks, "*it is the law itself which speaks through him*," the official is "spoken" by the law, since his "speech acts are totally regulated" by the symbolic order.[21] This is Hart's internal position with respect to the law.

On one level, this seems disingenuous. In the United States, literalist jurists rail against "activist" judges and claim merely to read texts without resort to external influences. It is just coincidence that the law they find always corresponds to their political presuppositions. Liberal critics, claiming to see through this, accuse them of disingenuousness. However, Lacanian insists *les non-dupes errant*:

> those who refuse to let themselves get caught in the symbolic fiction and believe only what they see with their own eyes are those who err most. What the cynic misses here is the efficiency of the symbolic fiction, the way it structures our (experience of) reality. A corrupt priest preaching on goodness may be hypocrite, but if people endow

> his words with the authority of the Church, they may inspire them to perform good deeds.[22]

It is as disingenuous for the critic to deny law's constraint as is for the literalist to insist on it. The very concept of judicial authority requires:

> "fetishistic disavowal": I know very well that things are the way I see them, that the person in front of me is a corrupt weakling, but I nonetheless treat him respectfully, since he wears the insignia of a judge, so that when he speaks, *it is the law itself which speaks through him*. So, in a way, I really do believe his words, not my eyes. This is where the cynic who believes only hard facts falls short: when a judge speaks there is a way more truth in his words (the words of the institution of law) than in the direct reality of the person of judge; if one limits oneself to what one sees, one simply misses the point.[23]

Even a judge who lies about his internal position may, in fact, be spoken by the law.

Kant is the true father of psychoanalysis, asserting that one cannot plumb the depths of one's own heart.[24] The usual reading is that since we can never know if we act out of duty to the moral law or out of pathology, then we must presume that all of our noble actions are smeared with immorality. Žižek offers an alternate account. Our inability to know our motives equally leads to the conclusion that all of our ignoble actions are smeared with morality.

> That is to say, in Kantian ethics, the true tension is not between the subject's idea that he is acting only for the sake of duty and the hidden fact that there was actually some pathological motivation at work, (vulgar psychoanalysis); the true tension is exactly the opposite one: the abysally free act is unbearable, traumatic, in that when we accomplish an act out of freedom, and in order to sustain it, we experience it as conditioned by some pathological motivation.[25]

Consequently, one reason we tell stories about our actions might be not that we can't bear the pain of our sin, but that we can't bear the *responsibility* for our morality. Better to pretend to have no choice. This is Hart's move. Proclaiming law separate from morality so that officials merely recognize law, he tries to exculpate them from guilt.

One of the paradoxes of Kant, indeed of Christianity, is that sin is the prerequisite of morality. Morality requires choice. The subject must adopt maxims congruent to the moral law and act in accordance with such maxims, not pathology. The problem is that we do not know the moral law. Indeed, if we could see the mind of God and know the moral law, we would become mere automatons.[26] Not being freely chosen, our actions might be empirically good (i.e., beneficial) but would have no moral purchase.

In other words, it is precisely our uncertainty of both the content of the moral law and our motives for acting that makes our choices free, endowing them with a moral dimension. Thus, Kant rewrites Original Sin. Before eating of the Tree of the Knowledge of Good and Evil, Adam and Eve – lacking such knowledge – were not capable of moral choice. It is only when they because capable of sin did they become capable of morality. As Žižek says "the bad news is that we are abandoned by God; the good news is that we are abandoned by God and left with our freedom."[27]

As a result, the making of a moral decision is unspeakably painful. We seek release in the three excuses Kant calls "radical evil": not profound or diabolical evil, but everyday banal evil lying at the root (*radix*) of human action.[28] All three are attempts to disavow responsibility.

The most venial evil is weakness: the claim that I couldn't help myself. Kant responds: of course you could; *du kannst, denn du sollst.*[29] All human actions are choices, albeit often forced choices. Lacan says even though the infant's "choice" of submitting to the law of prohibition establishing subjectivity is the equivalent of submitting to the gunman's demand "Your money or your life,"[30] nevertheless, she is morally responsible for it. After all, there are people who refuse to submit: i.e., psychotics.

Tellingly, in rejecting the command theory, Hart also, unwittingly, rejects Lacan's example of "forced choice." He asserts, "Law surely is not the gunman situation writ large, and legal order is surely not to be thus simply identified with compulsion."[31] Moreover, he claims that no moral code holds an individual liable for submitting to coercion.[32] As such, he acquits the citizenry for their participation in an immoral regime. Implicitly, "I was only following orders" is a valid *moral* defense to Hart. In doing so, Hart fails to recognize Kantianism as moral philosophy.

The next evil is impurity. The wicked subject knows she should obey the moral law but wishes to indulge her pathology. Consequently, she bends and stretches the law to interpret it as permitting her desires.

The most heinous radical evil is wickedness. This is the evil of which cynics accuse literalist judges: the false claim of following the law when one is really following one's desire. This is the official who says, "as much as it pains me to pronounce sentence, law is Law" when she secretly enjoys doing so.

If we never know why we act, it is only after the fact that we hypothesize reasons for our actions.[33] This is the judge's burden. Traditionalists such as Hart want to relieve the official of her guilt. She merely recognizes the law she must follow even if immoral. Thus the official claims to be weak (I had no choice) when she might actually be wicked (I wanted to do it). But the cynic who believes that all law is politics is equally wrong in thinking the law does not constrain the judge.

Nobody, including the judge, knows why she made her decision. However, she has a moral responsibility to own her decision: to justify it. Consequently, she must give reasons for her decision. The crit believes that this is cynicism. The literalist claims she is bound by her reasons. From a Žižekian perspective it is both and neither. The reasons given may or may not have caused the judicial decision. In Žižek's words:

> the true miracle of language is that it can *also* serve as a neutral medium which just designates a conceptual/ideal content. In other words, the true task is not to locate language as a neutral medium within a life-world practice, but to show how, within this life world, a neutral medium of designation can nonetheless emerge.[34]

Here we encounter the Hegelian–Žižekian retroactive understanding of freedom. Freedom is less the ability to make rational choices free from coercion – we don't know why we act and all of our choices are forced. It is the ability to retroactively adopt and take responsibilities for our actions.

> "Freedom" is thus inherently retroactive: at its most elementary, it is not simply a free act which, out of nowhere, starts a new causal link, but a retroactive act of determining which link or sequence of necessities will determine us.[35]

At first glance, there seems to be a parallel between Kant and Hart. At second look, however, Hart gets Kant backwards. Hart identifies morality with its known content. Law, in contrast, can only be identified formally through rules of recognition. In contrast, Kant argues that we cannot know the content of *morality*, although we can identify it by form: the categorical imperative of universality. Moreover, one distinction Hart draws between law and "morality" is that while law will occasionally impose forced choice, no system of morality will condemn a man for doing a "bad" act out of compulsion.[36] Yet Žižekian moral theory, following Kant, does precisely that.

The open texture of law

Hart is also both right and wrong about the completeness of law. On the one hand, Hart understands that law is linguistic in nature and, therefore, incomplete. It has an open texture. On the other hand, for the officials to merely *recognize* law, law must be complete and certain. That is, all law should fall within the core. How, then, to explain the penumbra in which officials must use discretion and bring a moral dimension back into law?[37]

Hart tries by suggesting that law's incompleteness is empirical rather than logical. It exists because we are "men not gods."[38] If parliament had sufficient time, knowledge, and wisdom it could anticipate every potential conflict and write a law to decide it. In our sub-lunar world this is impracticable and inefficient: better to leave unusual fact patterns for officials to adjudicate on a case-by-case basis.

Žižek unwittingly critiques Hart's position: "the limit pertaining to the form itself (to the categories used) is misperceived as a contingent empirical limitation."[39] He continues "what appears ... impossible only on account of our empirical limitations, is revealed to be impossible ... in its very notional-formal determinations.[40] Even an angelic Congress with infinite time could not weave a law whose texture was closed.

Žižek's metaphor turns Hart's inside out. The center of law is not certainty but an undigested hard kernel of non-law.[41] This is the real which is the symbolic's own internal limitation. The real is like "the grain of sand within the pearl. Positive law, including legislation, adjudication, and legal practice, is nothing but the attempt to build a shell of relative certainty around this uncertain center."[42]

Hart offered his metaphor to counter both the proponents and the opponents of legal realism. The realists, like the later "crits," thought law indeterminate. Many realists and critics assumed this implied that law never constrains officials. Objectivity was a sham; the law is what the judge ate for breakfast. Consequently, Hart describes realism as a "nightmare" to be contrasted to his "noble dream" of complete law.[43]

Hart chides both sides of this debate for assuming that determinacy is an either–or proposition.[44] Unfortunately, his metaphor replicates this mistake because it assumes that any individual case is either in the core (determinate) or penumbra (indeterminate).[45] From a Lacanian perspective, however, every legal decision, like every form of communication, has both a symbolic–objective and an imaginary–subjective moment.

Both to Hartian positivists and to literalist judges, reference to imagination and subjectivity reeks of arbitrariness and judicial activism. Is not the hallmark of democracy the government of laws and not men? But identifying a moment of free subjectivity in all judging – besides being accurate because its inevitable – does *not* mean law is not *also* objective or that one decision is as good as another. In deciding a case the judge is always interpreting objects – statutes, precedents, facts – that are before him. In other words, the reference to subjectivity does not mean that official imposes meaning from the outside. To paraphrase Bruce Fink, the problem of interpretation is not a lack, but a surfeit of meaning in a text.[46] The interpreter is forced to choose, determining the *best* permissible meaning. This is, of course, the theory of Hart's critic Ronald Dworkin, who insists that despite the ambiguity of law, nevertheless there is always one right answer.[47]

Hart's vision of law is imaginary in the Lacanian sense. The imaginary is not only the subjective order, it is the fantasy that there could be binary opposites resulting in closure and certainty. However, if Hart is wrong in thinking that law is completely determinate in the easy cases at the core, this does not mean that Hart's fantasy of law is deluded. The crit who thinks that he is not deluded when he criticizes the subjective moment of judging also errs. The symbolic cannot exist without the imaginary, as the imaginary is necessary for the signification of the law to congeal at least momentarily into meaning.

Hart imagines that he can fix the symbolic of law through a rule of recognition. As a positivist, he refuses to *define* what such a rule might be, merely *describing* its function. His one example – in the UK acts of Parliament are a source of law[48] – leads some to think they are genealogical in nature. However, language in his posthumous "Postscript" to the *Concept of Law* suggests that they could have a substantive component.[49] This can easily devolve into an infinite regress of rules recognizing rules recognizing rules of recognition, *ad infinitum*. As such, the concept of the rule of recognition merely replicates, rather than solves, the problem of signification. If each signified is itself a signifier referring to another signifier in an unending chain, how does fixed meaning, in Fink's language, "precipitate out"?[50]

Žižek's answer is that to confront the problem head-on is to solve it. Since signification will not stop itself, one must step in and stop it.

> A parallel with the flow of speech might be of some help here: the flow of speech cannot go on indefinitely, there has to be *le moment de conclure*, like the point that concludes a sentence. It is only the dot at the end that retroactively fixes or determines the meaning of the sentence. However, it is crucial to add that this dot is not a simple fixation which removes all risk, abolishing all ambiguity and openness. It is, on the contrary, the dotting itself, the cut, which release – sets free – meaning and interpretation: the dot always occurs contingently, as a surprise, it generates a surplus – why *here*?[51]

Law is an unending chain of texts, precedents, and novel fact patterns. Accordingly, every legal dispute is undetermined *ab initio* – that is precisely why there is a dispute. Hart captures the fact that, nevertheless, legal disputes are in fact eventually determined and there will often be a broad consensus that the determination is correct. In other words, it is not that the law is indeterminate, but that determination only exists in the future perfect tense. Law is not *pre*determined but someday it *will have been* determined.[52]

Psychoanalysis is a practice that depends on the belief that meaning can be produced through language. As I have stated, the problem is not that texts have no meaning, but that they have too much. The judge must choose a meaning, which is why we call a disposition of a case a "decision" and her explanation an "opinion." As Fink explains, whenever we read a sentence, we first encounter multiple ambiguities of language. But by the time we reach the end, we usually have resolved the ambiguity and assigned at least a tentative meaning.[53] In many everyday communications this happens so quickly that we are not conscious of the procedure. When reading difficult text, such as a Lacanian seminar or a complex legal opinion, it becomes all too obvious as we read and reread, trying out potential interpretations consistent with the text.

Morality and right

> *[M]orality itself is essentially criminal* – again, not only in the sense that the universal moral order necessarily "negates itself" in particular crimes, but, more radically, in the sense that *the way morality (and, in the case of theft, property) asserts itself is already in itself a crime.*[54]

To reiterate, Hart claims to separate law from morality – an immoral law is Law, albeit it might be too evil to obey. This primary rules of law cannot be identified by their moral, or other substantive, content but can only be recognized through the application of secondary rule. I argue above that although this correctly identifies one necessary moment of law – a master's discourse – Hart does not successfully divorce law from morality. By expelling morality from law, Hart makes morality into its object cause of law's desire – its very goal.

Hart is also correct that one cannot find morality by looking at positive law. Morality – or more broadly justice or right – is not a pre-existing fact that can be merely recognized. Right is impossible; it is real to the symbolic of positive law. It is the very limit to law itself.[55]

The relationship of right to positive law is the relationship of the real to law's symbolic.

> This means that the Real is not external to the Symbolic: the Real is the Symbolic itself in the modality of non-All, lacking an external Limit/Exception. In this precise sense, the line of separation between the Symbolic and the Real is not only a symbolic gesture *par excellence*, but the very founding gesture of the Symbolic and to step into the Real does not entail abandoning language, throwing oneself into the abyss of the chaotic Real, but, on the contrary, dropping the very allusion to some external point of reference which eludes the symbolic.[56]

It is commonly assumed that right pre-exists wrong. Wrong is a violation of the norm of right and justice consists in the re-establishment of right. This approach sees right as a static pre-existing thing: in Lacanian terminology, that right "exists."

Right, however, like Woman in Lacan and God in Hegel, does not exist. It insists.[57] How can I say that Hegel denies that God exists when Hegel speaks constantly about God (*Geist*)? One must understand how Hegel defines existence. Existence is characteristic of "things." To say that God exists is idolatrous – it is to attribute divinity to things, and reduce God to an object. Objects cease to be, but God does not.

One aspect that distinguishes Hegel from Kant is his understanding of the relationship between appearance and essences. Kant saw the inadequacy of appearance and assumed that there must be a hard kernel of essence underneath it. Hegel, instead, said that this inadequacy is essence itself. There is nothing beneath appearance – essence is the very limitations of appearance itself. Essence is real.[58]

If there is nothing below appearance so that appearance is essence, what is the difference between essence and semblance – between right and wrong? Semblance is the pretension that that which is contingent, impermanent, and changing is necessary, permanent, and static. It is the misunderstanding that there is a true essence that *exists* beneath appearance. Essence, in contrast, is the correct understanding of appearance.

This is the relationship of positive law and right. Right is not something that exists or pre-exists law, it is law's own limitation; its inevitable failure to achieve its goal. Consequently, it is wrong that pre-exists right, not the other way around.

At first glance, this might sound un-Hegelian. He did, after all, write the *Philosophy of Right*. He starts with an analysis of how property rights allow the abstract Kantian person to develop into a legal subject – the type of person who is capable of bearing legal rights and duties. Consequently, some American jurists assume that Hegel, like Locke, adopts a first-occupier theory of property.

This misses the point that Hegel is merely describing property's function. He does not define right per se, let alone establish when claims of rights are rightful. For example, he accurately identifies possession as a *claim* of first-in-time, first-in-right, but he is not specifying when and how such a claim could be justified.

Hegel only considers the issue of justification *after* he discusses wrong precisely because right only appears momentarily and retroactively in the righting of a pre-existing wrong. Indeed, Hegel gives (albeit in his trademark obscure manner) first-occupier claims of possession as an example of a wrong, not a right.

Hegel adopts a version of Kant's categorical imperative: "Be a person and respect others as persons."[59] It is, therefore, wrong to treat another person as a means to your ends rather than as an end in herself. To claim a right against another person is to treat her as a means and, therefore, wrong. This wrong can only retroactively become right if the person agrees and forms a common will so that each achieves her ends. Hegel gives contract as the most primitive form of this alchemy.

Consequently, Hart intuits correctly that we can not find morality, or in Hegel's account "right," by looking for it in the law. Right, to cite Žižek, is precisely that to which the law simultaneously has no access, as well as obstacle that prevents such access. Wrong, unlike right, does exist – it is a brute fact. Wrong is not the violation of right but its pre-condition. A claim to right is wrong because it is a semblance – it treats the contingent as necessary. Right only appears retroactively in the act of righting wrongs. Consequently, as is the case of Woman, the fact that right does not exist does not mean it is "*not* not there ... it is there in full."[60]

The obscene supplement to law

Finally, by rejecting the command theory, Hart tries to separate law from fear. But, by doing so, he does not do away with violence; he merely represses it. What is repressed in the symbolic returns in the real.[61] We see this when he damns the majority of mankind as beasts being herded to the abattoir. It is not just morality but *the immorality of law* that cannot be spoken within Hartian discourse.

This leads William MacNeil – no friend of formalism – to plead "Come back John Austin, all is forgiven – even if it means accepting the lawman-as-gunman into the cultural legal fold."[62] As I characterize McNeill's position elsewhere,

> Ironically, it is the Austinian subject, cringing before the violence of the law who at least retains the possibility of freedom.... As long as the subject complies with the external demands of the law, she is allowed to have her "inner space free." ... In contrast, Hart's official submits his very "h(e)art" to the sovereign.[63]

Moreover, by separating law from morality, Hart implicitly endorses one of Žižek's most controversial claims: that law always requires an obscene underside. We see this point in one of the earliest accounts of Law: *The Eumenides*, which ostensibly dramatizes the mythical moment when legal process supplanted vendetta. In fact, when the Erinyes – the personification of vengeance – leave the stage near the end of the play, it is only to take residence in a cave beneath the judicial bench. To Euripides, violence is *literally* the hidden support of law.[64]

To Hart, law is Law despite the fact of the violence that supports it. Indeed, Hart's position is not merely obscene, it is perverse. A pervert takes on the position of the object completely subjected to the law as subject,[65] in contrast to the ordinary neurotic subject who has a fraught relationship with law. The hysteric is never sure what the law wants from her. In contrast, the pervert – like Hart's officials – always knows what the law demands.[66]

But here I will stray from Žižek. Hart's attempt to expel "morality" from the law allows it – in the form of justice or what Hegel would call "right" –

to act as the legal subject's *object petit a*. It is the object of desire or goal that puts the entire chain of legal relations into motion. As such, if law has an obscene underside, it also has a divine one as well.

Notes

1 H.L.A. Hart, *The Concept of Law* (Oxford: Oxford University Press, 1994).
2 Ibid., p. 56.
3 Ibid., p. 57. This is in contrast to the command theory which merely posits that people follow rules because they predict that they will be punished if they disobey. Ibid., p. 84. Perhaps surprisingly, Žižek, following Hegel, makes a similar point.

> So it is quite clear to Hegel that appearing has nothing to do with conscious awareness: it does not matter what individuals' minds are preoccupied with while they are participating in a ceremony, the truth resides in the ceremony itself.

Slavoj Žižek, *The Parallax View* (Cambridge, MA: MIT Press, 2006), p. 406.
4 As Peter Fitzpatrick says, Hart initially suggests that "the internal aspect of rules [is] 'distinctive ... of human thought, speech and action'." Peter Fitzpatrick, *The Mythology of Modern Law* (Abingdon and New York: Routledge, 1992), p. 200. See also Jeanne L. Schroeder, *The Four Lacanian Discourses: or Turning Law Inside Out* (Abingdon: Routledge, 2008), p. 39 n. 47.
5 Hart (1994), p. 117.
6 Schroeder (2008), p. 32.
7 H.L.A Hart, "Positivism and the Separation of Law and Morals," *Harvard Law Review*, 71 (1958), pp. 593–629, p. 620.
8 Hart (1994), p. 100.
9 Ibid., p. 12.
10 Ibid., p. 123.
11 Bruce Fink, *The Lacanian Subject: Between Language and Jouissance* (Princeton: Princeton University Press, 1995), p. 132.
12 I set forth my analysis more fully in Schroeder (2008), pp. 30–52.
13 Fink (1995), p. 30.
14 Charles Dickens, *Oliver Twist* (London: Richard Bentley, 1838/2005). As Žižek says, "the master is defined as a subject who accepts ... he is a king because others treat him as a king, not the other way round – otherwise, if he thinks that he is a king 'in himself' he is a madman"; Slavoj Žižek, *Less than Nothing: Hegel and the Shadow of Dialectical Materialism* (London and New York: Verso, 2012), p. 422.
15 Schroeder (2008), p. 150.
16 Žižek (2012), p. 536.
17 Ibid., p. 537.
18 Ibid., p. 370. Elsewhere he states "As I have already hinted, one could also formulate this ... in terms of the Hegelian notion of tautology as the highest contradiction ... the form of identity contains utter heterogeneity." Slavoj Žižek, *The Indivisible Remainder: An Essay on Schelling and Related Matters* (London: Verso, 1996), pp. 100–101.
19 Žižek (2012), pp. 534–135.
20 Schroeder (2008), pp. 106, 127, 151–152.
21 Žižek (2012), p. 197.

22 Ibid., p. 517.
23 Ibid., p. 417.
24 Immanuel Kant, *The Metaphysics of Morals*, transl. Mary J. Gregor (Cambridge: Cambridge University Press, 1996), p. 155.
25 Žižek (2012), pp. 265–266.
26 Immanuel Kant, *Practical Philosophy*, transl. Mary J. Gregor (Cambridge and New York: Cambridge University Press, 1996), p. 123.
27 Žižek (2012), p. 111.
28 Kant (1998), p. 45.
29 Quoted in Žižek (2006), p. 92.
30 Bruce Fink, *Lacan to the Letter: Reading Écrits Closely* (Minneapolis: University of Minnesota Press, 2004), p. 181 n. 3 (citing Lacan, Seminar XI, 192–93/ 211–12).
31 Hart (1958), p. 603. See also Hart (1994), pp. 20–24, 40.
32 Hart (1994), pp. 178–179.
33 He states:

> It is interesting to note how the standard Kantian suspicion about an act being truly good or ethical is here weirdly mobilized in the opposite direction: we cannot be sure that an act really was "diabolically evil" that some pathological motivation did not make it a normal case of evil.
> [Žižek 2012, p. 318]

34 Ibid., p. 7 n. 4.
35 Ibid., p. 213.
36 Hart (1994), pp. 178–179.
37 Schroeder (2008), p. 118.
38 Hart (1994), p. 128. See also Schroeder (2008), pp. 119–120.
39 Žižek (2012), p. 284.
40 Ibid., p. 285.
41 Although we experience it in this way, "the Real is not a hard external kernel which resists symbolization, but the product of a deadlock in the process of symbolization." Žižek (1996), p. 110.
42 Schroeder (2008), p. 45.
43 H.L.A Hart, "American Jurisprudence Through English Eyes: The Nightmare and the Noble Dream," *Essays in Jurisprudence and Philosophy* (Oxford: Oxford University Press, 1983); Schroeder (2008), p. 147.
44 He refers to them as the Scylla and Charybdis of legal interpretation; Hart (1994), p. 47.
45 Schroeder (2008), p. 118.
46 As he says, specifically in the context of an analysand's discourse "there is only too much meaning there." Fink (2004), p. 88.
47 Ronald Dworkin, *Taking Rights Seriously* (London and New York: Bloomsbury Academic, 1977), pp. 119–141; Schroeder (2008), pp. 42, 117.
48 Hart (1994), p. 101.
49 Ibid., pp. 247, 249–250.
50 Fink (2004), p. 113.
51 Žižek (2012), p. 369.
52 That is, it is not determined *ex ante*, but it is determined *ex post*. Schroeder (2008), p. 115.
53 Fink states:

> The end of the sentence determines how the listener understands or "rereads" the beginning of the sentence; the end of the sentence fixes the

meanings, putting an end to the sliding (without necessarily reducing multiple meanings to one single meaning). And I may well play with my audience by generating assumptions early on in my sentence that I go on to undermine later in the sentence; indeed, much of humor works in this way.

[Fink (2004), p. 90]

54 Žižek (2012), p. 296.
55 Ibid., 535.
56 Slavoj Žižek, *The Puppet and the Dwarf: The Perverse Core of Christianity* (Cambridge, MA: MIT Press, 2003), pp. 68–70.
57 Jeanne L. Schroeder and David Gray Carlson, "Does God Exist? Hegel and Things," *Journal of the Unconscious*, 4 (2004), p. 1.
58 See David Gray Carlson, *A Commentary on Hegel's* Science of Logic (Basingstoke: Palgrave Macmillan, 2006), p. 48; Jeanne L. Schroeder and David Gray Carlson, "Law's Nonexisting Empire," *University of Miami Law Review*, 56 (2003), p. 2482.
59 G.W.F. Hegel, *Elements of the Philosophy of Right* (Cambridge: Cambridge University Press, 1981), p. 69.
60 Schroeder (2008), p. 43 (paraphrasing Lacan, Seminar I).
61 Lacan, Seminar III.
62 William P. MacNeil, *Lex Populi: The Jurisprudence of Popular Culture* (Stanford: Stanford University Press, 2007), p. 59.
63 Jeanne L. Schroeder, "The People's Court: A Review of MacNeil, *Lex Populi*," *Cardozo Legal Studies Research Papers* (2008), citing MacNeil (2007), p. 59.
64 Jeanne L. Schroeder, *The Triumph of Venus: The Erotics of the Market* (Oakland: University of California Press, 2004), pp. 286–290.
65 Lacan formalizes ordinary neurotic fantasy as $\$ \lozenge a$ – the barred subject has a relationship to the object cause of her desire. Perversion reverses this: $a \lozenge \$$. The pervert thinks he is the object cause of another's desire. Slavoj Žižek, *Looking Awry: An Introduction to Jacques Lacan through Popular Culture* (Cambridge, MA: MIT Press, 1991), p. 234.
66 Indeed, it is precisely the pervert's certainty about the law, and the hysteric's doubts, that differentiate the former from the latter. Slavoj Žižek, *The Ticklish Subject* (London: Verso, 1999), pp. 248–249.

Chapter 10

Afterword to transgression

Laurent de Sutter

Subversion and Co.

On 9 July 1962, in a room of the Laennec Hospital in Paris, Georges Bataille died to almost general indifference, the indifference usually reserved to the creators who prefer to deploy their work far from the labile excitations of the time.[1] A year later, in the pages of *Critique*, the magazine that he founded at the Editions du Chêne in 1946 and which was to resume at Editions de Minuit in 1949, some of those for whom Bataille's work did not deserve such indifference met at the time of a special issue.[2] There were Georges Delteil, Alfred Metraux, Michel Leiris, Raymond Queneau, André Masson, Jean Bruno, Jean Piel, Maurice Blanchot, Pierre Klossowski, Roland Barthes, Jean Wahl, Philippe Sollers – and Michel Foucault, who signed a text with an enigmatic title: "Preface to Transgression."[3] Foucault, at that time, was hardly better known than Bataille: after many difficulties, he had just published, at Plon, his *History of Madness in the Classical Age*, his second book, to which neither newspapers nor universities had paid more than polite attention.[4] It was the same with the other contributors to the issue: the homage paid to the founder of the magazine was the homage of personalities that history had not yet established as major figures of the literary and theoretical subversion appropriate to modernity. Moreover, as was shown with Foucault's text, it was not certain that such a canonization would have pleased them – they who, wrote Foucault, had found, in the work of Bataille, what they needed in order to do away with the easy terrors as well as with the cheap chills of subversion.[5] The magnitude of Bataille was that of a motion which, if it did not allow doing away with philosophy, still allowed doing away with the figure of the philosopher as bearer of the wisdom of the truth which would define its "clear and talkative identity."[6] This motion, Foucault argued, was precisely that of "transgression": that of what he called the "passage to the limit" of language and of the philosophical gesture that is supported by it – limits that the logic of subversion dreamed of breaking, whereas transgression was rather about "crossing" or "carrying" them.[7] Transgression is the motion by which we are brought to the limit of our consciousness, our language, and the law, the motion by which we never cease "to cross again and again a line that, behind (it), immediately closes as a wave of little memory, going backwards again to the horizon of the impassable."[8] This was what Foucault discovered in Bataille, and what he shared with the other authors of the issue number 195–196 (August–September 1963) of *Critique:* the idea that our relationship to the limit was not the horizontal relationship of frontal struggle but the vertical relationship of its extensive envelopment. Subversion was the dream of destroying the limit, whereas transgression was merely about *twisting* it, about turning it around in a game rendering it powerless through, like a cartoon magician, the intensification of the spiralling motion of envelopment in which it grabbed it and carried it.[9]

Ontology of the ruin

Against the philosophical tradition that established the truth of the philosopher as the category of subversion of all limits, the whirling thought of Bataille offered another possibility: that of acceptance – the acceptance of the fact that *there are limits.*[10] But the fact that there are limits does not imply that they compel us; on the contrary, the existence of limits is the very condition of any motion of transgression – that is to say, of any motion trying to give them intensity beyond the fact of their existence. A few months before Jacques Lacan eventually published his article on "Kant with Sade," Foucault had proposed a similar formula: Immanuel Kant was the one who affirmed the existence of the limit – an existence immediately intensified by Sade's sexual transgression, *the latter allowing the former.*[11] Without transgression, the limit is only a dead fact; it is a reality whose intensity can never, by itself, exceed the nullity of that of any state of fact as such – if you prefer: the nullity of any state of fact as it is a truth. Kant's truth of the finite and of the limit received some life only because of the Sadean transgression by which this limit was immediately overridden, enveloped and twisted, that is to say *fucked,* since that was precisely the name of Sade's motion, as well as that of Bataille. Just as Gilles Deleuze, in *Presentation of Sacher-Masoch,* talked about the Sadean art of "défoncement," Foucault saw in the work of the Divine Marquis the manifestation of an art of panic of the logic of foundation, of grounding, that no longer needed to go through its critique to take effect.[12] As grounding was always already without ground, limit was always already transgressed; strictly speaking, it was limit of nothing but itself, a pure form without content, a pure sign without meaning, a pure marker of a forever formal finitude. According to Foucault, it was this eternity of transgression, its eternal primacy, that the work of Bataille acutalized at the time of the death of God – and of which, unlike Sade, he offered the instruments of language likely to provide its adequate experience.[13] Whereas the architectures of the transgression of the limit developed by Sade incessantly replayed (and continued to rely on) the possibility that there was a subject, the language ecstasies of Bataille provided accounts of its disappearance or collapse. While there was a subject, it was not the limit as such that transgressed itself, but someone, somewhere, who inaugurated a battlefield trying to stage the limit as if it were an enemy to shoot from afar – from a point that was external to it. With Bataille, the limit became the subject itself, and vice versa; it was simply the empty name by which something remained from the subject becoming the limit transgressing the limit, and activating, under the mode of ecstatic intensification, its own spiraling motion. *The subject is a ruin* – a few shreds standing together only because of other shreds coming from language, and living only through the possibility that these fragments could still be shredded more, until passing to the limit by which they will finally lose their being.[14]

On the obscenity of life

Bataille's philosophy was therefore an anti-philosophy: it was the philosophy of the orgasm in which philosophy sank, sucked by the beyond that the limits it had set defined as its repulsive, unacceptable, obscene counterpart.[15] However, as noted by Foucault, this abyss was not second; it was first – transgression was opening rather than closing, creation rather than destruction, dawn rather than twilight, and beginning rather than end.[16] When, in turn, he decided to consider transgression as one of the major operators of his conception of law, Slavoj Žižek, too, though he almost never mentioned Bataille, suggested the same thing: for him, transgression came first.[17] It was not law that raised the limit of all things; it was not it that defined the separate territories of the authorized and the prohibited, the acceptable and the criminal; of this separation it was, itself, the *derivative product*, the epiphenomenon. Contrary to what St. Paul had claimed, there is no transgression because there is first a law defining a limit to transgress – just as there are limits only because something like an arch-transgression has set them.[18]

The relationship of the transgression to the limit, as the law constitutes the always singular and always local identity card, is a dual relationship, a dance – a dizzying dance, danced above the abyss, following an infinite motion of spiral, of spin. The primacy of transgression is not temporal: it is an intensive primacy; transgression is what intensifies the limit beyond zero; it is what gives the law an object that is not zero, flat, insignificant, or indifferent. Compared to the intensive nullity of the limit expressed in the law, transgression offers an infinite supplement: that of all the above or below zero intensities – all the intensities that can be modulated in more or less. This is the supplement that the law echoes every time it tries to formulate something like a possible occurrence of the limit – as a variation resulting from the spiraling motion by which transgression envelops it. The obscenity specific to law was therefore, for Bataille, the one specific to the limit as transgression intensified it: the more important the transgression was, the greater the obscenity limit itself became more important – and the more this magnitude was reflected in the law. If there was a primacy of transgression, it was in that this motion carried with it, in the same abysmal and obscene dance, the limit and the law, to which it gave life while withdrawing it from them – or rather, of which it *was* the life as it was withdrawing from them. Transgression was the life of law, the life of limit; it was what, by removing them from death, inscribed them to its register, as death constituted, so to speak, their natural environment, their ecology; it was what came to confer to death something like the grimace of life. Such was the nature of the obscene supplement that transgression came to bring to the limit and to the law in the motion of intensification at the heart of which they were taken: the supplement of life as the supreme obscenity in the face of death.

A controversy on exception

Although he agreed with Bataille's idea, according to which transgression enjoyed a sort of primacy within the capture device uniting it with the law and the limit, Slavoj Žižek did not defend the same conception of obscenity as the one that was at work within it.[19] In a way, one could even say that he shared the reluctance expressed by Gilles Deleuze against the idea of transgression – though, perhaps, this reluctance manifested itself in his work in a very different, more ironic, form. In his *Dialogues* with Claire Parnet, Deleuze described transgression as "too good a concept, good for seminarians under the rule of a pope or a priest, for cheaters," that is to say all those feeding on the very French worship for "dirty little secrets."[20] In his eyes, transgression, despite the fact that it twisted the law, was still whatever it might say or do under its conceptual ferule – it still was a part of the castrating machinery of the law and of its culture of resentment. Transgression, if you prefer, was the form that took resentment in order to give itself the impression that it was making the law dance, while it was the latter that remained the center of all of the former concerns and fantasies (the concept that Deleuze hated the most).[21] Obviously, Žižek, for his part, did not share the reservations expressed by Deleuze with regard to the concept of fantasy – nor did he share his deep-seated refusal to give any consideration to the law whatsoever. However, what he had in common with Deleuze was a form of suspicion raised against the kind of obscure omnipotence that Bataille recognized in transgression, in that it claimed to overcome the law even before it existed or was conscious of it.

The primacy of transgression, for Žižek, should be formulated in a subtler way than that of Bataille: the obscene supplement that it manifested was of a less vertiginous, less abysmal nature than he thought. According to Žižek, as he wrote, for example, in *The Puppet and the Dwarf*, transgression was "the very exception that sustains the Law"; "(Transgression) is the very intimate resistant core on account of which the subject experiences his relationship to the Law as that of subjection; it is that on account of which the Law has to appear to the subject as a foreign power crushing the subject."[22] The spiral described by Bataille, rather than a motion, became a point of view: the point of view of the observation satellite by which an individual lying on Earth suddenly realizes how his situation is framed, normalized, defined by the law. Unlike what was the case in Bataille, transgression, according to Žižek, is not a stranger to the law – or, at least, it does not constitute the original dimension of strangeness at the heart of law, the dimension in which the law would live a non-null life. No. Transgression *is* the law; the intensive obscenity of life that envelops the limit exposed by the law constitutes its true essence; it determines what Žižek calls its " 'normal' functioning."[23] This is to say that *it is its dimension of subjection itself*.

The duff up theorem

To consider transgression as a perspective on the law belonging to the law itself, and not as a radical exteriority putting it always already in crisis, it was necessary to make a jump: that of epistemology – and of the policy that accompanies it. For Žižek, knowledge is not that which is achieved through a direct confrontation with reality – or, rather, knowledge that is obtained in this way belonging to the realm of academic sterility, the realm of knowledge at its most frozen, at its steepest, at its most violent. Just as Foucault said of Bataille, what is interesting is not direct confrontation with reality: it is rather to make reality *spill the beans* by panicking it to the point where it unveils the default to the armor of knowledge with which it bards itself. The knowledge that Žižek seeks is, if you will, a kind of "non-knowledge" (to use another concept of Bataille), the knowledge of a truth always escaping from the massiveness of identity that the big machineries of knowledge try to assign to it. This is not a coincidence: the place where Bataille's doctrine of "non-knowledge" was forged is also the place where the Lacanian doctrine of truth as "*mi-dite*" (or "half-truth") was forged – Lacan who, as everyone knows, followed with Bataille the classes that Alexandre Kojève, replacing Alexandre Koyré, gave at the Ecole des Hautes Etudes.[24] In the vocabulary of Žižek, however, the doctrine of non-knowledge or half-truth involves a device of perception: knowledge or truth belonging more to the order of the sensitive than to the order of the intelligible – to the order of the image more than to that of concept. This is why, in his recent work (starting with *The Parallax View*), Žižek has embarked on the development of something of a new strategy, whose name precisely is "parallax view," the biased vision.[25] Rather than the frontal gaze, knowledge, in the negative form whose object would be half-truth itself, can only be obtained by a sideways glance, by vigilance with regard to what happens at the extreme margins of the field of vision and, usually, is abandoned there. Parallax is the strategy of vision by which the parasites of vision, the signs unrecognized in advance as signifiers, carry with them all of what there is to see elsewhere – it envelops them with a supplement ruining the pre-ordained claims to meaning. If you prefer, parallax is a strategy similar to the one that the theoreticians of Russian formalism tried to define with the word "defamiliarization," and that one could formulate approximately as an attempt to see what is otherwise rather than what it is.[26] *What is never is what it is*: the tautology of being that was defended by the university is what the strategy of "parallax view" defeated, replacing it with a kind of dehiscence in which the spectacle that being presents becomes that of a *duffing up*. But it was precisely in this that, for Žižek, the transgression operated: it duffed up the being of the limit and of the law – that is to say, it embodied the parallax view by showing their essential inadequacy to themselves, inadequacy of which it was the name.

To end up with love

The central paradox of the understanding of transgression and the law suggested by Žižek was as follows: transgression was what ruined the claim of the law to identity – but, in ruining this claim, it also offered its only possible foundation.[27] Indeed, it was clear that, as Deleuze said of Sade, this was an ungrounded foundation, a grounding without ground in the metaphysical sense; it nevertheless remained that there was, thanks to transgression, something like a possible foundation to the law. It was necessary to argue by contradiction, and to imagine the hypothesis according to which the law would succeed one day in presenting to the world an image that would be consistent with its being: this hypothesis was the very name of the most horrible nightmare – the one illustrated in the novels of Franz Kafka, for example.[28] A law that would be Law in the most transcendent sense would be a strictly unlivable, insufferable law; it would be an inhuman law, or at least a law from which humanity would have been expelled only to leave behind it what Victor Hugo called the "frowning over the sun," the eyebrow of God. The parallax of transgression was therefore the point of view from which one could see the separation of the law and the Law (e.g., in Kant, the separation of positive law and moral law), that is, the separation of the law relative to transgression itself. For it was the dimension of the Law, in its ogresque transcendence, that was embodied by transgression, and that, by incarnating it, it made possible to see as active in the heart of the concrete law of legislation, of what Žižek called, using quotation marks, " 'mere legality.' "[29] In truth, the "mere legality" does not exist: there is legality only as *passed through* by transgression as the embodiment of the majuscule Law – the Law of which Žižek also said, pushing further his reading of St. Paul, that one of the possible names was that of Love.[30] What makes the law unbearable is not the fact that it is the law: it is the fact that it is Love – or, rather, that it is enveloped by the unlivable supplement of Love, a Love whose inhuman demands could never be satisfied. So the laws embodying the Law (such as the maxims of the Kantian moral law) are laws aiming at establishing nothing more than the overall culpability of all subjects, a pure culpability without fault, without action and without intention.[31] There were two faces of the law: the adequate, inhuman, and unbearable face of the Law, being both Love and transgression; and the inadequate, human, and laughable face of the law, as failure of Love and of its inexorable appetite. The first of these faces was that of authenticity, where the second was that of the inauthentic – but, contrarily to what we had learned from the philosophical tradition, it was the inauthentic that was, for Žižek, the only possible (that is to say impossible) foundation of the law in its ordinary sense. It was useless to seek a truth of the Law, except to experience that this truth, by collapsing under its own obscenity, eventually designates its opposite as a fairer truth – that is, the half-truth that the law is the very place of inauthenticity and of its awkward dance.

Law's nothing

To the anti-philosophy of transgression developed by Bataille and praised by Foucault, Žižek opposed, in his twisted and indirect way, an anti-philosophy of law whose almost stubborn pragmatism made Bataille's pathos ridiculous. Because it was indeed a kind pragmatism: demonstrating the equation by which Law, transgression, and Love balanced one another, it was in the daily, mundane, and imperfect remainder of its motion of spin that he finished by delivering the ambiguous eulogy. Much more than the great organ of the moral law, or the Dionysian laughter of the Grand Transgressor, it was the frowning of the official who eventually embodies the almost ideal face of the law – as could be the case in Hegel's *Philosophy of Law*.[32] Perhaps, however, it all could be summarized as a war of trenches: that between two possible readings of Hegel, one inherited from Kojève and paradoxically twisting the text towards Nietzsche; and the other, on the contrary, inherited from Lacan and twisting the text, equally paradoxically, towards Kant. Whereas Bataille considered the law from the standpoint of the abstract universal (and its ruin), Žižek considered it from the point of view of the concrete universal – from the daily operations whose dailiness was the only possible connection to the absolute. The law was, for him, a kind of contradictory refuge whose violence of subjection did not depend on itself but on the obscene supplement that prevented it from being itself, and without which it proved to be a delicate almost nothing. *The law is a nothing* – anyway, if anything, it is not this violent monster that some theoretical traditions passing through the twentieth century (traditions that an easy reflex could lead to connect to Žižek) claimed that it was. Or rather, if it was a violent monster, it was insofar as its "normal" functioning was immediately seized and invested by a supplement conjuring its normality and turning it into a nightmare, as evidenced by the example of administration. For Žižek, it was indeed the insignificant public servant driving his interlocutor crazy, coming to obtain this or that form and not ever getting it, that best embodied this unbalanced amphiboly of law, both small mundane machine and fussy love monster.[33] One will never get a love gesture from a public servant; always, we will end up in default with respect thereto; at the same time, this defect also is the failure of the law on which the public servant himself bases him- or herself – this defect is what frees us to be in default. But this scene, as everyone has experienced it, is a comic scene; it even is, in many ways, the paradigm of every comic scene – an almost too obvious illustration of the famous definition of what arouses laughter given by Henri Bergson.[34] The mechanical encrusted on the living: this could be a definition of administration – except that, contrary to what Bergson thought, it is not the mechanical that is the obscene supplement causing laughter, but life itself (as, on another hand, Bataille had perfectly understood it).

After critique

Once he had published "Preface to Transgression," Foucault only seldom returned to Bataille's thought: just as it had occupied him in the first years of his work, its usefulness for him seemed to shrink with the development of his own thought.[35] To the pathos of transgression and the law, and to the massiveness of the logic of illegality it illustrated, Foucault preferred to substitute the clinical coldness of an analysis of small "illegalisms," as Deleuze called it in the little book that he devoted to his colleague.[36] Yet despite this shift from "molar" to "molecular," the deflation of the concept of law proposed by Foucault (or Deleuze) always inscribed itself within the possible horizon of its ruin: the law, in a dark, not thematized, way, remained the enemy. Moreover, Foucault (and Deleuze) were not the only ones to have engaged in such a move; Louis Althusser, Jean-François Lyotard, Jacques Derrida, Pierre Bourdieu, and many others from so many disciplines were also working towards a systematic critique of the law.[37] While this critique may eventually have led to unexpected openings, such as the amazing clinic of law developed by Deleuze, the inaugural moment of the theory of law was produced by this generation of thinkers – and by their disciples. The surprise that could be caused by the additional twist suggested by Žižek should be even greater since, often, his work has been described as being involved in the tradition that, concerning law, had made anti-legalism its motto. In fact, Žižek's anti-philosophy of law is not an anti-legal anti-philosophy; rather, it is anti-philosophy as it is anti-legalistic – it rises against the obscene omnipotence of Law acting in the heart of the law, the Law that so many philosophers have defended. This was the case, among others, with the philosophers of anti-legalism: their criticism of the law was to take place only in the name of another law, as superior as it is secret, which would come to redeem its nullity and that philosophy alone could formulate. One only had to think of the laws of historical materialism in Althusser, for example, or the law of infinite justice in Derrida, or the law of the face in Levinas: in all these cases, it is about redeeming the concrete law by an abstract Law. Žižek's proposed path, on the other hand, is the opposite: it consists, in a convoluted way, in redeeming the abstract Law by the concrete law – the former existing only through the latter, but ruining it by the mere fact that it provides its own existence to it. From this point of view, Žižek's anti-philosophy of law is a theory that reverses both the various doctrines of liberalism (from Habermas to Rawls through Lefort) and those of anti-liberalism, as represented by those that we continue to wrongly call "poststructuralist." To both camps, it opposes something like a banality: it replaces the theater of the Law, of the *lex*, by the domesticity of what one finally has to call with its own name – that is, the name, the "grave and beautiful name," as Françoise Sagan (the writer of the end of the story, according to Kojève) put it of sadness, that is the name of *ius*.

Notes

1 Michel Surya, *Georges Bataille, la mort à l'oeuvre*, 2nd edn, Paris, Gallimard, 1992.
2 *Critique*, "Tribute to Georges Bataille," No. 195–196, August–September 1963. On this issue and its place in the history of the journal, see Sylvie Patron, *Critique (1946–1996). Une encyclopédie de l'esprit moderne*, Paris, IMEC, 1999.
3 Michel Foucault, "Postface à la transgression," *Critique*, *loc. cit.*, pp. 751ff. The text was included in Michel Foucault, *Dits et écrits. I. 1954–1975*, ed. D. Defert and F. Ewald, Paris, Gallimard, 2001, p. 261; then was published separately as Michel Foucault, *Postface à la transgression*, Paris, Lignes, 2012. This is the edition that will be mentioned from now on, abbreviated as PT.
4 Michel Foucault, *Histoire de la folie à l'âge classique. Folie et déraison* Paris, Gallimard, 1972. On the reception of this work and its various editions, see the biography of Foucault by David Macey, *Michel Foucault*, trans. P.-E. Dauzat, Paris, Gallimard, 1994.
5 PT, p. 19.
6 PT, p. 31.
7 PT, p. 8. The canonical presentation of the concept of transgression is given in Georges Bataille, *L'érotisme*, Paris, Minuit, 1957, pp. 71ff.
8 PT, p. 16.

9 PT, p. 18.
10 PT, p. 16.
11 PT, p. 20.
12 PT, p. 20.
13 PT, p. 25.
14 PT, p. 26.
15 For a definition of anti-philosophy, see Alain Badiou, *Le séminaire. Lacan. L'antiphilosophie 3. 1994–1995*, ed. V. Pineau, Paris, Fayard, 2013, *passim.*
16 PT, p. 35.
17 Slavoj Žižek, *The Puppet and the Dwarf: The Perverse Core of Christianity*, Cambridge, MA, MIT Press, 2003, pp. 110ff, hereinafter abbreviated as PD. For a different but concurring view with the one presented here, see Jodi Dean, *Žižek's Politics*, London, Routledge, 2006, pp. 135ff.
18 PD, pp. 111ff. On the Žižekian interpretation of St. Paul, and its differences with those of Alain Badiou and Giorgio Agamben, see Adam Kotsko, *Žižek and Theology*, London, Continuum, 2008, *passim.*
19 PD, p. 113.
20 Gilles Deleuze and Claire Parnet, *Dialogues*, 2nd edn, Paris, Flammarion, 1996, p. 58.
21 Ibid., p. 59. For a commentary, see Laurent de Sutter, "The Law and the Maiden: A Short Introduction to Legal Pornology," *New York Law School Law Review*, 2012, vol. 57, pp. 125ff.
22 PD, pp. 116–117.
23 PD, p. 113.
24 Elisabeth Roudinesco, *Jacques Lacan. Esquisse d'une vie, histoire d'un système de pensée*, Paris, Fayard, 1993, pp. 125ff.
25 Slavoj Žižek, *The Parallax View*, Cambridge, MA, MIT Press, 2006, *passim.*
26 Victor Shklovsky, "Art as Process," in Tzvetan Todorov, *Théorie de la littérature. Textes des formalistes russes*, Paris, Seuil, 1965, pp. 76ff.
27 PD, p. 117.
28 PD, p. 120.
29 PD, p. 120.
30 PD, p. 114.
31 PD, p. 120. Cf. Gilles Deleuze, *Présentation de Sacher-Masoch. Le froid et le cruel*, Paris, Minuit, 1967, pp. 72ff. For a discussion, see Laurent de Sutter, *Deleuze. La pratique du droit*, Paris, Michalon, 2009.
32 PD, p. 120. We still need a detailed study of Žižek's sustained dialogue with Hegel's *Philosophy of Law*, a dialogue that has undergone major changes between *Le plus sublime des hystériques. Hegel passe*, Paris, Point Hors Ligne, 1988 (reissue Paris, PUF, 2011), and *Less than Nothing: Hegel and the Shadow of Dialectical Materialism*, London, Verso, 2012.
33 PD, p. 120.
34 Henri Bergson, *Le rire*, ed. Sibertin G. Blanc, Paris, PUF, 2011.
35 Francis Marmande, "Ceci n'est pas une préface," in Michel Foucault, PT, pp. 85ff.
36 Gilles Deleuze, *Foucault*, Paris, Minuit, 1986.
37 For an example, see the contributions collected in *Althusser and Law*, ed. Laurent de Sutter, London, Routledge, 2013.

Chapter 11

Sonorous law II

The refrain[1]

Anne Bottomley and Nathan Moore

Part one

To the extent that it makes a systematized appearance in his work, Žižek considers law to be an institutional issue. The possibility of, for instance, both contract and convention are subsumed within this institutional framing, so that the humour we might associate with contract, and the satire of convention, disappears into a generalized irony of the institution.[2] This irony is apparent in two interlocking ways. First, the irony of the institution sets before us a choice to be made, but with the understanding that what will be chosen will not be selected through anything like free will; because there is, truly, only one option, inevitably and necessarily. Second, that what it is in any case impossible to do must be prohibited as such, precisely because it is impossible. These are the twin poles of the legal institution: a choice that is no choice, and the prohibition on what it is impossible to do. Through these devices, a legal subject is secreted by the institution in such a way that both can indulge themselves in the appearance of free will (seemingly holding the capacity of choice)[3] and of possessing a possible omnipotence or fusion with the real (since powers are only limited by prohibition).[4]

This is well demonstrated in Žižek's example of the institution of marriage, which is concerned not to strip away the twin "illusions" of choice and fusion but rather to reconcile those who commit themselves to it, and thereby to those "illusions." This is crucial for two, again interlinked, reasons: first, that the institution of marriage allows the subject(s) to transcribe their desire within the symbolic realm and thereby give desire its proper form or structure, and inevitably so; and, second, that the idea of transgressing the institution is revealed as a naive and futile gesture that takes all too seriously the possibility of fusing with the object of desire beyond the constraints of what marriage prohibits. Consequently:

> public proclamation is what marriage is ultimately all about: a symbolic commitment, not just an expression of our (fluctuating) emotions – in the marriage ceremony, one makes a vow, one gives one's

> word.... So, although one should, of course, defend the right to divorce, one should nonetheless insist that marriage should be conceived of as valid forever and essentially indissoluble: if divorce occurs, it does not mean that a marriage is simply over but rather and more radically that the marriage never really existed.[5]

Žižek, rightly in our view, rejects any radical or critical possibility so far as transgression is concerned, a point he reiterates in this collection.[6] Rather, the radicalness of marriage, as Žižek presents it, lies in its rejection of the possibility of the big Other: the big Other does not exist as a completed or whole unity, which can condone and legitimate by seeing, in the sense of recognizing and thereby registering, the married couple.[7] This is why the public pronouncement of marriage is so important: it is a proclamation necessitated by the point that there is no gaze *to see* the marriage bond, and thereby legitimate it externally, from without. Rather the proclamation comes from within the bond, as a sort of puncture or a resounding Badiouian fidelity. At the same time, he argues, one does not, cannot, join with the big Other by "breaking out" of marriage. This emphasizes an important point: not only is transgression no weapon when it comes to fighting capitalism; rather transgression is the capitalistic weapon *par excellence*, inasmuch as it discards fidelity and activates irony, not as the necessary condition of and for world-making but as the excuse to *unmake* the world by refusing the compulsion of any possibility for commitment or responsibility.

Curiously, in making this crucial point, Žižek follows, to the letter, the teaching of Deleuze and Guattari. Under control (or axiomatic capital[8]), breaking out of institutions and confinements is no longer the problem, because this is exactly the agenda of control as it sets about freeing us so that we might finally become self-determining, under such rubrics as "getting in touch with the real thing at last." Control operates by breaking institutions open.[9] Deleuze and Guattari's concept of the apparatus is key here, for thinking of how to respond to such breakings open (and down).[10] However, for his part, and in an explicitly legal register, Žižek suggests a sort of supra-institutional *right* of distress, a right to protest or revolt, a superior law.[11] In this, Žižek seems to coincide with Sade,[12] but also – and more problematically – it seems little more than an inversion of Schmitt's famous formula, such that the "sovereign is he who decides on the right of distress." The institution becomes suspended in the light of a decision about when, where, and how to seize the vital, material necessities for life (along with, of course, the decision about what constitutes such necessities). In this sense, it is a de-institutionalizing gesture, but one which is not aligned with the purposes of control; rather, it is self-evident, an irrefutable, "of course" responding to the dilemma of those who do not have enough to sustain themselves.

However, this notion of (a right to) distress, to the extent that it exemplifies that tickling object[13] which brings the institutionalized subject "face-to-face" with the uncanny, with that which is apparently lacking in the institution, calls for a preparatory question: does the form of law determine the form of the institution, or *vice versa*? Which comes first, the law or the institution? Of course, they come together, and it is perhaps not too trite to point out why: both law and institution share, along with the unconscious (to which they are both isomorphic), the fact of being structured like a language. In this sense, to be given the choice to do what is inevitable corresponds to a pole which we might call metaphoric; while prohibiting what is impossible can be considered as metonymic.[14] It then seems as if we do, indeed, choose one link in the chain rather than another (a decision as the substitute for the other decisions which could have been made), and that we could achieve a complete signification if only we were not prohibited from doing so (that our power could otherwise extend throughout the chains of signification).

Considering the institution in this way – as being structured like a language – then encourages us to ask: how is it that the subject is related to the institution? What is the point of linkage between subject and law? It is the parallax view, the *object petite a* which ties body to law, while being absent from both. This is why Žižek is clear that it is not enough to simply gather up perspectives, because one cannot add institutions up to arrive at a complete super-institution, and neither can one simply "break out." The parallax view is unavoidable, even if we imagine that is does not exist. It is this which impels the metonymic-metaphoric binding of the institution, so that the subject might then gain the decisive imaginary-symbolic screen in front of which it can then claim that the *object* does not exist.

If this is so, then law is to be diagrammed in the following way: the institution and the subject are "connected" by way of the *object petit a*, which belongs to neither of them. The institution operates between two poles: metaphor (the illusion of free choice) and metonymy (the illusion of omnipotence). These two poles allow the subject to exist as such, and the institution "holds" the subject, providing a *katechon* warding off the diabolic forces of the *object*. The parallax view can then be taken as that moment of dislocation when the *object* (as it were) comes into view, revealing not the secret knot or connection between subject and institution but rather their alterity, their mutual misrecognition of each other and thus of themselves. Mladen Dolar relates this specifically to the anomic state of exception and, as noted above, it seems right to us that the present diagram corresponds with that of Schmitt's, and the expansion made upon this by Agamben.[15]

It therefore seems that everything is set up so as to expel the virtual: on the one hand, the exclusion of choice is necessary so that the very undecidability at the heart of the decision is warded off; while on the other, the imperative to decide at the heart of omnipotence is kept at bay. What do we mean by "the virtual" in this context? Simply and crucially: the difference which is not lacking. Why is this important? Because it allows for a thinking of law that is not limited to the state of exception. For us, this is an essential movement of stepping back from a critical legal brink: law is not the big Other which either condemns or frees us. Rather, it is an assemblage of operations, and only if we grasp this do we begin to understand the full insight of Foucault's point that, in the eighteenth century, law became a tactic – a means to an end.

To formulate and underscore this point, we proceed by way of music. This may seem, initially, counter-intuitive. However, it becomes less so if, for the purposes of this analysis, we understand there to have been three epochs of law, sequential and yet nevertheless existing simultaneously, which can be considered as marked by a certain musicality or, better, *refrain*. Thus, just as there is classical, romantic, and modern music, so too there is classical, romantic, and modern law. The thesis of our chapter is simple: the majority of critical legal scholars have not yet thought law, been able to think law, in its modern register. The main symptom of this failure is an obsession with the origins and founding of law, sometimes encoded as "legal ontology." We are tempted to refer to scholars still fixated on origins as legal romantics, but we can only do so by pointing out that Schmitt was both right and wrong to define the romantic as incapable of any meaningful decision or action.[16] Without doubt, the legal romantic resides in the realm of discussion and representation, focused upon the never-ending (because undecidable) debate regarding the law's origin; yet it is not quite right to say that action is subsequently necessarily absent, or even that the actions taken are the "wrong" or most ineffective actions. Rather, it is a question of romantic relations or territory, and this is why it is useful now to turn to "the refrain."

Part two

Classical law – leaving to one side the rather unfortunate similes that proliferate between music and architecture – can be thought of as architectural in the sense that it involves a firm hierarchy of interdependence between norms, the relations of which are organized according to the requirements of good proportion and balance, and grounded on solid foundations. Unsurprisingly, it is best typified by the point at which it begins to become undone, to deterritorialize, in Kantian legalism. It is, in fact, a constant tension between imposing a firm order on relations, the classical, and the deformation of order by relations, the baroque (Kant and Kafka).[17] However, this doubled movement does not undermine anything but rather provides the necessary twin poles through which the classical (and the baroque) are able to function as such: one must decide according to the proper procedures, while the illusion of omnipotence is warded off by the internalization of infinity through the monad. The romantic appears at that point when the foundations themselves are called into question, as if the present foundations were merely arbitrary and as if either an alternative foundation might be available or there is a deeper, more truthful foundation, repressed and concealed by that which is currently presented as foundational. We can see then why Schmitt is wary of this romance, to the extent that any decisive act related to the present foundation is de-legitimated in advance, irrespective of its efficacy or effect. From such a perspective, all acts become mere representations or, even, simulacra.

However, we do not consider the romantic to be necessarily ineffectual and withdrawn, even though *he* is in constant danger of so becoming. Deleuze and Guattari describe two elements of romanticism which we are predisposed to look benignly upon. First, romanticism, by uprooting the foundations, institutes a new kind of movement, one no longer pulsing or throbbing in the deformations of the baroque, but a vector which constantly sweeps back and forth across the earth, always gathering and distributing plots and shares in the name of a universal humanity. Second, the romantic calls forth a new people.[18] To be clear, it does not institute or found a new people but rather points to the absence of a people (we might even say, a "community") through the act of calling forth. That is, the romantic evidences the necessity of deterritorialization as the condition of any territory.[19]

It follows from this that the romantic is not quite as ineffectual as Schmitt would have us believe: there are romantic acts to the extent that new distributions are carried out, and the consistency of a territory is maintained through that which escapes it. In more familiar legal terms, this latter point is well illustrated by the relationship between the normal and the abnormal: as a statistical assemblage, derived from mass observations of itself, the population is constantly redistributed between the poles of the normal and the abnormal, precisely because the former can only be extracted from the latter.[20] Schmitt is correct to understand this as a challenge to the form of the decision as he understands it, but he is wrong to consider it as not forming a new type of decision, a new possibility for action.

With this in mind, we can return to Žižek and ask: what is the difference between the *object petit a* and the refrain? The short answer, in the musical register, is timbre: that is, the concreteness of sound, its presence. However, this is not presence in the way in which we might like to imagine that the big Other can be made present through some "act" of transgression. Nor, and more importantly, is it the uncanny glimpse of the *object* around which the institution gravitates, as if around a tiny black hole of lack. Rather, the concreteness of timbre requires us to reformulate the idea of presence, in complete detachment from the pairing of presence–absence. Consequently, it is a disappointment that Žižek's account of music focuses only upon opera, emphasizing its libretto and narrative; further, to the extent that the music itself is discussed, it is as no more than a counterpoint to the libretto and, even more problematically, only in the registers of melody and harmony. Remaining in the domain of the word, Žižek does not reach (out to) the sense of music. Consequently, he is in danger of being that kind of romantic criticized by Schmitt who, unable to act, simply proposes a "deeper" law (such as a right of distress).

Part three

If we understand rhythm to be a pulse in time, then timbre cannot be dissociated from rhythm: they are always in a reciprocal relationship. The representation of sound through the Fourier transform evidences this: "the timbre of a sound is constituted by the regularities that define it." By regularity, we must understand the change in wavelength over time, such that it is the contraction of time, in listening, which gives the frequency or pitch of the sound. More than this, the shape of the wavelength gives the quality of the sound – the sound of a violin, of a snare drum, and so on. This shape is also of time, so that timbre is always pitched. The Fourier transform is the representation and analysis of timbre through a decomposition of the complexity of the shape of the wave. It is evident that timbre (and pitch) are themselves of time, of pulse, and thus of rhythm.[21] Furthermore, if we consider timbre through the Fourier transform, what also becomes evident is that sound can be understood as a sort of auto-interference: the composition of waves into a specific shape and timbre suggests that timbre results from an internal divergence or difference from (within) itself. In this we begin to understand, again, Deleuze and Guattari's point about the connection between the refrain and the territory, inasmuch as the territory is constituted by that which escapes it (lines of flight).[22] At the same time, territory is never any-territory-whatever, but is always specific or consistent. Differing from itself does not cause it to become "anything at all" but rather to become a specific quality, affect, or perception contracted from, and in, movement.

In a different key, the ramifications of this have been admirably set out by Jean-Luc Nancy, and it is in his account that we can begin to understand a concept of a presence other than that formulated in the presence–absence pair. Nancy's initial distinction is between hearing and listening: the sound of the voice is both heard (and understood) and listened to and, in the latter, not so much understood as strained towards, as if the ear were trying to reach the sense of sound. Significance is carried by sound, but the latter remains distinct, not being insignificant or even meaningless but directional, in movement – a question of *sense*. Just as for

Deleuze there is sense outside of the triad of denotation, signification, and manifestation,[23] so too for Nancy there is a sense which resounds as the condition of meaning typified by the sonorous. However, the direction of this sense is, perhaps, rather chaotic inasmuch as it rebounds, echoes back on and into itself, such that sense is first and foremost spacing, the vibration of an environment that would have to be thought of as ecological. Sense is the difference that makes a difference.[24]

Nancy writes:

> Approach to the self: neither to a proper self (I), nor to the self of an other, but to the form or structure of *self* as such, that is to say, to the form, structure, and movement of an infinite referral, since it refers to something (itself) that is nothing outside of the referral. When one is listening, one is on the lookout for a subject, something (itself) that identifies *itself* by resonating from self to self, in itself and for itself, hence outside of itself, at once the same as and other than itself, one in the echo of the other, and this echo is like the very sound of its sense. But the sound of sense is how it refers to *itself* or how it *sends back to itself* or *addresses itself*, and thus how it makes sense.[25]

The sonorous courses through a circuit which involves the ear, the vibration of the air, and the space of the vibration as well as its duration. Analytically, we can isolate each point in this circuit, but we must not think that they are simply ready-made components that are then slotted into their proper positions, for that would be the more structural arrangement of meaning as differential referral. Rather, the sonorous circuit emerges only from the mutual implication of each of these points in a shared resonance, not as pure sound but as a jumble of waves and interferences, so that sound coincides with itself, and interferes with itself. Again, it is possible to understand this in the abstract, as an address that is transmitted and then received (the relationship of signal to noise), but the point is that it cannot occur in the abstract: sound needs its materiality, its ecology, its territory. The refrain is always concrete.

Is it then just a matter of lapsing into a naive notion of presence? This is the particular value of Nancy's account for us: it is not the imagined presence of the big Other, but the concrete structure of presence, of a presencing:

> This presence is thus not the position of a being-present: it is precisely not that. It is presence in the sense of an "in the presence of" that, itself, is not an "in view of" or a "vis-à-vis." It is an "in the presence of" that does not let itself be objectified or projected outward. That is why it is first of all presence in the sense of *present* that is not a being ... but rather a *coming* and a *passing*, an *extending* and a *penetrating*.[26]

This presence is not contrasted with absence – it is not either here or there (nowhere) – but rather, it is the presencing of the possibility of the present–absent difference, the concrete possibility of meaning. If we stay with the idea of spacing, sound (which is only heard in its jumble of interferences) is a sort of folding that brings into contact, short-circuits, that which seems held apart as a vibration that runs through bodies and is transformed by them in the process, while also transforming them. At the same time, the echo of sound is never heard in the instant but comes and goes, rising and falling, in contractions of time and the "shape" of the sound. This is timbre, the material space–time of sound.

Part four

What enables us to hold that sound, the refrain, is something different to *object petit a*? Here, we need to consider how music is different from the voice. Dolar's investigation of the object voice in *A Voice and Nothing More*[27] is exemplary; however, for us, an ambiguity runs throughout his account: the ambiguity of the difference between voice and music. It is as if sound must, from the psychoanalytical perspective, remain all-too-human, so that music itself is reduced, in distinction to the object voice, to mere aestheticization, to fetishism. However, the difference between voice and music needs to be pushed further, because only then is it possible to escape what we might call the bad (or weak) romance of critical legal studies: that is, the fixation on the origin.

Of course, psychoanalysis recognizes the dependence of meaning upon the voice, and Dolar's account begins from the point at which the voice outlives the meaning it conveys; as something that does not simply do "good work and die," but rather persists even after meaning has been conveyed. The voice "produces a remainder which cannot be made a signifier or disappear in meaning; the remainder that doesn't make sense, a left-over, a cast-off – shall we say an excrement of the signifier?"[28] This is excrement on the run, set loose as the impossible juncture of body and language, subject and Other, *phone* and *logos*, *zoe* and *bios*. The voice binds both elements together, while being of neither of them. This is voice as *object petit a*, as parallax view which, institutionally, separates the poles of decision and omnipotence. It seems as if we are close to the resounding space-time described by Nancy, particularly when Dolar writes, of the pre-symbolic scream:

> it appears that we are dealing with a voice external to structure, yet this apparent exteriority hits the core of the structure: it epitomizes the signifying gesture precisely by not signifying anything in particular.... For the signifier in general, as such, is possible only as a non-signifier.[29]

Post-symbolically, the singing voice serves only to conceal the voice by clamping it into "intense attention" and "aesthetic pleasure."[30] However, Dolar rightly holds that the musical voice is more ambivalent than this; that music "evokes the object voice and obfuscates it; it fetishizes it, but also opens the gap that cannot be filled."[31] What Dolar is pointing to here is what Deleuze and Guattari call the refrain: that is, the *affect* of music. This affect is the constitution of the territory, the binding of the institution, the spacing of the echo. It is the specific, concrete presencing which is not a question of filling the gap but rather of "gapping," creating the gap through the resounding space-time of the echo. However, within the register of psychoanalysis, it could appear that we remain caught within our own fetishes in asserting this – as if we could take decisions and do whatever we have not been prohibited from doing. In short, it seems as if we are narcissists by insisting upon the refrain, by insisting upon the musical voice over and above the object voice.[32]

However, this is only the case if a particular understanding of affect is heard. Specifically, if affect is caught as the supplement to meaning, it remains the thing that, up to a point, can carry meaning and even reinforce it but that, if carried too far, if strained towards too much, threatens to undermine meaning, to explode out of the structure of negative referral. Dolar illustrates the point well by reviewing the more or less constant fear of music evident throughout history; however, he does so by a creating an equivalence between music and voice, as if they were the same thing. Dolar is aware that music should, in analytical terms, be treated differently; yet he always comes back to a consideration of music as either aesthetic fetishization or, as with his more sustained account of the fear of music, by making it indistinguishable from voice:

> music, *and in particular the voice*, should not stray away from words which endow it with sense; as soon as it departs from its textual anchorage, *the voice* becomes senseless and threatening – all the more so because of its seductive and intoxicating powers.[33]

Music of itself seems to offer a dangerous and excessive (non)meaning within the psychoanalytical account, a point underscored precisely by the fact that music is understood only in contrast to language: it is either *pre-* or *post-*symbolic. The structure-like-a-language here seems inevitable, and it is no coincidence that the paradigmatic form of music for Dolar, as it is for Žižek, is opera. However, a formula subsequently put forward by Dolar strikes us as potentially more interesting, and we will return to it below: law is structured less like a language, and more as a *lalangue* or llanguage. For the moment, it is enough to say, here, that we are interested in this potential only on condition that music is not "beyond the word,"[34] but rather understood and valued as a logic of its own, as the spacing refrain or, perhaps, to adopt another configuration of Dolar's, as a matter of "the voice against the voice."[35]

Part five

The acousmatic voice – the voice which has no visible source – is directly linked to the law. Not knowing where it comes from, the voice without source takes on the role of source: its origin-less-ness is the condition for it becoming (treated as if) an origin. Its very hiddenness to the eye constitutes its authority: to hear is to obey.[36] The psychoanalytic formulation suggests something else: that there is a silence of the voice, more profound than that of the invisibility of its source, such that we might say that there is a silence of the ear that outweighs the silence of the eye. This point is a point of divergence for us. For psychoanalysis, the silence of the ear is not simply the excrement of the signifier, the voice that survives its message; rather, it is something *non-sonorous*, an echoing silence that returns in response to the word, in response to, and – crucially – as the result of, the symbolic, *after* the signifier. Nevertheless, the non-sonorous here reverberates, keeping open the non-coincidence of language and body.[37] In this, we would argue that psychoanalysis remains romantic, the non-sonorous reverberation being the silence of the big Other, calling for a new foundation, a new beginning, and a future to come. This is not to say that it is the bad or weak romance of the origin fixation – in fact, in Dolar's account, this is precisely not the case: the opening of silence is the silence of the people *who do not yet exist*. It is, therefore, the potential redistribution, the founding of a new earth, which is that which Deleuze and Guattari characterize as central to the ethos and logic of the romantic. Nevertheless, a divergence for us is necessary because we do not wish to remain caught in the romantic, even in its "good" or stronger form. Rather, for us, it is a question of becoming modern, and here we must return to philosophy.

Nancy's account of silence tends to another direction. For him, silence is not non-sonorous, but is, rather, "still a sonority – or, if you prefer, an arch-sonority."[38] Silence is "an arrangement of resonance,"[39] which is nothing less than the differing of timbre from itself, the auto-interference by which it is shaped as a specific sound, a particular spatio-temporal arrangement. It is presencing, or the present silence achieved when the difference of the present-absent pair is silenced. This presence is the straining to hear, the expectation of sense (consistency) that is concrete because it carries the potential to incorporate:

> The possibility of sense is identified with the possibility of resonance, or of sonority itself. More precisely, the perceived possibility of sense ... is overlaid with the resonant possibility of sound: that is, when all is

> said and done, with the possibility of an echo or a return of sound to self in self.[40]

This means that voice and music cannot be quickly aligned. While the object voice might be the silence of the signifier, this does not displace a sort of primacy of the sonorous, of a refrain, which assembles elements together into a territory, a territory which will be crucial if a subject is to be seen and heard. For this reason, Nancy refuses to let the sonorous be treated solely as something "left-over" from meaning, after the signifier. If silence is a resonance (not non-sonorous), this is because what sounds is always first something concrete, meaning that it is always, necessarily, in the middle of things.[41] How it breaks, and what it breaks, is dependent entirely upon the territory and its refrains. Nancy is explicit:

> going once again toward music … without letting ourselves be restrained by a primacy of language and signification that remains dependent on a whole onto-theological prevalence and even on what we can call a philosophical *anesthesia* or *apathy*.[42]

It is as if there were only a chaos of sound, of an infinite interpenetration of sonorities, towards which there is only, first and foremost, straining to listen and, through this straining, a selection, a subtraction from chaos, so that a territory might be formed – the universe not as celestial harmony but as discordance, even a detuniverse, from which a refrain is pulled out: not simply as something uncanny, as a merely structural point of impossible conjunction (*object petit a*), but rather as the possibility of sense, the echoing back of what sense will or can be. To be clear: not anything at all, not omnipotence, or even a choice; but a compulsion or seizure. The refrain, in its specificity, makes things resonate.

Part six

At this point we remain romantic, inasmuch as the refrain is, itself, the calling up of a people to come and the distribution of new resonances and vibrations. At what point, then, does the refrain become modern? When it is no longer a new earth – a new foundation – to be called forth, but the forces of the cosmos, which are to be captured.[43] This is not a move into a non-differentiated "wholeness," nor the illusion of the profundity of transgression, but the refining of materials and techniques, a sort of minimalization through which the specific is put into touch with the universal.[44] As Deleuze and Guattari point out, this is a question of technique, of developing, distilling, and filtering practices so that, we might say, the arch-sonorous might be heard. What is modern is to listen for, and to render audible, the sonority of the echo itself:

> Music molecularizes sound matter and in so doing becomes capable of harnessing nonsonorous forces such as Duration and Intensity. *Render Duration sonorous.* Let us recall Nietzsche's idea of the eternal return as a little ditty, a refrain, but which captures the mute and unthinkable forces of the Cosmos.... If this machine must have an assemblage, it is the synthesizer ... [which] makes audible the sound process itself, the production of that process ... its synthesis is of the molecular and the cosmic, material and force, not form and matter, *Grund* and territory.[45]

To begin with the concrete, with what is to hand, is to no longer seek to redistribute or re-found but to experiment, to subject the concrete materiality to stresses, breakdowns, re-combinations, and so on, in order to see what can be captured or harnessed: "To be an artisan and no longer an artist, creator, or founder, is the only way to become cosmic, to leave the milieus and the earth behind."[46]

For this reason, it does not seem to us that Žižek is right when he contrasts Schoenberg with Webern. That is, it is not enough to say that to be modern is to have done with the big Other:[47]

Although Schoenberg, already totally resigned to the fact that no actual public can directly respond to his work, still counted on the symbolic fiction of the one purely hypothetical, imagined listener, which was needed for his composition to function properly, Webern renounced even this purely theoretical supposition and fully accepted that there is no big Other, no ideal listener for him.[48]

In accepting that there is no big Other, we must accept that the institution does not function from the outside in, through the imposition of choice and prohibition; rather, it is a question of the object voice, the tiny black hole of the *object petit a*, that arranges elements around itself, not as the first term, but as that left-over, uncanny silence through which the non-sonorous reverberates. This need not be the bad weak romance of a fixation on origins (although we do consider that Žižek's theorization of the right of distress sees him become a weak-bad romantic), but it is, nevertheless, romantic. This is to say nothing about either Schoenberg or Webern but rather that, in problematizing composition with reference to the listener – whether it be the last listener or the absent one – Žižek remains within the realm of the earth, of redistributing forces and calling forth a new people (the listener(s) to come).[49]

Part seven

The romantic *nomos*, to seek the founding of a new earth and its distributions and enclosures, is not an inherently bad thing. But consider whether, rather than an artist or creator, what we need today, especially in legal theory, are artisans: that is, modernists. We noted above that, for Schmitt, the romantic condition was marked by an inability to act. Rather than a complete absence of decision, the romantic, in this formulation, has decided in favor of interminable discussion, deferred revolution, and a sort of idealized withdrawal from the reality of the world. The romantic seems overcome, consequently, by the basis of decision – what would, what could, legitimate action? Schmitt's solution is, of course, well known to every critical legal scholar – it is the exception that "grounds" the decision, being both interior and exterior to the right (or rather, the ability) to decide. We have already noted Dolar's linking of the voice to the Schmittian exception, and it is worth returning now to that in some detail. Dolar writes:

> The letter of the law, in order to acquire authority, has to rely, at a certain point, on the tacitly presupposed voice; it is the structural element of the voice which ensures that the letter is not "the dead letter," but exerts power and can be enacted. … *the voice is structurally in the same position as sovereignty*, which means that it can suspend the validity of the law and inaugurate the state of emergency.… The emergency is the emergence of the voice in the commanding position, where its concealed existence suddenly becomes overwhelming and devastating.[50]

When things are normal, the voice functions to breathe life into the otherwise dead letter of the law. The voice is heard, but nobody listens to it. The emergency is then the reversal of this, inasmuch as the law ceases to be heard, and one begins to strain to listen for it. Precisely, such a listening, in this circumstance, is the calling forth of a new earth: the sudden perception of the territory as lacking any support, of the law becoming ungrounded or even dethroned. If so, then we return to an earlier point, but now reversed: the notion of the exception is inherently romantic. This is why we argue that critical legal scholarship, to the extent that it remains within the compass of the Schmittian exception (whether consciously or not), is romantic. This is particularly so in the case of the espousal of rights and, even more so, in a focus on "radical" rights, such as Žižek's right to distress, or a right to resist or revolt, or a right to the city, and so on. To the extent that such murmurings are heard through the void at the heart of the institution of law, that is, heard, here and in this case, through the silent object voice of *petit object a*, then we must contend that the legal *object* is romantic, and not modern. For what the *object* does is to raise up the question of the foundation, and thereby articulate towards the possibility of a new foundation, of a foundation "yet to come." It is the weak romance of a short circuit between *object petit a* and the big Other.

If we limit ourselves to the silent, non-sonorous reverberation of the object voice, perhaps things are not so bad: we find ourselves to be the recipients of the mute excess of our own institutional discourse. However, what if the reverberation is not silent, what if it is the very echo of what comes back to us, the clearing of the space-time in which we present ourselves as subjects? What if silence is not non-sonorous, but in fact the presencing of the concrete in its possibilities, that is, the echoing of timbre? Then we are faced with a decision: either a choice for the problem of legitimacy, and the assertion of a superior right to come (the weak-bad romance), or the choice for a Spinozist power that is not content to simply call forth a new earth, or to even redistribute powers, but rather insists on the need to investigate what a body can do. This is the choice for the modern which, quite clearly, is not necessarily "distinct" or separate from the romantic, but which quickly comes to operate (requires it to operate) within its own register: resonating through the refining of techniques and the developing of artifices, focussing ever more minutely on the molecules of space–time (the cosmic), and thereby fashioning from these new arrangements and new combinations. It is the difference between, on the one hand, an abstract process of transcendental withdrawal (as in the gesture of romance) and, on the other, of an immanent world-making (the modernist capture of the cosmos in a territory).

To that end, the problem is not where to begin, but how to engage with what is already happening, to listen to that which already resounds. This requires a new training of the ear, so that we can begin to hear the timbre of those concrete artifices that are so rife in areas such as property law, contracts, intellectual property, and so on. What we find through an engagement with the sonorous is that sound does not wait for an origin, for a foundation or legitimation, before it "begins" to resound. It is caught up in a constant becoming-timbre, which activates both the possibility of the romantic as well as, crucially, that of the potential of the modern. If the modern has not yet been fully grasped – at least in the register of (a) legal hearing – it is because the techniques necessary to achieve it have not yet been developed. Critical legal scholarship has remained caught within the romantic imaginary: seeking new pasts, rather than creating futures, we can expect it to become increasingly fixated with its own archiving.

We do not finally agree that law is structured like a language, because the big Other is not, finally, our issue. We prefer to say that it is structured like llanguage [*lalangue*], inasmuch as there is a concrete remainder to the signifier; although, how this remainder arises, and how it operates institutionally, we can follow only so far. Not the non-sonorous reverberation for us, but rather the arch-sonority of the echo. We draw close to Dolar when he writes:

> The antinomy of the signifier and the voice, which we have been pursuing from the outset, thus turns into the inner divergence [of *lalangue*] which precludes the separation of the signifier versus voice,

with the consequence that we can no longer isolate the signifier on the basis of "it speaks."[51]

Yet it is still a matter of internalizing a difference, a lack. The voice penetrates the signifier as a function of the present–absent pair, creating an impossible and interminable circuit. It is a game of the ideal (signifier) and the material (voice). However, for us, it is necessary to push further, to strain towards virtuality and the presencing of the present–absent pair: it is not a question of silence coming back, of its uncanny and mute reverberation in "response" to our words, our questions; but rather how silence sounds at the limit of (in)audibility, how it catches things up in a becoming-inaudible. We must, in this, understand silence as a matter of selection, of rendering (in)audible, and of unfolding at the point where the solution is not yet known, where further work is required, where a sense remains to be fabricated or "artisaned." Before voice and signifier, there is musicality, the refrain.

If the signifier leads to a sort of disablement, inasmuch as it raises, inevitably, the silence of what was not said, of what could not be en-acted, then there hangs over all language the spectre of what could not be, the impossibility which, precisely, must be prohibited.[52] We are therefore led, continuously, to think in terms of presence–absence. Yet the silence of the arch-sonority is different inasmuch as it comes first, as a great block of white noise, from which arrangements, refrains, and decisions are extracted. This is what the artisan does: not content to call forth a new earth and a new people (that is, to hear the silence of the signifier; the strong romanticism), it is a matter of extracting and making consistent another concept, affect, or function. However, we must be careful, because consistency does not mean essence, or identity, or lack of change. Rather, consistency is the duration of an affect, in both space and time, against the chaos-cosmos of arch-sonority which, at this point, we can usefully consider as white noise. Here, silence is a doubled movement of subtraction, in that one begins with the pure perception[53] of white noise as the resounding and concrete silence of the virtual; and then it is also the extraction of a cosmic force, through the silencing of what is (too) chaotic: that is, the silencing of silence. In truth, it is never one and then the other, but both simultaneously: there is a folding of silence, in the same way as there is a folding of metal for the blacksmith, and a folding of sound (echoes) for the musician.

Hence the significance of the synthesizer for Deleuze and Guattari.[54] More specifically, it is the analogue synthesizer which is crucial here, due to its subtractive functioning. It begins with a block of sound from which frequencies and harmonics are subtracted in order to leave an affective sound, a sound resonant to the territory in which one operates, either as "reinforcement" (forming a territory) or escape (leaving the territory) or, of course, both simultaneously. By filtering and using specific envelopes to *shape* sound, what is actually happening is that a sonority (a refrain) is being extracted from the chaos-cosmos of silence (or white noise): "What is added from one filter to the next are intensive subtractions ... it is thus an addition of subtractions."[55] The refrain is the result of this "addition of subtractions," so that, in each subtraction, a small piece of the cosmos is harnessed to a particular spatio-temporal sonority. It is a question of following the refrain, of finding those points of subtraction that can be made relevant or active, giving the sound a consistent and affective timbre, or force, overall. Extracting by adding subtractions, or presencing the present–absent pair – they are the same process.

Part eight

The link between the decision and the exception, and the resulting weak-bad romanticism of the origin, is only necessary when the decision is located in the realm of the romantic. Then it inevitably becomes a question of asking: who can decide? On what basis is there authority to decide? To what does the decision refer back? What is the decision meant to achieve? Schmitt needs the category of the exception at that point at which the older legitimations of the earth are ceasing to function, the point at which it becomes impossible to consider oneself as an autochthon. However, while hearing the call, Schmitt refuses to become modern, instead seeking to re-ground the law in a new earth, a new *nomos*. Therefore, to the extent that the modern appears in Schmitt's work, it is to be warded off – as the *nomos* of the sea (to an extent), the air, and finally of the astronautical.[56] In distinction, for us, to be(come) modern is to forge the astro-song, the cosmic refrain – in law, it is therefore a question of forging and following the astronomos.

We must have done with the exception as a romantic category, whether in the form of the sovereign or of those who "oppose." The category of the decision must be de-linked from the problematizations of legitimacy and intention, from the continued return of the foundation. Most crucially, these problematizations cannot be used to artificially limit the consequences of decisions, as if certain outcomes were to be considered merely as "externalities," or "side-effects," or as "unintended." In such cases, it is always a matter of referring the decision back to the point of its deciding, as if this point were its only flash of existence, and its sole explanation. In such an operation, the decision is like the *object petit a*, and everything becomes an interminable question of the signifier and the voice, as Dolar clearly shows. No, now it is the consistency of decisions which must be encountered, their spatio-temporal resonances, their refrains, their territories and lines of flight. The modernist *follows* decisions, not in the sense of automatically applying them again and again (in which case there is no need to follow the decision because it doesn't go anywhere), but of extracting potentialities, new affects, new possibilities of life. To what extent can decisions be extended or varied, when and where must they be cut back and circumvented … at what point does counterpoint become a completely new key center?

Rather than a "law story," it might be better to think of a "law score," but even this runs into difficulties to the extent that the score might be considered as, reduced to, a representation. More to the point, it is a question of dealing with law-sonorities, with concrete blocks, that are never decided once and for all, but which echo constantly, giving an ever varying legal timbre. Not a free-for-all, not a false choice, not a fusion, not the uncanny … not even a hearing, but just a listening.

Notes

1 This chapter extends a presentation and performance entitled *Sonorous Law I: Our Theme is Echo*, given at the Law and the Senses Conference, Westminster University, London, April 2013. Our thanks to Andreas, Andrea, Victoria, Danilo, and others at that conference.

2 For more on the humorous and ironic dimensions of the law, see Nathan Moore (2012), "Image and affect: Between neo-Baroque sadism and masochism," *New York School of Law Review* 57 (1), pp. 97–113.

3 Slavoj Žižek and Mladen Dolar (2002), *Opera's Second Death*, Abingdon and New York: Routledge, p. 112. It is at this pole that Žižek locates contract – see p. 113.

4 Žižek and Dolar (2002), p. 125:

> The true trauma is thus not the intervention of external reality, which interrupts the blissful immersion, but the inversion of this joy – objective reality intervenes to externalise the inherent impediment, to sustain the illusion that without its intervention the blissful immersion would have gone on to its ecstatic climax.

5 Ibid., p. 133.

6 Slavoj Žižek (2015), "The Rule of Law Between Obscenity and the Right of Distress," *Žižek and Law*, Abingdon and New York: Routledge.

7 Žižek and Dolar (2002), pp. 221–223.

8 See Anne Bottomley and Nathan Moore (2012), "Law, Diagram, Film: Critique Exhausted," *Law and Critique* 23 (2), pp. 163–182.

9 Moore (2012).

10 Bottomley and Moore (2012).

11 Žižek (2015).

12 Moore (2012).

13 Slavoj Žižek (2009), *The Parallax View*, Cambridge, MA: MIT Press, p. 17.

14 Lorenzo Chiesa (2007), *Subjectivity and Otherness: A Philosophical Reading of Lacan*, Cambridge, MA, and London: MIT Press, Chapter 2.

15 Mladen Dolar (2006): *A Voice and Nothing More*, Cambridge, MA: MIT Press, p. 119.

16 Carl Schmitt (1991), *Political Romanticism*, trans. G. Oakes, Cambridge, MA: MIT Press.

17 Heinrich Wofflin (1964), *Renaissance and Baroque*, trans. K. Simon, London: Collins. In this sense, it is interesting, in musical terms, to imagine a sort of short circuit, by which Bach enters into direct relation with his true successors:

Reich, Glass and Riley. See also Gilles Deleuze and Felix Guattari, *Capitalism and Schizophrenia: A Thousand Plateaus* (1988), trans. B. Massumi, London: The Athlone Press, p. 338; and Anne Bottomley (2010), "Lines of Perspective, Lines of Flight: Belly of an Architect," *Cardozo Law Review*, 31 (4), p. 1055.

18 Beethoven, obviously, but also more recent artists, such as John Coltrane (from *A Love Supreme* onwards), or even the Mahavishnu Orchestra. We would contend that dubstep also falls within the category of the romantic, as opposed to the more cosmic (and modern) expression of drum and bass, calling forth as it does an urban landscape in which the people are lacking. The crucial point is that the romantic is concerned with a sort of musical *nomos* of the earth. For the differences between Schmitt's understanding of *nomos*, and that of Deleuze and Guattari, see Moore (2012).

19 See Deleuze and Guattari (1988), pp. 340–341. Such deterritorialization is well evident in Schubert's *Die Winterreise*, as well as Britten's *Billy Budd*, to pick two examples. Importantly, in both, the score does not serve to support or contextualize the voice, but precisely begins to unground it, always threatening to send it skittering across the surface of the ice or sea. In *Beau Travail*, not only does Claire Denis bring the deterritorialization vectors in *Billy Budd* to the fore, she also uses the work as one element in her film, thereby extracting, and harnessing, extra-territorial forces, of which more below.

20 See Nathan Moore (2013), "Diagramming control," in P. Rawes, ed., *Relational Architectural Ecologies: Architecture, Nature and Subjectivity*, Abingdon: Routledge; and Francois Ewald (1991) "Norms, discipline, and the law," in R. Post, ed., *Law and the Order of Culture*, Berkeley: University of California Press. In the register of Deleuze and Guattari's language, we would need to speak of the abnormal as becoming-minor.

21 Aden Evans (2005), *Sound Ideas*, Minneapolis: University of Minnesota Press, pp. 2–5.

22 Deleuze and Guattari (1988), pp. 508–510.

23 Gilles Deleuze (1990), *The Logic of Sense*, trans. M. Lester and C. Stivale, New York: Columbia University Press. See, in particular, "Third Series of the Proposition."

24 Gregory Bateson (1972), *Steps Towards an Ecology of Mind*, London: University of Chicago Press.

25 Jean-Luc Nancy (2007), *Listening*, trans. C. Mandell, New York: Fordham University Press, p. 9.

26 Nancy (2007), p. 13

27 Dolar (2006).

28 Ibid., p. 20.

29 Ibid., pp. 28–29.

30 Ibid., p. 30.

31 Ibid., p. 31.

32 See the discussion of narcissism, ibid., pp. 39–41.

33 Ibid., p. 43. Our emphases.

34 Ibid., p. 50.

35 Ibid., p. 55.

36 Ibid., pp. 62–63.

37 Ibid., pp. 160–162.

38 Nancy (2007), p. 29.

39 Ibid., p. 21.

40 Ibid., pp. 29–30.

41 See Nathan Moore (2012) "The Perception of the Middle," in L. de Sutter and K. MacGee, eds, *Deleuze and Law*, Edinburgh: Edinburgh University Press.

42 Nancy (2007), p. 30. Italics in the original.

43 Deleuze and Guattari (1988), p. 342. We consider the cosmos, in distinction from the earth, not as a foundation, from which good proportion and aesthetic pleasure might rise up (as so many redistributions and plots), but as a complex of seething forces, constantly passing through each other. The cosmic is self-organizing non-linearity: formations, patterns and assemblages in movement, which nevertheless have specificity. See M. Mitchell Waldrop (1992), *Complexity*, London: Penguin Books, pp. 65–66; and Anne Bottomley and Nathan Moore (2008) "Blind Stuttering: Diagrammatic City," *Griffith Law Review* 17 (2), pp. 559–579.

44 "He's trying to get further out (more abstract) and yet more basic (funkier) at the same time": drummer Tony Williams referring to Miles Davis's "electric" period, as related in the biography of Davis by Ian Carr, and quoted in Colin Harper (2014), *Bathed in Lightning*, London: Jawbone, p. 344.

45 Deleuze and Guattari (1988), p. 343. We might well imagine other forms of "modern" music in this sense, with perhaps the extended techniques of free improvisation being an obvious contender. However, the perils of collapse, in the face of the cosmos, are such that perhaps at least a degree of composition is usually necessary, irrespective of whether this exists as written passages or agreed directions prior to performance, or editing post-performance.

46 Ibid., p. 345.

47 Žižek and Dolar (2002), p. 221.

48 Ibid., pp. 221–2.

49 Admirably, for this reason, Žižek remains resolutely Wagnerian.

50 Dolar (2006), p. 120. Italics in the original.

51 Ibid., p. 144.

52 Or, through *lalangue*, a silence to at least be enjoyed: ibid.

53 See the discussion of Bergson in Moore (2012).

54 See Deleuze and Guattari (1988).

55 Gilles Deleuze (2004), *Francis Bacon: The Logic of Sensation*, trans. D. Smith, London: Continuum, p. 117.

56 Carl Schmitt (1997), *Land and Sea*, trans. S. Draghici, Washington: Plutarch Press.

Postscript

The rule of law between obscenity and the right to distress

Slavoj Žižek

The obscene underside of the law

According to legend, Alfred Hitchcock (himself a Catholic) was once driving through a small Swiss town. All of a sudden, he pointed his finger at something through the car window and said: "This is the most terrifying scene I've ever seen!" A friend sitting at his side looked in the direction pointed out by Hitchcock with surprise: there was nothing remarkable out there, just a priest who, while talking to a young boy, put his hand onto the boy's arm. Hitchcock halted the car, rolled down the window and shouted: "Run, boy, save your life!" While this anecdote could be taken as a display of Hitchcock's eccentric showmanship, it does bring us to the "heart of darkness" of the Catholic Church – how?

Ritualized violence

Let's take a short detour. One of the terrifying effects of the non-contemporaneity of different levels of social life is the rise of the violence against women – not just random violence, but systematic violence, violence which is specific to a certain social context, follows a pattern, and transmits a clear message. While we were right to be terrified at the gang rapes in India, the worldwide echo of these cases is nonetheless suspicious – as Arundhati Roy pointed out, the cause of this unanimous outburst of moral outrage was that the rapists were poor, from the lower strata. So, perhaps, it would be commendable to widen our perception and include other similar phenomena. The serial killings of women in Ciudad Juárez at the border with Texas are not just private pathologies but a ritualized activity, part of the subculture of local gangs (first gang rape, then torture to death which includes cutting off nipples with scissors, etc.), and directed at single young women working in new assembling factories – a clear case of the macho reaction to the new class of independent working women.[1] Even more unexpected are serial rapes and murders of aboriginal women in Western Canada, close to reservations around Vancouver, belying Canada's claim to be a model tolerant welfare state: a group of white men abduct, rape, and kill a woman, and then deposit the mutilated body just within the reservation territory, which puts it legally under the jurisdiction of the tribal police totally unprepared to deal with such cases. When Canadian authorities are contacted, they as a rule limit their investigation to the native community in order to present the crime as a case of local family violence due to drugs and alcohol.[2] In all these cases, the social dislocation due to fast industrialization and modernization provokes a brutal reaction of males who experience this development as a threat.

And the same perverted social-ritual logic is at work in the cases of pedophilia which continuously shatter the Catholic Church: when the Church representatives insist that these cases, deplorable as they are, are the Church's internal problem, and display great reluctance to collaborate with police in their investigation, they are, in a way, right – the pedophilia of Catholic priests is not something that concerns merely the persons who happened to choose the profession of a priest because of incidental reasons of private history with no relation to the Church as an institution; it is a phenomenon that concerns the Catholic Church as such, that is inscribed into its very functioning as a socio-symbolic institution. It does not concern the "private" unconscious of individuals, but the "unconscious" of the institution itself: it is not something that happens because the Institution has to accommodate itself to the pathological realities of libidinal life in order to survive, but something that the institution itself needs in order to reproduce itself. One can well imagine a "straight" (not pedophiliac) priest who, after years of service, gets involved in pedophilia because the very logic of the institution seduces him into it. Such an *institutional Unconscious* designates the obscene disavowed underside that, precisely as disavowed, sustains the public institution. (In the army, this underside consists of the obscene sexualized rituals of fragging etc. which sustain the group solidarity.) In other words, it is not simply that, for conformist reasons, the Church tries to hush up the embarrassing pedophile scandals; in defending itself, the Church defends its innermost obscene secret. What this means is that identifying oneself with this secret side is a key constituent of the very identity of a Christian priest: if a priest seriously (not just rhetorically) denounces these scandals, he thereby excludes himself from the ecclesiastic community, he is no longer "one of us" (in exactly the same way a citizen of a town in the South of the US in the 1920s, if he denounced Ku Klux Klan to the police, excluded himself from his community, i.e., betrayed its fundamental solidarity).

Consequently, the answer to the Church's reluctance should be not only that we are dealing with criminal cases and that, if the Church does not fully participate in their investigation, it is an accomplice after the fact; more than this, the Church as such, as an institution, should be investigated with regard to the way it systematically creates conditions for such crimes. That is to say, what makes these crimes so disturbing is that they did not just happen in religious surroundings – these surroundings were part of them, directly mobilized as the instrument of seduction:

> the seduction technique employs religion. Almost always some sort of prayer has been used as foreplay. The very places where the molestation occurs are redolent of religion – the sacristy, the confessional, the rectory, Catholic schools and clubs with sacred pictures on the walls. ... a conjunction of the overstrict sexual instruction of the Church (e.g., on the mortal sinfulness of masturbation, when even one occurrence of which can, if not confessed, send one to hell) and a guide who can free one of inexplicably dark teaching by inexplicably sacred exceptions. [The predator] uses religion to sanction what he is up to, when calling sex part of his priestly ministry.[3]

Religion is not just invoked in order to provide a *frisson* of the forbidden, i.e., to heighten the pleasure by making sex an act of transgression; on the contrary, sex itself is presented in religious terms, as the religious cure of the sin (of masturbation). The pedophile priests were not liberals who seduced boys by claiming that gay sexuality is healthy and permitted – in a masterful use of the reversal called by Lacan *point de capiton*, they first insisted that the confessed sin of a boy (masturbation) really is mortal, and then they offered gay acts (say, mutual masturbation) – i.e., what cannot but appear an even stronger sin – as a healing procedure. The key resides in this mysterious transubstantiation, by means of which the prohibiting Law which makes us feel guilty apropos of an ordinary sin is enacted in the guise of a much stronger sin – as if, in a kind of Hegelian coincidence of the opposites, the Law coincides with the strongest transgression. And is the present US politics, in its inherent structure, not a kind of political equivalent of Catholic pedophilia? The problem of its new moral vigor is not just that morality is manipulatively exploited, but that it is directly mobilized; the problem with its appeal to democracy is that it is not simply hypocrisy and external manipulation, but that it directly mobilizes and relies on sincere democratic strivings.

In the summer of 2012, there occurred in Slovenia an almost clinically pure display of the Catholic Church's obscenity. It involved two actors, the conservative cardinal Franc Rode, a Slovene with the highest place in the Church *nomenklatura*, and Alojz Uran, the archbishop who was first deposed by the Vatican and then even ordered to immediately leave Slovenia until accusations against him were clarified. Since Uran was very popular among Catholic believers, rumors started to circulate about the reasons for this extraordinarily harsh punishment. After a week or so of embarrassing silence, the Church authorities grudgingly proclaimed that Uran is suspected of fathering an illegitimate child – an explanation which, for a series of reasons, was met with widespread disbelief. First, rumors about Uran's paternity had circulated already for decades, so why did the Church not take measures years before, when Uran was nominated the archbishop of Slovenia? Second, Uran himself publicly proclaimed that he was ready to undergo DNA or any other tests to prove that he has no children. Last but not least, it is well known that, in the Slovene Church, a struggle has been going on for many years between conservatives (among them Rode) and moderates (among them Uran). But whatever the truth, the public was shocked by the double standards displayed by the Catholic *nomenklatura*: while Uran was ordered to leave Slovenia due to a mere *suspicion* of fathering a child, the reaction of the Church was infinitely milder in the numerous cases of pedophilia among the priests – the cases were never reported to the police, the responsible priest was never punished but just moved to another part of Slovenia, there was pressure on the parents of the abused children to keep things under the carpet, etc.[4]

What made things even worse was the open cynical "realism" displayed by Cardinal Rode: in one of his radio interviews, he said that "statistically, this is an *irrelevant* problem – one or at the utmost two out of hundred priests had a kind of adventure." What immediately drew the attention of the public was the term "a kind of adventure" used as an euphemism for pedophilia: a brutal crime of raping children was thus presented as a normal display of adventurous "vivacity" (another term used by Rode), and, as Rode quipped in another interview: "In forty-years time you would expect some small sins to occur, wouldn't you?" This is Catholic obscenity at its purest: no solidarity with the victims (children), what we find beneath the morally upright posture is just the barely concealed solidarity with the perpetrators on behalf of cynical realism (that's how life is, we are all red under our skin, priests can also be adventurous and vivacious...), so that, in the end, the only true victims appear to be the Church and the perpetrators themselves exposed to the unfair and malicious media campaign. The lines are thus clearly drawn: pedophilia is ours, our own dirty secret, and as such normalized, the secret foundation of our normality, while fathering a child is a true violation to be ruthlessly rejected – or, as G.K. Chesterton put it in his *Orthodoxy* a century ago (unaware of the full consequences of his words, of course):

> The outer ring of Christianity is a rigid guard of ethical abnegations and professional priests; but inside that inhuman guard you will find the old human life dancing like children, and drinking wine like men; for Christianity is the only frame for pagan freedom.

The perverse conclusion is unavoidable here: you want to enjoy the pagan dream of pleasurable life without paying the price of melancholic sadness for it? Choose Christianity! We can discern the traces of this paradox up to the well-known Catholic figure of the priest (or nun) as the ultimate bearer of sexual wisdom. Recall what is arguably the most powerful scene in *The Sound of Music*: after Maria escapes from the von Trapp family back to the monastery, unable to deal with her sexual attraction towards Baron von Trapp, she cannot find peace there, since she still longs for the Baron; in a memorable scene, the Mother Superior summons her and advises her to return to the von Trapp family and sort out her relationship with the Baron. She delivers this message in the weird song "Climb every mountain!," whose surprising motif is: Do it! Take the risk and try everything your heart wants! Do not allow petty considerations to stand in your way! The uncanny power of this scene resides in its unexpected display of the spectacle of desire, which renders the scene literally *embarrassing*: the very person one would expect to preach abstinence and renunciation turns out to be the agent of fidelity to one's desire. Today, with cases of pedophilia popping up all around in the Catholic Church, one can easily imagine a new version of the scene from *The Sound of Music*: a young priest approaches the abbot, complaining that he is still tortured by desires for young boys, and demanding further punishment; the abbot then answers by singing "Climb every young boy ..."

One has to draw a further distinction here, between adult male homosexuality and pedophilia. Recent outbursts of homophobia in East European post-communist states should give us pause to think: in gay parades which took place over the last years in Serbia and Croatia (Belgrade, Split), the police were unable to protect participants who were ferociously attacked by thousands of violent Christian fundamentalists – how to combine this wrath with the fact that the main force behind the anti-gay movement in Croatia is the Catholic Church, so well-known for numerous paedophile scandals? (A Croat gay activist sarcastically remarked how the error of the gays is that their partners are adult men and not children ...). A parallel with the army, the other type of organized crowd mentioned by Freud in the same series with the church, shows us the way. From my own experience of military service in 1975, I remember how the old infamous Yugoslav People's Army was homophobic to the extreme – when someone was discovered to have homosexual inclinations, he was instantly turned into a pariah, treated as a non-person, before being formally dismissed from the Army. Yet, at the same time, everyday army life was excessively permeated with the atmosphere of homosexual innuendo. How is this weird coincidence of the opposites possible? The mechanism was described by Robert Pfaller:

> As Freud observed, the very acts that are forbidden by religion are practiced in the name of religion. In such cases – as, for instance, murder in the name of religion – religion also can do entirely without

> miniaturization. Those adamantly militant advocates of human life, for example, who oppose abortion, will not stop short of actually murdering clinic personnel. Radical right-wing opponents of male homosexuality in the USA act in a similar way. They organize so-called "gay bashings" in the course of which they beat up and finally rape gays. The ultimate homicidal or homosexual gratification of drives can therefore also be attained, if it only fulfills the condition of evoking the semblance of a counter-measure. What seems to be "opposition" then has the effect that the x to be fended off can appear itself and be taken for a non-x.[5]

What we encounter here is a textbook case of the Hegelian "oppositional determination": in the figure of the gay basher raping a homosexual, the homosexual encounters himself in its oppositional determination, i.e., tautology (self-identity) appears as the highest contradiction. This is the immanent contradiction at the very core of the Church's identity, making it the main anti-Christian force today. Legend has it that when, in 1804, the Pope approached Napoleon to put the Emperor's crown on his head, Napoleon took the crown from his hands and put it on his head alone; the Pope quipped: "I know your aim is to destroy Christianity. But believe me, Sire, you will fail – the Church has tried to do this for 2000 years and still hasn't succeeded."

The prohibited prohibition

This inherent inconsistency of the ideologico-legal order is not limited to church institutions – one of its most conspicuous cases today is that of China. How do official communist theorists react when confronted with the all too obvious contradiction: a Communist Party which still legitimizes itself in Marxist terms, but renounces Marxism's basic premise, that of workers' self-organization as a revolutionary force in order to overthrow capitalism? It is difficult to avoid the impression that all the resources of the legendary form of Chinese politeness are mobilized here: it is considered impolite to directly raise (or insist on) these questions. This resort to politeness is necessary, since it is the only way to combine what cannot be combined: to enforce Marxism as official ideology while openly prohibiting its central axioms would cause the collapse of the entire ideological edifice, thereby rendering it meaningless. The result is thus that, while certain things are clearly prohibited, this prohibition cannot be publicly stated, but is itself prohibited: it is not merely prohibited to raise the question of workers' self-organization against capitalist exploitation as the central tenet of Marxism, it is also prohibited to publicly claim that it is prohibited to raise this question.[6] In this way, we violate what Kant called the "transcendental formula of public law": "All actions relating to the right of other men are unjust if their maxim is not consistent with publicity." A secret law, a law unknown to its subjects, would legitimize the arbitrary despotism of those who exercise it – compare with this formula the title of a recent report on China: "Even what's Secret is a Secret in China."[7] Troublesome intellectuals who report on political oppression, ecological catastrophes, rural poverty, etc., were sentenced to years of prison for betraying a state secret. The catch is that many of the laws and regulations that make up the state-secret regime are themselves classified, making it difficult for individuals to know how and when they're in violation.

This secrecy of the prohibition itself serves two different purposes that should not be confused. Its commonly admitted role is that of universalizing guilt and fear: if you do not know what is prohibited, you cannot even know when you are violating a prohibition, which makes you potentially guilty all the time. Except of course at the height of the Stalinist purges when, effectively, everyone could be found guilty, people *do* know when they are doing something that will annoy those in power. The function of prohibiting prohibitions is thus not to give raise to "irrational" fear, but to let the potential dissidents (who think they can get away with their critical activity, since they are not breaking any laws, but only doing what laws guarantee for them – freedom of the press, etc.) know that, if they annoy those in power too much, they can be punished at the power's will. In ex-Yugoslavia, the infamous Article 133 of the penal code could always be invoked to prosecute writers and journalists. It criminalized any text that falsely presented the achievements of the socialist revolution or that *might arouse tension and discontent among the public* for the way it dealt with political, social, or other topics. This last category is obviously not only infinitely plastic, but also conveniently self-relating: doesn't the very fact that you are accused by those in power equal the fact that you "*aroused tension and discontent among the public*"? In those years, I remember asking a Slovene politician how he justified this law. He just smiled and, with a wink, told me: "Well, we have to have some tool to discipline those who annoy us without worrying about legal niceties!"

But there is another function of prohibiting prohibitions which is no less crucial: that of *maintaining appearances* – and we all know how absolutely crucial appearances were under Stalinism; the Stalinist regime reacted with total panic whenever there was a threat that appearances would be disturbed: in the Soviet media, there were no black chronicles, no reports on crimes and prostitution, not to mention workers or public protests. This prohibiting of prohibitions is far from being limited to Communist regimes: it is also operative in today's "permissive" capitalism. A "postmodern" boss insists that he is not a master but just a coordinator of our joint creative efforts, the first among equals; there should be no formalities among us, we should address him by his nickname, he shares a dirty joke with us … but in all this, he *remains our master*. In such a social link, relations of domination function through their denial: we are not only obliged to obey our masters, we are also obliged to act as if we are free and equal, as if there is no domination – which, of course, makes the situation even more humiliating. Paradoxically, in such a situation, the first act of liberation is to demand from the master that he acts as one: one should reject false collegiality from the master and insist that he treats us with cold distance, as a master.... No wonder then that all this sounds vaguely Kafkaesque – Kafka effectively wrote that "it is an extremely painful thing to be ruled by laws that one does not know,"[8] thereby bringing out the implicit superego obscenity of the famous legal principle that "ignorance (of the law) is not an excuse."[9] Derrida is thus fully justified in emphasizing the self-reflexivity of the prohibition with regard to the Law – the Law not only prohibits, it is ITSELF prohibited:

> The law is prohibition: this does not mean that it prohibits, but that it is itself prohibited, a prohibited place ... one cannot reach the law, and in order to have a rapport of respect with it, one must not have a rapport with the law, one must interrupt the relation. One must enter into relation only with the law's representatives, its examples, its guardians. These are interrupters as much as messengers. One must not know who or what or where the law is.[10]

In one of his short fragments, Kafka himself pointed out how the ultimate secret of the Law is that *it does not exist* – another case of what Lacan called the inexistence of the big Other. This inexistence, of course, does not simply reduce the Law to an empty imaginary chimera; it rather makes it into an impossible Real, a void which nonetheless functions, exerts influence, causes effects, curves the symbolic space, and this curvature opens up the space for ideological manipulations, for turning the letter of the law against itself.

Save the appearances!

Here is an exemplary case of such manipulation: in a letter to *Los Angeles Times*, Kathryn Bigelow justified *Zero Dark Thirty*'s depiction of the torture methods used by government agents to catch and kill Osama bin Laden:

> Those of us who work in the arts know that depiction is not endorsement. If it was, no artist would be able to paint inhumane practices, no author could write about them, and no filmmaker could delve into the thorny subjects of our time.

Really? Without acting like abstract moralist idealists, and fully aware of the unpredictable urgencies of fighting terrorist attacks, should we not at least add that torturing a human being is in itself something so profoundly shattering that to depict it neutrally – i.e., to neutralize this shattering dimension – already *is* a kind of endorsement?

More precisely, the catch is: *how* is torture depicted? Since the topic is so sensitive, any kind of actual neutrality in the film's texture is here a fake – a certain stance towards the topic is always discernible. Imagine a documentary on the Holocaust depicting it in a cool disinterested way as a big industrial-logistic operation, dealing with the technical problems (transport, disposal of the bodies, preventing panic among the prisoners to be gassed …) – such a film would either embody a perverse and deeply immoral fascination with its topic, or it would count on the very obscene neutrality of its style to engender dismay and horror in spectators. Where is Bigelow here?

Definitely and with no shadow of a doubt on the side of the normalization of torture. When Maya, the film's heroine, first witnesses boarding, she is a little bit shocked, but she quickly learns the game – later in the film she coldly blackmails a high-level Arab prisoner with the threat "if you don't talk to us, we will deliver you to Israel." Her fanatical pursuit of bin Laden helps to neutralize any ordinary moral qualms. Much more ominous is her partner, a young bearded CIA agent who masters perfectly the art of passing glibly from torture to friendliness after the victim is broken (lighting his cigarette and sharing jokes). There is something deeply disturbing in how, later in the film, he smoothly changes from bearded torturer in jeans to a well-dressed Washington bureaucrat. *This* is normalization at its purest and most efficient – a little bit of uneasiness, more about hurt sensitivity than about ethics, but the job has to be done. We are therefore far from films like *Dirty Harry* or *Rambo* where a brutal vigilante macho hero tortures with obvious pleasure and a depraved smile. However, the very fact, underlined by many a critic, that Bigelow depicts torture as a disturbing experience which leaves a bitter taste (but only in Maya, not in her male partner-torturer who doesn't have any qualms), not as an activity done with sadistic pleasure, is what makes the film so problematic. This awareness of the hurt sensitivity as the (main) human cost of torture makes it sure that the film is not cheap Rightist propaganda: the psychological complexity is properly depicted, so that well-meaning liberals can enjoy the film without feeling guilty. This is why *Zero Dark Thirty* is much worse than *24*, where Jack Bauer at least breaks down in the series' finale.

As to the replacement of the word "torture" by "enhanced interrogation technique," one should note that we are dealing here with an extension of Politically Correct logic: in exactly the same way that "disabled" becomes "physically challenged," "torture" becomes "enhanced interrogation technique" (and, why not, "rape" could become "enhanced seduction technique"). The crucial point is that torture – brutal violence practiced by the state – was made publicly acceptable at the very moment that public language was rendered Politically Correct in order to protect victims from symbolic violence. These two phenomena are the two sides of the same coin.

The most obscene defense of the film is the claim that Bigelow rejects cheap moralism and soberly presents the reality of the anti-terrorist struggle, raising difficult questions and thus compelling us to think (plus, some critics add, she "deconstructs" feminine clichés – Maya displays no sexual interests or sentimentality, she is tough and dedicated to her task, like a man). Our answer should be that, precisely apropos a topic like torture, one should not "think." A parallel with rape imposes itself here: what if a film were to show a brutal rape in the same neutral way, claiming that one should avoid cheap moralism and start to think about rape in all its complexity? Our guts tell us that there is something terribly wrong here: I would like to live in a society where rape is simply considered unacceptable, so that anyone who argues for it appears an eccentric idiot, not in a society where one has to argue against it – and the same goes for torture: a sign of ethical progress is the fact that torture is "dogmatically" rejected as repulsive, without any need for argumentation.

The debate about waterboarding being torture or not should be dropped as an obvious nonsense: why, if not by causing pain and fear of death, does boarding make hardened terrorist-suspects talk? This is why one should reject the "realist" argument according to which waterboarding is a mere "mental trickery torture" where the prisoner thinks he is going to drown but actually isn't in much danger: we should weigh the benefit and potentially life-saving effect of the information that can be obtained through such trickery versus the wrong of the trickery itself. However, boarding is experienced by its victim as a real threat of drowning, in the same way that a mock ritual of shooting a prisoner (described long ago by Dostoyevsky) is a terrifying experience even if the prisoner thinks he is going to be shot but actually isn't in any danger. So we are back at the utilitarian calculus – the brief suffering of one against the death of many.

So what about the "realist" argument: torture was always going on, if anything even more in the (near) past, so is it not better to at least talk publicly about it? This, exactly, is the problem: if torture was always going on, *why are those in power now telling us openly about it?* There is only one answer: to normalize it, i.e., to lower our ethical standards. Therein resides the central point: one can well imagine desperate situations where one succumbs to the temptation of torturing one to save thousands, but it is crucial that one doesn't normalize such extreme situations into standard procedure, because such normalization blinds us to the horror of what we are doing. Does torture save lives? Maybe, but for sure it loses souls – and its most obscene justification is to claim that a true hero is ready to forsake his/her soul to save the lives of his/her countrymen. The normalization of torture in *Zero Dark Thirty* is therefore a sign of the moral vacuum we are gradually approaching. If there is any doubt about this, just try to imagine a major Hollywood film depicting torture in a similar way 20 or 30 years ago – it is unthinkable.

The cynic's naivety

The last resort of those who try to justify such relativization of the law is cynicism. The cynicism of those in power is today often so direct and open that there seems to be no need for the critique of ideology: why should we lose time and engage in arduous "symptomal reading," discerning gaps and repressions in the public discourse of those in power, when this discourse more or less openly and shamelessly admits its particular interests? There are nonetheless multiple problems with this thesis. However, such a cynical notion of society in which those in power brutally admit what they are doing is by far insufficient: precisely when they openly and "realistically" admit that it is ultimately all about power, money, influence, or whatever, they err in the extreme, their realism without illusions is the very form of their blindness. What they fatefully underestimate is the efficiency of illusions that structure and sustain their ruthless power games or financial speculations. At the beginning of Hitler's rule, it was the big capitalist cynics who told themselves "let's allow Hitler to take over and get us rid of the Left, and then we'll get rid of him." The financial crisis of 2008 was not brought about by the cynical bankers who acted upon the "greed is good" principle, nor by blinded idealists. Therein resides the limit of Sloterdijk's old formula of cynical reason "they know what they are doing, and they are nonetheless doing it": they are blind for the illusions inherent to the brutal "realist" stance.

Recall Marx's brilliant analysis of how, in the French revolution of 1848, the conservative–republican Party of Order functioned as the coalition of the two branches of royalism (Orleanists and legitimists) in the "anonymous kingdom of the Republic."[11] The parliamentary deputies of the Party of Order perceived their republicanism as a mockery: in parliamentary debates, they continuously generated royalist slips of tongue and ridiculed the Republic to let it be known that their true aim was to restore the kingdom. What they were not aware of is that they themselves were duped as to the true social impact of their rule. What they were effectively doing was establishing the conditions of bourgeois republican order that they despised so much (by for instance guaranteeing the safety of private property). So it is not that they were royalists who were just wearing a republican mask: although they experienced themselves as such, their very "inner" royalist conviction was the deceptive front masking their true social role. In short, far from being the hidden truth of their public republicanism, their sincere royalism was the fantasmatic support of their actual republicanism – the royalists

> deceived themselves concerning the fact of their united rule. They did not comprehend that if each of their factions, regarded separately, by itself, was royalist, the product of their chemical combination had necessarily to be *republican*.... Thus we find these royalists in the beginning believing in an immediate restoration, later preserving the republican form with foaming rage and deadly invective against it on their lips, and finally confessing that they can endure each other only in the republic and *postponing the restoration indefinitely* [*die Restauration aufs Unbestimmte vertagen*]. The *enjoyment* of the united rule [*der Genuß der vereinigten Herrschaft*] itself strengthened each of the two factions, and made each of them still more unable and unwilling to subordinate itself to the other, that is, to restore the monarchy.[12]

Marx describes here a precise case of perverted libidinal economy: there is a Goal (restoration of the monarchy) which members of the group experience as their true goal, but which, for tactical reasons, has to be publicly disavowed; however, what brings enjoyment are not multiple ways of obscenely making fun of the ideology they have to follow publicly (rage and invectives again republicanism), but the very indefinite postponement of the realization of their official Goal (which allows them to rule united). Recall how it is when, in the private sphere, I am unhappily married, I mock my wife all the time, declaring my intention to abandon her for my mistress whom I really love, and while I get small pleasures from invectives against my wife, the enjoyment that sustains me is generated by the indefinite postponement of really leaving my wife for my mistress. And, back to politics, were today's Party of Order not the US Republicans during the time of Ronald Reagan? Their Orleanists were neoliberal capitalists, and their legitimists Tea Party fundamentalists – they hated each other, but they knew they could only rule together, so each of them endlessly postponed the measures they really cared about (ban on abortion, etc.). This is the formula of today's cynical politics: its true dupes are the cynics themselves, who are not aware that their truth is in what they are mocking, not in their hidden belief. As such, cynicism is a perverted attitude: it transposes onto its other (non-cynical dupes) its own division. This is why, as Freud pointed out, the perverse activity is not an open display of the unconscious, but its greatest obfuscation.

There is one thing about Henry Kissinger, the ultimate cynical *Realpolitiker*, which cannot but strike the eye of all observers: how utterly wrong all his predictions were. When news reached the West about the 1991 anti-Gorbachev military coup, he immediately accepted the new regime (which ignominiously collapsed three days later) as a fact – in short, when socialist regimes were already a living corpse, he was counting on a long-term pact with them. What this example perfectly demonstrates is the limitation of the cynical attitude: cynics are *les non-dupes* who *errent*; what they fail to recognize is the symbolic efficiency of the illusions, the way they regulate activity which generates social reality. The position of cynicism is that of wisdom – the paradigmatic cynic tells you privately, in a confidential low-key voice: "But don't you get it that it is all really about … [money, power, sex], that all high principles and values are just empty phrases which count for nothing?" In this sense, philosophers effectively "believe in the power of ideas," they believe that "ideas rule the world," cynics are fully justified in accusing them of this sin – however, what the cynics don't see is their own naivety, the naivety of their cynical wisdom. It is the philosophers who are the true realists: they are well aware that the cynical position is impossible and inconsistent, that cynics effectively follow the principle they publicly mock. Stalin was a cynic if there ever was one – but precisely as such, he sincerely believed in communism.

The right of distress and emancipatory violence

How, then, should radical emancipatory politics deal with the inconsistency of the existing legal order? The first lesson is that it should not focus on the overthrowing of the existing legal order; it should rather begin with violating prohibited prohibition, the unwritten rules, the in-existing Law. An exemplary case of such a confrontation of prohibited prohibitions with direct emancipatory violence is provided by Christopher Nolan's *The Dark Knight Rises*. Here is the film's (simplified) storyline. Eight years after the events in *The Dark Knight*, law and order prevail in Gotham City: under the extraordinary legal powers granted by the Dent Act, Commissioner Gordon has nearly eradicated violent and organized crime. He nonetheless feels guilty about the cover-up of Harvey Dent's crimes (when Dent tried to kill Gordon's son before Batman saved him, Dent fell to his death, and Batman took the fall for the Dent myth, allowing himself to be demonized as Gotham's villain), and plans to admit to the conspiracy at a public event celebrating Dent, but decides that the city is not ready to hear the truth. No longer active as Batman, Bruce Wayne lives isolated in his Manor while his company is crumbling after he invested in a clean energy project designed to harness fusion power but shut it down after learning that the core could be modified to become a nuclear weapon. The beautiful Miranda Tate, a member of the Wayne Enterprises executive board, encourages Wayne to rejoin society and continue his philanthropic works.

Here enters the (first) villain of the film: Bane, a terrorist leader who was a member of the League of Shadows, gets hold of the copy of Gordon's speech. After Bane's financial machinations bring Wayne's company close to bankruptcy, Wayne entrusts Miranda with his enterprise and also engages in a brief love affair with her. (In this she competes with Selina Kyle, a cat burglar who steals from the rich in order to redistribute wealth, but finally rejoins Wayne and the forces of law and order.) Learning that Bane has also got hold of his fusion core, Wayne returns as Batman and confronts Bane, who says that he took over the League of Shadows after Ra's al Ghul's death. Crippling Batman in close combat, Bane detains him in a prison from which escape is virtually impossible: inmates tell Wayne the story of the only person to ever successfully escape from the prison, a child driven by necessity and sheer force of will. While the imprisoned Wayne recovers from his injuries and re-trains himself to be Batman, Bane succeeds in turning Gotham City into an isolated city-state. He first lures most of Gotham's police force underground and traps them there; then he sets off explosions which destroy most of the bridges connecting Gotham City to the mainland, announcing that any attempt to leave the city will result in the detonation of Wayne's fusion core, which has been converted into a bomb.

Here we reach the crucial moment of the film: Bane's takeover is accompanied by a vast politico-ideological offensive. Bane publicly reveals the cover-up of Dent's death and releases the prisoners locked up under the Dent Act. Condemning the rich and powerful, he promises to restore the power of the people, calling on the common people to "take your city back" – Bane reveals himself to be "the ultimate Wall Street Occupier, calling on the 99% to band together and overthrow societal elites."[13] What follows is the film's idea of people's power: summary show trials and executions of the rich, streets littered with crime and villainy –

> After a few months, Wayne successfully escapes prison, returns to Gotham as Batman, and enlists his friends to help liberate the city and stop the fusion bomb before it explodes. Batman confronts and subdues Bane, but Miranda intervenes and stabs Batman – the societal benefactor reveals herself to be Talia al Ghul, the daughter of Ra's al Ghul: it was she who escaped the prison as a child, and Bane was the one person who aided in her escape. After announcing her plan to complete her father's work by destroying Gotham, Talia escapes. In the ensuing mayhem, Gordon cuts off the bomb's ability to be remotely detonated while Selina kills Bane, allowing Batman to chase Talia. He tries to force her to take the bomb to the fusion chamber where it can be stabilized, but she floods the chamber. Talia dies when her truck crashes off the road, confident that the bomb cannot be stopped. Using a special helicopter, Batman hauls the bomb beyond the city limits, where it detonates over the ocean and presumably kills him.

Batman is now celebrated as a hero whose sacrifice saved Gotham City, while Wayne is believed to have died in the riots. As his estate is divided up, Alfred witnesses Wayne and Selina together alive in a cafe in Florence, while Blake, a young honest policeman who knew about Batman's identity, inherits the Batcave. In short, "Batman saves the day, emerges unscathed and moves on with a normal life, with someone else to replace his role defending the system."[14]

Batman, Joker, Bane

The first clue to the ideological underpinnings of this ending is provided by Alfred, Wayne's faithful butler, who, at Wayne's (would-be) burial, reads the last lines from Dickens's *Tale of Two Cities*: "It is a far, far better thing that I do, than I have ever done; it is a far, far better rest that I go to than I have ever known." Some reviewers of the film took this quote as an indication that it

> rises to the noblest level of Western art. The film appeals to the center of America's tradition – the ideal of noble sacrifice for the common people. Batman must humble himself to be exalted, and lay down his life to find a new one.... An ultimate Christ-figure, Batman sacrifices himself to save others ... the film does not primarily champion one political philosophy over another, but presents the central premise of Western civilization.[15]

And, effectively, from this perspective, there is only one step back from Dickens to Christ at Calvary: "For whosoever will save his life shall lose it: and whosoever will lose his life for my sake shall find it. For what is a man profited, if he shall gain the whole world, and lose his own soul?" (*Matthew* 16:25/26.) Is Batman's sacrifice the repetition of Christ's death? Is this idea not compromised by the film's last scene (Wayne with Selina in a Florence café)? Is the religious counterpart of this ending not rather the well-known blasphemous idea that Christ really survived his crucifixion and lived a long peaceful life (in India or even Tibet, according to some sources)? The only way to redeem this final scene would have been to read it as a daydream (hallucination) of Alfred while sitting alone in the Florence café.

The further Dickensian feature of the film is a de-politicized complaint about the gap between the rich and the poor – early in the film, Selina whispers to Wayne while they are dancing at an exclusive upper-class gala:

> A storm is coming, Mr. Wayne. You and your friends better batten down the hatches. Because when it hits, you're all going to wonder how you thought you could live so large, and leave so little for the rest of us.

Nolan, like every good liberal, is "worried" about this disparity and he admits that this worry penetrates the film:

> what I see in the film that relates to the real world is the idea of dishonesty. The film is all about that coming to a head.... The notion of economic fairness creeps into the film, and the reason is twofold. One, Bruce Wayne is a billionaire. It has to be addressed.... But two, there are a lot of things in life, and economics is one of them, where we have to take a lot of what we're told on trust, because most of us feel like we don't have the analytical tools to know what's going on ... I don't feel there's a left or right perspective in the film. What is there is just an honest assessment or honest exploration of the world we live in – things that worry us.[16]

Although viewers know Wayne is mega-rich, they tend to forget where his wealth comes from: arms manufacturing plus stock-market speculations, which is why Bane's stock-exchange games can destroy his empire – arms dealer and speculator, *this* is the true secret beneath the Batman mask. How does the film deal with it? By resuscitating the archetypal Dickensian topic of a good capitalist who engages in financing orphanages (Wayne) versus a bad greedy capitalist (Stryver, as in Dickens). In such Dickensian over-moralization, the economic disparity is translated into "dishonesty" which should be "honestly" analyzed, although we lack any reliable cognitive mapping, and such an "honest" approach leads to a further parallel with Dickens – as Christopher Nolan's brother Jonathan (who co-wrote the scenario) put it bluntly:

> *Tale of Two Cities* to me was the most sort of harrowing portrait of a relatable recognizable civilization that had completely fallen to pieces. The terrors in Paris, in France in that period, it's not hard to imagine that things could go that bad and wrong.[17]

The scenes of the vengeful populist uprising in the film (a mob that thirsts for the blood of the rich who have neglected and exploited them) evoke Dickens' description of the Reign of Terror, so that, although the film has nothing to do with politics, it follows Dickens' novel in "honestly" portraying revolutionaries as possessed fanatics, and thus provides

> the caricature of what in real life would be an ideologically committed revolutionary fighting structural injustice. Hollywood tells what the establishments want you to know – revolutionaries are brutal creatures, with utter disregard for human life. Despite emancipatory rhetoric on liberation, they have sinister designs behind. Thus, whatever might be their reasons, they need to be eliminated.[18]

Tom Charity was right to note "the movie's defense of the establishment in the form of philanthropic billionaires and an incorruptible police"[19] – in its distrust of the people taking things into their own hands, the film "demonstrates both a desire for social justice and a fear of what that can actually look like in the hands of a mob."[20] Karthick raises here a perspicuous question with regard to the immense popularity of the Joker figure from the previous film: why such a harsh disposition towards Bane when the Joker was dealt with so leniently in the earlier movie? The answer is simple and convincing:

> The Joker, calling for anarchy in its purest form, critically underscores the hypocrisies of bourgeois civilization as it exists, but his views are unable to translate into mass action. Bane, on the other hand poses an existential threat to the system of oppression.... His strength is not just his physique but also his ability to command people and mobilize them to achieve a political goal. He represents the vanguard, the organized representative of the oppressed that wages political struggle in their name to bring about structural changes. Such a force, with the greatest subversive potential, the system cannot accommodate. It needs to be eliminated.[21]

However, even if Bane lacks the fascinating strength of Heath Ledger's Joker, there is a feature that distinguishes him from the latter: unconditional love, the very source of his hardness. In a short but touching scene, he tells Wayne how, in an act of love in the midst of terrible suffering, he saved the child Talia, not caring for consequences and paying a terrible price for it (Bane was beaten within an inch of his life while defending her).[22] Karthick is totally justified in locating this event in the long tradition, from Christ to Che Guevara, which extols violence as a "work of love," as in the famous lines from Che Guevara's diary: "Let me say, with the risk of appearing ridiculous, that the true revolutionary is guided by strong feelings of love. It is impossible to think of an authentic revolutionary without this quality."[23] What we encounter here is not so much the "Christification of Che" but rather a "Cheization" of Christ himself – the Christ whose "scandalous" words from Luke ("if anyone comes to me and does not hate his father and his mother, his wife and children, his brothers and sisters – yes even his own life – he cannot be my disciple"(14:26)) point in exactly the same direction as Che's famous quote: "You may have to be tough, but do not lose your tenderness." The statement that "the true revolutionary is guided by a great feeling of love" should be read together with Guevara's much more "problematic" statement on revolutionaries as "killing machines":

> Hatred is an element of struggle; relentless hatred of the enemy that impels us over and beyond the natural limitations of man and transforms

> us into effective, violent, selective, and cold killing machines. Our soldiers must be thus; a people without hatred cannot vanquish a brutal enemy.[24]

Or, to paraphrase Kant and Robespierre yet again: love without cruelty is powerless; cruelty without love is blind, a short-lived passion which loses its persistent edge. Guevara is here paraphrasing Christ's declarations on the unity of love and sword – in both cases, the underlying paradox is that what makes love angelic, what elevates it over mere unstable and pathetic sentimentality, is its cruelty itself, its link with violence – it is this link which raises love over and beyond the natural limitations of man and thus transforms it into an unconditional drive. So while Guevara certainly believed in the transformative power of love, he would never have been heard humming "all you need is love" – what you need is to *love with hatred*, or, as Kierkegaard put it long ago: the necessary consequence (the "truth") of the Christian demand to *love one's enemy* is

> the demand to *hate the beloved* out of love and in love.... So high – humanly speaking to a kind of madness – can Christianity press the demand of love if love is to be the fulfilling of the law. Therefore it teaches that the Christian shall, if it is demanded, be capable of hating his father and mother and sister and beloved.[25]

In contrast to erotic love, this notion of love should be given here all its Paulinian weight: *the domain of pure violence*, the domain outside of law (legal power), the domain of the violence which is neither law-founding nor law-sustaining, *is the domain of agape*.[26] Consequently, we are not dealing here with a simple brutal hatred demanded by a cruel and jealous God: the "hatred" enjoined by Christ is not a kind of pseudo-dialectical opposite to love, but a direct expression of *agape* – it is love itself that enjoins us to "unplug" from our organic community into which we were born, or, as St. Paul put it, for a Christian, there are neither men nor women, neither Jews nor Greeks.... So, again, if the acts of revolutionary violence are "works of love" in the strictest Kierkegaardian sense of the term, it is not because the revolutionary violence "really" aims at establishing a non-violent harmony; on the contrary, the authentic revolutionary liberation is much more directly identified with violence – it is violence as such (the violent gesture of discarding, of establishing a difference, of drawing a line of separation) which liberates. Freedom is not a blissfully neutral state of harmony and balance, but the very violent act that disturbs this balance. This is why, in *The Dark Knight Rises*, the only authentic love in the film is Bane's, the "terrorist's," in clear contrast to Batman.

Along the same lines, the figure of Ra's al Ghul, Talia's father, deserves a closer look. Ra's, an agent of virtuous terror fighting to counterbalance corrupted Western civilization, has a mixture of Arab and Oriental features. He is played by Liam Neeson, an actor whose screen-persona usually radiates dignified goodness and wisdom (he is Zeus in *Clash of the Titans*), and who also plays Qui-Gon Jinn in *The Phantom Menace*, the first episode of the *Star Wars* series. Qui-Gon is a Jedi knight, the mentor of Obi-Wan Kenobi as well as the one who discovers Anakin Skywalker, believing that Anakin is the Chosen One who will restore the balance of the universe, ignoring Yoda's warnings about Anakin's unstable nature; at the end of *The Phantom Menace*, Qui-Gon is killed by Darth Maul.[27]

In the *Batman* trilogy, Ra's is also the teacher of the young Wayne: in *Batman Begins*, he finds Wayne in a Chinese prison; introducing himself as "Henri Ducard," he offers the boy a "path." After Wayne is freed, he climbs to the home of the League of Shadows, where Ra's is waiting, although presenting himself as the servant of another man who calls himself Ra's al Ghul. At the end of a long and painful training, Ra's explains that Bruce must do what is necessary to fight evil, while revealing that they have trained Bruce with the intention of him leading the League to destroy Gotham City, which they believe has become hopelessly corrupt. Months later, Ra's unexpectedly reappears, and reveals that he was not Henri Ducard, but Ra's al Ghul. In the ensuing confrontation, Ra's elaborates on the League of Shadows' exploits throughout history (sacking Rome, spreading the Black Death, and starting the Great Fire of London). He explains that the destruction of Gotham City is merely another mission by the League to correct humanity's recurring fits of decadence and presumably protect the environment. Ra's then has his henchmen burn down Wayne Manor with the intent of killing Bruce, stating "Justice is balance, you burnt my home and left me for dead, consider us even." Wayne survives the fire, and confronts Ra's as Batman; after overpowering him, he leaves Ra's for dead on a train which falls into a car garage and explodes; Ra's uses his last moment to meditate, and is presumed dead, though no body is found in the wreckage … Ra's is thus not a simple embodiment of Evil: he stands for the combination of virtue and terror, for the egalitarian discipline fighting a corrupted empire, and thus belongs to a line that stretches (in recent fiction) from Paul Atreides in *Dune* to Leonidas in *300*. And it is crucial that Wayne is his disciple: Wayne was made into Batman by him.

Violence, which violence?

Two common-sense reproaches impose themselves here. First, there *were* monstrous mass killings and violence in actual revolutions, from Stalinism to the Khmer Rouge, so the film is clearly not just engaging in reactionary imagination. The second, opposite reproach: the actual Occupy Wall Street (OWS) movement was not violent, its goal was definitely not a new reign of terror; insofar as Bane's revolt is supposed to extrapolate the immanent tendency of the OWS movement, the film thus ridiculously misrepresents its aims and strategies. The ongoing anti-globalist protests are the very opposite of Bane's brutal terror: Bane stands for the mirror-image of state terror, for a murderous fundamentalist sect taking over and ruling by terror, not for its overcoming through popular self-organization.... What both reproaches share is the rejection of the figure of Bane. The reply to these two reproaches is multiple.

First, one should make clear the actual scope of violence. The best answer to the claim that the violent mob reaction to oppression is worse than the original oppression itself was the one provided long ago by Mark Twain in *A Connecticut Yankee in King Arthur's Court*:

> There were two "Reigns of Terror" if we would remember it and consider it; the one wrought in hot passion, the other in heartless cold blood ... our shudders are all for the "horrors" of the minor Terror, the momentary Terror, so to speak, whereas, what is the horror of swift death by the axe compared with lifelong death from hunger, cold, insult, cruelty, and heartbreak? A city cemetery could contain the coffins filled by that brief Terror which we have all been so diligently taught to shiver at and mourn over; but all France could hardly contain the coffins filled by that older and real Terror, that unspeakably bitter and awful Terror, which none of us have been taught to see in its vastness or pity as it deserves.

In order to grasp this parallax nature of violence, one should focus on short-circuits between different levels, say, between power and social violence: an economic crisis that causes devastation is experienced as uncontrollable quasi-natural power, but it SHOULD be experienced as VIOLENCE.

Then it is not only Nolan's film which was not able to imagine authentic people's power – the "real" radical-emancipatory movements themselves were also not able to do it, they remained caught in the coordinates of the old society, which is why the actual "people's power" often was such a violent horror.

One should, then, demystify the problem of violence, rejecting simplistic claims that twentieth-century communism used too much excessive murderous violence and that we should be careful not to fall into this trap again. As a fact, this is, of course, terrifyingly true – but such a direct focus on violence obfuscates the underlying question: what was wrong in the twentieth-century communist project as such, which immanent weakness of this project pushed the communists (not only those) in power to unrestrained violence? In other words, it is not enough to say that communists "neglected the problem of violence": it was a deeper socio-political failure that pushed them to violence. (The same goes for the notion that communists "neglected democracy": their overall project of social transformation enforced on them this "neglect.")

And, last but not least, it is all too simple to claim that there is no violent potential in OWS and similar movements – there *is* violence at work in every authentic emancipatory process: the problem with the film is that it wrongly translated this violence into murderous terror. Let me clarify this point with the detour through my critics who, when they are forced to admit that my statement that Hitler wasn't violent enough is not meant as a call for even more terrifying massive killing, tend to turn around their reproach: I just use provocative language in order to make a common-sense uninteresting point. Here is what one of them wrote apropos of my claim that Gandhi was more violent than Hitler:

> Žižek is here using language in a way that is designed to be provocative and to confuse people. He doesn't *actually* mean that Gandhi was more violent than Hitler.... What he means to do instead is to alter the typical understanding of the word "violent" so that Gandhi's non-violent means of protest against the British will be considered more violent than Hitler's incredibly violent attempts at world domination and genocide. Violence, for Žižek in this particular instance, actually means that which causes massive social upheaval. In that way, he consider Gandhi to be more violent than Hitler. But this, like so much of what Žižek writes, is actually nothing new or interesting or surprising. And that's why he writes it in the provocative, confusing, and bizarre manner that he chooses instead of a straightforward manner. If he would have written that Gandhi accomplished more through non-violence that aimed at systemic change than Hitler accomplished through violent means, we would all agree ... but we would also all know that there is nothing profound in such a statement. Instead, Žižek attempts to shock us and, in doing so, he covers up the completely humdrum conclusion about Gandhi and Hitler that everyone already believed to be true before they read Žižek.[28]

In short, I try to sell the common thesis that Gandhi aimed at changing the system, not destroying people, but since this is a commonplace, I formulate it more provocatively, weirdly expanding the meaning of the word violence to include institutional changes. So why call Gandhi's attempts to undermine the British state in India more violent than Hitler's mass killings? To draw attention to the fundamental violence that sustains a normal functioning of the state (Benjamin called it mythic violence), and the no less fundamental violence that sustains every attempt to undermine the functioning of the state (Benjamin's divine violence).[29] This is why the reaction of state power to those who endanger it is so brutal, and why, in its very brutality, this reaction is precisely reactive, protective. So, far from eccentricity, the extension of the notion of violence is based on a key theoretical insight, and it is the limitation of violence to its directly visible physical aspect which, far from being normal, relies on an ideological distortion. This is also why the reproach that I am fascinated by some ultra-radical violence with comparison to which Hitler and Khmer Rouge didn't go far enough misses the point, which is not to go further in *this* type of violence but to change the entire terrain. It is difficult to be really violent, to perform an act that violently disturbs the basic parameters of social life. When Bertolt Brecht saw a Japanese mask of an evil demon, he wrote how its swollen veins and hideous grimaces "all betake / what an exhausting effort it takes / To be evil." The same holds for violence which has any effect on the system. The Chinese Cultural Revolution serves as a lesson here: destroying old monuments proved not to be a true negation of the past. It was rather an impotent *passage a l'acte*, an acting out that bore witness to the failure to get rid of the past. There is a kind of poetic justice in the fact that the final result of Mao's Cultural Revolution is the current unmatched explosion of capitalist dynamics in China: a profound structural homology exists between Maoist permanent self-revolutionizing, the permanent struggle against the ossification of State structures, and the inherent dynamics of capitalism. One is tempted to paraphrase Brecht again here: "What is the robbing of a bank compared to the founding of a new bank?": what were the violent and destructive outbursts of a Red Guardist caught in the Cultural Revolution compared to the true Cultural Revolution, the permanent dissolution of all life-forms which capitalist reproduction dictates?

Traces of utopia

Back to Nolan's Batman trilogy: we can see now how it clearly follows an immanent logic.[30] In *Batman Begins*, the hero remains within the constraints of a liberal order: the system can be defended with morally acceptable methods. *The Dark Knight* is effectively a new version of the two John Ford western classics (*Fort Apache* and *The Man Who Shot Liberty Valance*) which deploy how, in order to civilize the Wild West, one has to "print the legend" and ignore the truth – in short, how our civilization has to be grounded on a Lie: one has to break the rules in order to defend the system.[31] Or, to put it in another way, in *Batman Begins*, the hero is simply a classic figure of the urban vigilante who punishes the criminals where police cannot do so; the problem is that the police, the official law-enforcement agency, relates ambiguously to Batman's help: while admitting its efficiency, it nonetheless perceives Batman as a threat to its monopoly on power and a testimony of its own inefficiency. However, Batman's transgression is here purely formal; it resides in acting on behalf of the law without being legitimized to do it: in his acts, he never violates the law. *The Dark Knight* changes these coordinates: Batman's true rival is not Joker, his opponent, but Harvey Dent, the "white knight," the aggressive new District Attorney, a kind of official vigilante whose fanatical battle against crime leads him to kill innocent people and destroys him. It is as if Dent is the reply of the legal order to Batman's threat: against Batman's vigilante struggle, the system generates its own illegal excess, its own vigilante, much more violent than Batman, in direct violation of the law. There is thus poetic justice in the fact that, when Bruce plans to publicly reveal his identity as Batman, Dent jumps in and instead names himself as Batman – he *is* "more Batman than Batman himself," actualizing the temptation Batman was still able to resist. So when, at the film's end, Batman takes upon himself the crimes committed by Dent to save the reputation of the popular hero who embodies hope for ordinary people, his self-effacing act contains a grain of truth, Batman in a way returns the favor to Dent. His act is a gesture of symbolic exchange: first Dent takes upon himself the identity of Batman, then Wayne – the real Batman – takes upon himself Dent's crimes.

Finally, *The Dark Knight Rises* pushes things even further: is Bane not Dent brought to an extreme, to its self-negation? Is it not Dent who draws the conclusion that the system itself is unjust, so that in order to effectively fight injustice one has to turn directly against the system and destroy it? And, as part of the same move, is it not Dent who loses his final inhibitions and is ready to use murderous brutality to achieve this goal? The rise of such a figure changes the entire constellation: for all participants, Batman included, morality is relativized, it becomes a matter of convenience, something determined by circumstances: it's open class warfare, everything is permitted to defend the system when we are dealing not just with mad gangsters but with a popular uprising.

Is this, then, all? Should the film be flatly rejected by those who are engaged in radical emancipatory struggles? Things are more ambiguous, and one has to read the film in the way one has to interpret a Chinese political poem: absences and surprising presences count. Recall the old French story about a wife who complains that her husband's best friend is making illicit sexual advances towards her: it takes some time until the surprised friend gets the point – in this twisted way, she is inviting him to seduce her.... It is like the Freudian unconscious which knows no negation: what matters is not a negative judgment of something, but the mere fact that this something is even mentioned – in *The Dark Knight Rises*, people's power IS HERE, staged as an Event, in a key step forward from Batman's usual opponents (criminal mega-capitalists, gangsters and terrorists).

Here we get the first clue – the prospect of the OWS movement taking power and establishing a people's democracy in Manhattan is so patently absurd, so utterly non-realist, that one cannot but raise the question: WHY THEN DOES A MAJOR HOLLYWOOD BLOCKBUSTER DREAM ABOUT IT, WHY DOES IT EVOKE THIS SPECTER? Why even dream about OWS exploding into a violent takeover? The obvious answer (to smear OWS with accusations that it harbors a terrorist-totalitarian potential) is not enough to account for the strange attraction exerted by this prospect of "people's power." No wonder that the proper functioning of this power remains blank, absent: no details are given about how this people's power functions, what the mobilized people are doing (remember that Bane tells the people they can do what they want – he is not imposing on them his own order). One can even talk of necessary *censorship* here: any depiction of the self-organization of the people during Bane's reign would have ruined the effect of the film, laying bare its inconsistency.

This is why the film deserves a close reading: the Event – the "people's republic of Gotham City," dictatorship of the proletariat on Manhattan – is *immanent* to the film, it is (to use the worn-out expression from the 1970s) its "absent center." This is why external critique of the film ("its depiction of the OWS reign is a ridiculous caricature") is not enough – the critique has to be immanent, it has to locate within the film itself a multitude of signs that point towards the authentic Event. (Recall, for example, that Bane is not just a brutal terrorist, but a person of deep love and sacrifice.) In short, pure ideology is not possible; Bane's authenticity HAS to leave its trace in the film's texture.

And one should also not shirk from imagining an alternate version of the film, something like what Ralph Fiennes did with *Coriolanus*: in his film, it is as if Coriolanus, obviously out of place in the delicate hierarchy of Rome, only becomes what he is, gains his freedom, when he joins the Volscians (with their leader Aufidius playing the role of Bane). He does not join them simply in order to take revenge on Rome, he joins them because he belongs there. In joining the Volscians, Coriolanus does not betray Rome out of a sense of petty revenge, but he regains his integrity – his only act of betrayal occurs at the end when, instead of leading the Volscian army into Rome, he organizes a peace treaty between the Volscians and Rome, breaking down under the pressure of his mother, the true figure of superego Evil. This is why he returns to the Volscians, fully aware what awaits him there: the well-deserved punishment for his betrayal.[32] So what about imagining a Batman who rejoins Bane's forces in Gotham City; after helping them to almost defeat the state power, he breaks down, mediates an armistice, and then goes back to the rebels, knowing he will be killed for his betrayal?

"The right of distress"

Our conclusion should thus not be simply that people have the right to a violent overthrow of the existing legal order – one should be more precise here: the conflict is inherent to the sphere of the law, i.e., the right to a revolution is an uncanny legal principle that overrides other such principles. Hegel pointed the way here in his account of the "right of distress (*Notrecht*)"[33]:

> *§127* The particularity of the interests of the natural will, taken in their entirety as a single whole, is personal existence or life. In extreme danger and in conflict with the rightful property of someone else, this life may claim (as a right, not a mercy) a right of distress [*Notrecht*], because in such a situation there is on the one hand an infinite injury to a man's existence and the consequent loss of rights altogether, and on the other hand only an injury to a single restricted embodiment of freedom, and this implies a recognition both of right as such and also of the injured man's capacity for rights, because the injury affects only this property of his.
>
> *Remark:* The right of distress is the basis of *beneficium competentiae* whereby a debtor is allowed to retain of his tools, farming implements, clothes, or, in short, of his resources, i.e., of his creditor's property, so much as is regarded as indispensable if he is to continue to support life – to support it, of course, on his own social level.
>
> *Addition:* Life as the sum of ends has a right against abstract right. If for example it is only by stealing bread that the wolf can be kept from the door, the action is of course an encroachment on someone's property, but it would be wrong to treat this action as an ordinary theft. To refuse to allow a man in jeopardy of his life to take such steps for self-preservation would be to stigmatize him as without rights, and since he would be deprived of his life, his freedom would be annulled altogether....
>
> *§128* This distress reveals the finitude and therefore the contingency of both right and welfare of right as the abstract embodiment of freedom without embodying the particular person, and of welfare as the sphere of the particular will without the universality of right.

Hegel does not talk here about humanitarian considerations that should temper our legalistic zeal (if an impoverished father steals bread to feed his starving child, we should show mercy and understanding even if he broke the law), but about a basic legal right, a right which is *as a right* superior to other particular legal rights. In other words, we are not dealing simply with the conflict between the demands of life and the constraints of the legal system of rights, but with a right (to life) that overcomes all formal rights, i.e., with *a conflict inherent to the sphere of rights*, a conflict which is unavoidable and *necessary* insofar as it serves as an indication of the finitude, inconsistency, and "abstract" character of the system of legal rights as such. "To refuse to allow a man in jeopardy of his life to take such steps for self-preservation [such as stealing the food necessary for his survival] would be to *stigmatize him as without rights*" – so, again, the point is not that the punishment for justified stealing would deprive the subject of his life but that it would exclude him from the domain of rights, i.e., that it would reduce him to bare life outside the domain of law, of the legal order. In other words, this refusal deprives the subject of his very *right to have rights*. Furthermore, the quoted *Remark* applies this logic to the situation of a debtor, claiming that he should be allowed to retain of his resources so much as is regarded as indispensable if he is to continue with his life not just at the level of bare survival but "on his own social level" – a claim that is today fully relevant with regard to the situation of the impoverished majority in indebted states such as Greece. However, the key question here is: can we universalize this "right of distress," extending it to an entire social class and its acts against the property of another class? Although Hegel does not directly address this question, a positive answer imposes itself from Hegel's description of "rabble" as a group/class whose exclusion from the domain of social recognition is *systematic*: "*§ 244, Addition:* Against nature man can claim no right, but once society is established, poverty immediately takes the form of a wrong done to one class by another." In such a situation in which a whole class of people is systematically pushed beneath the level of dignified survival, to refuse to allow them to take "steps for self-preservation" (which, in this case, can only mean the open rebellion against the established legal order) is to *stigmatize them as without rights*.

Notes

1 See Sergio Gonzales Rodriguez, *The Femicide Machine*, Los Angeles: Semiotext(e), 2012.
2 See Wally T. Oppal, *Forsaken: The Report of the Missing Women Commission of Inquiry*, 19 November 2012, available online at www.missingwomeninquiry.ca/wp-content/uploads/2010/10/Forsaken-ES-web-RGB.pdf.
3 Gary Wills, "Scandal," *The New York Review of Books*, 23 May 2002, p. 6.
4 Another cynical strategy is to blame the enemy: the US Catholic authorities referred to a research whose alleged result was that the sexual permissiveness from the 1960s on is to be held responsible for the widespread pedophilia in the Church.
5 Robert Pfaller, "The Potential of Thresholds to Obstruct and to Facilitate: On the Operation of Displacement in Obsessional Neurosis and Perversion" (unpublished paper, 2002).
6 What one usually gets from theorists is a private admission that, of course, this is contradictory, but that, nonetheless, such a contradictory ideological edifice *works*, and works spectacularly: it is the only way to ensure fast economic growth and stability in China. Need we add that this is the "private use of reason" at its purest?
7 See "Even what's Secret is a Secret in China," *The Japan Times*, 16 June 2007, p. 17.

8 Franz Kafka, "The Problem of Our Laws," in *The Complete Stories*, New York: Schocken Books, 1995, p. 437.
9 The EU pressure on Greece in 2011 and 2012 to implement them fits perfectly what psychoanalysis calls superego. Superego is not an ethical agency proper, but a sadistic agent which bombards the subject with impossible demands, obscenely enjoying the subject's failure to comply with them; the paradox of the superego is that, as Freud saw it clearly, the more we obey its demands, the more we feel guilty. Imagine a vicious teacher who gives to his pupils impossible tasks, and then sadistically jeers when he sees their anxiety and panic. This is what is so terribly wrong with the EU demands/commands: they don't even give a chance to Greece, their failure is part of the game.
10 Jacques Derrida, *Acts of Literature*, New York: Routledge, 1992, p. 201.
11 See Karl Marx, "Class Struggles in France," *Collected Works*, vol. 10, London: Lawrence and Wishart, 1978, p. 95.
12 Ibid.
13 Tyler O'Neil, "Dark Knight and Occupy Wall Street: The Humble Rise," *Hillsdale Natural Law Review*, 21 July 2012, available online at http://hillsdalenaturallawreview.com/2012/07/21/dark-knight-and-occupy-wall-street-the-humble-rise/.
14 R.M. Karthick, "The Dark Knight rises a 'Fascist'?," *Society and Culture*, 21 July 2012, available online at http://wavesunceasing.wordpress.com/2012/07/21/the-dark-knight-rises-a-fascist/.
15 O'Neil, op. cit.
16 Christopher Nolan, interview in *Entertainment* 1216, July 2012, p. 34.
17 www.buzzinefilm.com/interviews/film-interview-dark-knight-rises-christopher-nolan-jonathan-nolan-07192012.
18 Karthick, op. cit.
19 http://edition.cnn.com/2012/07/19/showbiz/movies/dark-knight-rises-review-charity/index.html?iref=obinsite.
20 Forrest Whitman, "The Dickensian Aspects of The Dark Knight Rises," 21 July 2012, available online at www.slate.com/blogs/browbeat/2012/07/23/the_dark_knight_rises_and_the_end_of_counterprogramming_why_batman_had_no_competition_at_the_box_office.html.
21 Op. cit.
22 Tom Hardy, the actor who plays Bane, also played Charles Bronson/Michael Peterson, the legendary British prisoner known for the mixture of violence, the quest for justice and the artistic sense which makes him similar to Bane, in *Bronson* (2010).
23 Quoted from Jon Lee Anderson, *Che Guevara: A Revolutionary Life*, New York: Grove, 1997, pp. 636–637.
24 Quoted from ibid.
25 Soeren Kierkegaard, *Works of Love*, New York: Harper & Row, 1962, p. 114.
26 A supreme literary example of such "killing out of love" is Toni Morrison's *Beloved*, where the heroine kills her daughter to prevent her falling into slavery.
27 One should note the irony of the fact that Neeson's son is a devoted Shia Muslim, and that Neeson himself often talks about his forthcoming conversion to Islam.
28 http://lazersilberstein.tumblr.com/post/26499132966/according-to-slavoj-zizek-no-one-understands-slavoj-zizek.
29 There is a homologous procedure in our language. In the domain of politics, one often uses (ironically) the passive form of an active verb – say, when a politician who is forced to voluntarily step down, one comments on it that he was stepped down. In China, during the Cultural Revolution, one even used the neutral form – like struggle – in an artificial passive or active version; when a

cadre accused of revisionism was submitted to a session of ideological struggle, it was said that he was struggled, or that the revolutionary group was struggling him (here, the intransitive verb was changed into a transitive one: we not only struggle, we struggle *someone*). Such distortions of normal grammar adequately expressed the underlying logic; consequently, instead of rejecting them as violent distortions of normal use of language, we should praise them as disclosures of the violence that underlies this normal use.

30 I rely here on an idea developed by Srecko Horvat (Zagreb).

31 For a more detailed analysis of *The Dark Knight*, see Chapter 1 of Slavoj Žižek, *Living at the End Times*, London: Verso Books, 2010.

32 For a more detailed reading of Fiennes's Coriolanus, see Chapter 9 of Slavoj Žižek, *The Year of Dreaming Dangerously*, London: Verso Books, 2012.

33 I owe this reference to Hegel's *Notrecht* to Costas Douzinas, who developed it in his intervention "The Right to Revolution?" at the Hegel colloquium "The Actuality of the Absolute," organized by the Birkbeck School of Law in London, 10–12 May 2013. Passages from Hegel's *Philosophy of Right* are quoted from www.marxists.org/reference/archive/hegel/works/pr/prconten.htm.

Index

Printed in Great Britain
by Amazon

49115200R00151